IGN TOURING AND LEISURE GUIDES

BRITTANY

This guidebook forms part of a new series of
regional touring and leisure guides to France
and is produced in association with the French
national mapping agency, the
Institut Géographique National.
Feature articles trace the history, culture and
architecture of each region and detail the prime sports and
leisure pursuits available to holidaymakers. These are
complemented by a gazetteer section which provides
information on resorts and places of interest.
Through the exclusive use of IGN's superb topographical
mapping, the motoring tours and walks outlined in each
guide aim to help you discover new aspects of France.
Above all, though, it is our hope that these guides open the
door to your own discoveries.

**Published by Robertson McCarta in association with
THE INSTITUT GEOGRAPHIQUE NATIONAL**

We particularly thank the staff of the Comité Régional de Tourisme de Bretagne for their assistance and Patrick Goyet and Pauline Hallam of the French Tourist Office in London.

First published in 1991 by

Robertson McCarta Limited
17–18 Angel Gate
City Road
London EC1V 2PT

in association with

Institut Géographique National
136 bis, rue de Grenelle
75700 Paris

Publishing Director Henderson McCartney
IGN Coordinator Nathalie Marthe
Series Editor Catharine Hutton
Project Coordinators Folly Marland, Ruth Keshishian
Editors Christian Senan, Catherine Bray, Daphne Terry
Contributors Keith Spence, Albert Coquil
Art Director Prue Bucknall
Design Assistant Alison Shackleton
Line maps and illustrations Paul Bryant
Research Stephane Chemouilli, Marie-Claire Faliu, Lucy Deedes-Vincke
Photo Research Christine Altur
Production Bob Towell, Grahame Griffiths
Typeset by Columns Limited, Reading
Printed and bound by Grafedit, SpA. Bergamo, Italy

British Library Cataloguing in Publication Data
Brittany. – (IGN touring and leisure guides. Regional guides to France).
1. France. Brittany – Visitors' guides
I. Institut Géographique National
II. Series
914.4104839

ISBN 1–85365–242–3

Photographic credits
C.R.T.B. 35, 39 (bottom), 53, 76, 85, 97, 105 (bottom), 108, 111, Monique BICHET 51, J. P. CORBEL 21, 113, GALLON 12, 14, 55 (bottom), 105, 107 (top), LEXONIL 83, PINHEIRA 42, 74, 88, 102, RAINON 34, 48, 50, VIGNERON 26, 110; **EXPLORER** 22, 23, BERTHOULE 17, Francis BOIZOT 63, Thierry BORREDON 23, CAMBAZARD 20, S. CORDIER 31, 55 (top), Christian CUNY 82, DESMARTEAU 78, Brigitte & Jose DUPONT 4 (left), 8, 24, 40, 44, 64, 65, 72, FREDERIC 67, Alain GILLOU 7, Luc GIRARD 18, Jean-Paul HERVY 16, 29, 58, 59, HUG 6, Francois JALAIN 89, Jean-Michel LABAT 112, Rene LANAUD 81, Gilbert LA COSSE 99, Rene LANAUD 101, Michel LE COZ 15, Alain LE TOQUIN 71, Patrick LORNE 11, 70, Jean-Paul NACIVET 44, 69, 84, Alain NICOLAS 32, N. PINAKOTHEK 93, RIBIERAS 9, Philippe ROY 4 (top), 66, 79 (bottom), 87, Ex ROY 92, Louis SALOU 95, Henri VEILLER 94 (top & bottom), Villegier 39 (top), Alain WEISS 13; Marie-Claire FALIU 1 (Title Page), 15, 58, 64, 79 (top), 88, 107 (top), 109

CONTENTS

AN INTRODUCTION TO BRITTANY

The thick granite promontory of Brittany separates the Channel from the Atlantic, jutting west in a wriggling 1,200-km coastline of long beaches, coves, cliff faces and busy little fishing ports.

Brittany is primarily sea country, an ideal holiday world of sunny sands, rock pools to be explored, headlands scrambled, of sailing and river cruising. It is the land where young children, abroad maybe for the first time, come to form their earliest memories of holidays in France.

It is also a region of outstanding historical and architectural heritage, a land steeped in the Breton traditions which ensure its continued individuality and great popularity.

TITLE PAGE A FISHING BOAT AT ROSCOFF
LEFT THE LIGHTHOUSE AT PLOUMANAC'H
ABOVE TRADITIONAL BRETON HEADDRESSES

ARMOR AND ARGOAT

A land both ancient and modern

Brittany's deeply indented coast, 1,200 km or 750 miles long and cut into hundreds of creeks and small inlets by the relentless power of wind and wave, looks on the map like the head and shoulders of a strange monster jutting from the western edge of Europe. In earlier centuries the Bretons looked outwards to the sea for their livelihood, venturing in small sailing boats to the Newfoundland fishing banks, or harrying the world's merchant shipping vessels as far afield as the Indian Ocean. Since the middle of the 19th century, Brittany's coast has become one of northern Europe's most popular holiday playgrounds – a process accelerated in recent years by a massive road-building programme across the interior of the country and, as far as visitors from Britain are concerned, by a vastly improved cross-Channel car-ferry service to St-Malo and Roscoff.

In the ancient Breton language which was spoken long before the Romans conquered the country in 55 BC, this coastal region was known as 'Ar-Mor', meaning 'The Sea'. The Romans adopted this name, calling the province of north-west Gaul 'Gallia Armorica'. In 1990 the name was officially revived for one of Brittany's four *départements* or administrative regions, when the Côtes-du-Nord, which stretches along much of the northern edge of the region, was renamed Côtes-d'Armor.

Inland from Armor lay 'Ar-Goat' pronounced argwat, meaning 'Woodland', a dense forest covering the interior of Brittany. Down the centuries the land has been gradually cleared for agriculture and industry, until little of the ancient woodland now remains. Like their fellow Celts in Wales and the western counties of England, farmers in the interior of Brittany have had a hard struggle to produce crops from their thin soil. So, not surprisingly, the country people of Argoat, like the coast-dwellers of Armor, have turned enthusiastically to the new opportunities offered by tourism, welcoming

WHITE HORSES AT ROSCOFF

holidaymakers to a varied landscape which ranges from peaceful lakes and rivers to wild, rocky uplands where the granite bones of the land break through the barren surface.

Anyone wanting to get the true feel of Brittany must know something of both Armor and Argoat, ideally in all parts of the region. Apart from the Côtes-d'Armor, Brittany has three other *départements*: Ille-et-Vilaine on the Normandy border, Finistère in the far west and Morbihan in the south and east. Until the reorganization of French local government in the 1960s, Brittany had a fifth *département*, Loire-Atlantique, with its capital at Nantes. This now forms part of the adjoining Pays de la Loire region.

Though all these *départements* share that indefinable quality one might call 'Breton-ness', each of them has its own distinct character. The eastern side of Brittany might be anywhere in North France, but as you head west the landscape gradually changes, becoming more hilly, windswept and typically Breton, until you reach the Pointe du Raz and the other ocean-battered headlands and there is nothing but ocean between you and North America.

This introduction will take a brief look at the *départements* in anti-clockwise order, beginning with Ille-et-Vilaine, the first taste of Brittany for most visitors arriving either by road or by sea, continuing with Côtes-d'Armor, Finistère and Morbihan, and ending just across the Brittany border with the unique fenland of the Grande Brière, now in Loire-Atlantique.

Ille-et-Vilaine

In the centre of Ille-et-Vilaine's short stretch of coast is the fortress-harbour of St-Malo, guarded by a fringe of reefs and rocky islets. Traditionally it has been the first sight of Brittany for anyone coming by sea, and it is still the ideal approach, especially in early morning when the grey shape of the little town, crowned by a tall spire, appears through the mist like a ship at anchor. St-Malo is the key both to the resorts of north-east Brittany, and to the inland riches of Ille-et-Vilaine.

Westward across the tidal barrage of the Rance is the sophisticated resort of Dinard, popular with the British since the 1850s, with outlying smaller holiday centres like St-Lunaire and St-Briac-sur-Mer. On its eastern side, St-Malo merges with the resorts of Paramé and Rothéneuf. Some 12 km farther, at the Pointe du Grouin, the coast turns abruptly south, protecting the muddy Baie du Mont-St-Michel. Famed for their quality, oysters grow to prodigious size in the rich alluvial silt here, lovingly tended by the oyster-growers of Cancale, and eaten equally lovingly by gourmets in the restaurants that line its little harbour.

A DISTANT VIEW OF MONT ST-MICHEL

The abbey of Mont-St-Michel, rising above the bay on its rocky island, is no longer in Brittany, though it used to be until the River Couesnon that separates Normandy from Brittany changed its course. Known simply as *La Merveille*, it is one of North Europe's architectural wonders, and no-one visiting this part of the world should fail to climb the hill that leads to its soaring Gothic grandeur.

Compared with the other *départements*, Ille-et-Vilaine is badly off for coastline; but it more than makes up for this by the riches that lie inland. Its name is derived from its two main rivers which meet at Rennes. From Dinan the Ille flows south, joining the Vilaine at Rennes; at this point the Vilaine meanders southwards, finally reaching the sea near the Golfe du Morbihan. Rennes is the capital both of the *département* and of Brittany as a whole, and though it is not the most exciting of French cities it does possess fine museums, art galleries and public gardens. Most of medieval Rennes was burnt down in a disastrous fire in 1720, and so the city centre is mainly in sober classical style. The outskirts, however, are thoroughly up-to-date with a flourishing university and expanding hi-tech industries.

In contrast to the stolid prosperity of Rennes are the medieval frontier towns of Fougères and Vitré, both dominated by mighty castles whose battlements and turrets still look strong enough to withstand a siege. Throughout the Middle Ages this part of the country formed a buffer zone between France and the Duchy of Brittany and was the scene of constant warfare, as the French monarchy struggled to win ascendancy over the fiercely independent Breton dukes. There are plenty of fine smaller towns as well, such as Dol with its strangely lopsided

cathedral, and Combourg, home of the great 18th-century writer Chateaubriand.

Apart from its towns and villages, Ille-et-Vilaine has more remote countryside than any other part of Brittany. It also has more remnants of the ancient Argoat forest, notably the Forêt de Rennes north-east of the city, and the Forêt de Paimpont on the extreme western edge of the *département*. Once part of the vast Forêt de Brocéliande, it is full of haunting memories from Brittany's remote and mythical past. Before the Romans came, the Druids had their 'university' among its groves of oak trees, where they underwent a twenty-year apprenticeship. And after the Romans left, Brocéliande was one of the legendary kingdoms of Arthur and the Knights of the Round Table, whose memory lives on today in many of the placenames, peopling the lakes and woodland around Paimpont with the ghosts of Lancelot, Guinevere, Merlin and King Arthur himself.

Côtes-d'Armor
As one would expect from its name, the Côtes-d'Armor has the most varied and fascinating coastline in the whole of Brittany. As you go from east to west this consists of the Côte d'Emeraude or Emerald Coast, the Baie de St-Brieuc, and the Côte de Granit Rose or Pink Granite Coast. The Côte d'Emeraude, which also includes St-Malo and Dinard, is full of little sandy coves, contrasting with sweeping beaches like those round Sables-d'Or-les-Pins and the fishing port of Erquy. The Baie de St-

Brieuc is a yachtsman's paradise, with small, sheltered pleasure-boat harbours and new marinas lining its western side from St-Brieuc up to the busy port of Paimpol.

Far more dramatic than either of these is the Côte de Granit Rose, Brittany's northernmost rock bastion. Along this rugged coastline, cut by the estuaries of the rivers Trieux and Jaudy, which reach far inland, are small bays fringed with shattered moon landscapes of rock, and offshore islands that are the home of thousands of gulls, cormorants and other sea birds. Around Perros-Guirec and Trégastel – the only resorts of any size in Côtes-d'Armor – are the pinkish-coloured rocks that have given the whole coast its name, eroded by countless centuries of wind and tide into extraordinary humanoid and animal shapes.

Inland, too, the Côtes-d'Armor is enormously varied. In its south-west corner, on the border with Finistère, are the wild and remote Montagnes Noires or Black Mountains. It has beauty spots too, like the Lac de Guerlédan, popular with windsurfers and other watersports enthusiasts, and the wilderness of giant tumbled boulders known as the Gorge de Toul-Goulic, where an underground river roars deep below. Large areas are almost without main roads, and have managed to preserve their rural remoteness.

The Côte-d'Armor's splendid old towns include Lamballe, which has one of the main stud farms of North France; Tréguier, whose cathedral spire is pierced with holes to lessen its resistance to the wind; and Dinan, whose streets of medieval half-timbered houses, dropping down to the banks of the Rance, make it the most picturesque medieval town in the whole of Brittany.

For centuries the Côtes-d'Armor was the borderland where the two halves of Brittany met – the *francisant* or French-speaking half to the east, and the *bretonnant* or Breton-speaking half to the west. Nowadays, when so few people speak Breton, the distinction has little meaning. Nevertheless, this *département* shares with Finistère the feeling of being Breton in the ancient way, far more so than Ille-et-Vilaine to the east or Morbihan to the south.

Finistère

In Finistère the qualities that go to make up 'Breton-ness' reach their culmination. Its Latin name, *Finis terrae*, means 'world's end' as does its Breton name, Pen ar Bed. Just as Cornwall in England feels quite different from the rest of the West Country, so Finistère feels quite different from the rest of Brittany. It even has its own 'Cornwall', the area known as Cornouaille, centring on the ancient capital of Quimper.

Much of Finistère's countryside is harsher and more windswept than the rest of Brittany. Its people seem more conscious too of their Breton heritage, with more Breton spoken and more traditional costumes worn by its elderly

POINTE DE PEN-HIR, FINISTERE

countrywomen. The buildings have evolved into forms suitable to the hard granite from which they were built, and the hard climate they have to withstand. Churches bristle with spiky pinnacles and crockets, while the older cottages that dot the uplands crouch low against winter storms sweeping in from the Atlantic.

On the map, Finistère is a highly irregular rectangle, cut into three separate peninsulas on its western side by the Rade de Brest and the Baie de Douarnenez. With the Atlantic on three of its four sides, its history has not surprisingly been largely shaped by the sea. The oldest coastal towns, such as Quimper and Morlaix, grew up on estuaries, at the first practicable place to build a bridge across the river, and became wealthy from sea-borne trade. Apart from the major centres, almost every creek has its small fishing harbour which fell into decay before being revived, to some degree during summer at least, by today's small-boat sailors.

In spite of its enormous length of coast, Finistère does not have many seaside resorts, except on its comparatively short southern side. Its long north-facing coast, the Côte des Abers et de Léon, has few resorts of any consequence apart from Carantec, half-way between Morlaix and Roscoff, and is very much a haven for away-from-it-all holidaymakers who are happy with rocks, sea and minimal tourist facilities. On Finistère's western coast, between the headlands of the Pointe de St Mathieu and the Pointe du Raz, has the sheltered presqu'île de Crozon or Crozon peninsula has the popular resort of Morgat, unusual for this part of Brittany in being south-facing.

If Finistère is the most Breton part of Brittany, then the Bigouden area round Pont-l'Abbé in its south-west corner is the part of Finistère that clings most tenaciously to the old Breton traditions of language and dress. From here proceeding east, the coast faces south and its curving beaches are thus a good deal sunnier and warmer than those farther north. Naturally the main seaside resorts of the *département* are clustered here – Bénodet, Beg-Meil and Fouesnant. Concarneau, with its medieval *Ville Close* or walled city surrounded by sea, and Pont-Aven, centre for Gauguin and a group of fellow painters in the late 19th century, and still very much an artists' village, are other lures that draw visitors to the southern coast of Finistère.

Inland is Brittany's only range of hills that remotely resemble mountains; the Monts d'Arrée, whose highest point is well under 400 m or 1,300 ft above sea-level. These immensely ancient hills are the eroded remains of the Armorican Massif which heaved up from the ocean-bed about 500 million years ago, and are thus ten times older than the Alps or Himalayas. They now form part of the Armorique Regional Nature Park, which also includes the offshore islands of Ouessant and Molène, part of the Crozon peninsula and the Aulne estuary.

Since the establishment of the park in 1968, inland Finistère has undergone a steady process of recovery after centuries of neglect and indifference. Regional craft centres and *écomusées* or ecological museums have been set up, where centuries-old rural skills can be studied, along with all aspects of the environment from minerals to wildlife. On the edge of the park the little town of Huelgoat, in an idyllic setting of lake, rock and woodland, is now a popular centre for holidays.

Finistère has made a unique contribution to European architecture in the form of the *enclos paroissiaux* or parish closes, of which the finest lie along the Elorn river, inland from Landerneau. These extraordinary complexes of church, triumphal arch, charnel house and carved calvary are often on such a scale as to dwarf the surrounding houses in the small villages in which they stand.

Morbihan

Unlike Finistère, the Morbihan is better known for its coastal region than for anything that lies inland. It takes its name from the most characteristic feature of this southern coast – the wide island-studded gulf, known to the Bretons as 'Mor-Bihan' or 'Little Sea', that brings a sub-tropical mildness to the villages round its edge and to the splendid city of Vannes, capital of the Morbihan, at its inner extremity. Its lagoon-like waters are ideal for beginners learning how to sail, and also for bird-watchers as it has one of the highest concentrations of sea birds along the whole Atlantic coast of France.

A single narrow channel from the Golfe du Morbihan leads out into the Baie de Quiberon, protected from the force of the Atlantic by the inward-curving finger of the Quiberon peninsula, some 15 km long and joined to the mainland by a narrow sandy isthmus. Its rocky western side, constantly pounded by the sea, is dangerous for swimmers, but its eastern side is far calmer, with long sandy beaches facing a bay that on fine summer days is alive with bright-sailed dinghies and skimming windsurfers.

Quiberon Bay is lined with the resorts of the Côte des Megalithes, so called from the giant stones placed around its fringes by Neolithic man. From about 3000 BC the local peoples chose this part of Brittany to bury their leaders in stone chambers mounded high with soil, and set up thousands of standing stones, either singly or in groups. Like the alignments at Carnac which have puzzled archeologists for more than 200 years, many of the stones are now embedded in modern holiday developments, but the contrast only serves to emphasize their atmosphere of time-worn mystery.

About 16 km in from the coast the rolling, gorse-covered heathland of the Landes de Lanvaux, one of the least populated parts of Brittany, forms a low ridge along the spine of the Morbihan. Inland again, the town of Pontivy, renamed briefly Napoléonville at the beginning of the 19th century, stands right at the centre of Brittany, at the hub of a network of canals once important commercially but now mainly given over to pleasure craft. Pontivy has an imposing medieval castle; but only 32 km away, at Josselin, is Brittany's best-preserved castle, as fine as any of the more famous châteaux along the banks of the Loire.

Just across the River Vilaine, in the north-western corner of Loire-Atlantique, is the extra-ordinary expanse of fenland, criss-crossed by canals and dotted with marshland villages, known as the Grande Brière. Covering about 7,000 ha or 17,500 acres, it forms part of a Regional Nature Park. Before the park was set up in 1970 the Brière had been in decline, suffering from depopulation, a progressive neglect of its watercourses and buildings, and a loss of traditional fishing and boating skills. Over the past twenty years, however, the Brière, like the Monts d'Arrée in Finistère, has begun to recover, largely due to the boom in tourism. Derelict cottages have been renovated, small museums have been opened with active craftsmen taking part, and visitors can explore the quiet waterways in *chalands* or flat-bottomed punts, enjoying the scenery and wildlife of this peaceful backwater.

THE GRANDE BRIERE

BRITTANY'S ISLANDS

A fragile necklace in the ocean

The string of islands which fringe the Brittany coastline are known as the Iles du Ponant. A unique group in Europe, these twelve islands can all be visited and, since the majority forbid cars, they are best discovered on foot or by bicycle, and ideally off-season.

Listed below as they would be encountered on a north to south journey around the coast, they vary from the tiny and minimally populated, perfect for those seeking solitude, to those which attract ferryloads of summer holidaymakers for their attractive landscapes and lively resort atmosphere.

A variety of accommodation possibilities are offered, and details can be obtained by contacting the Office de Tourisme usually at the mainland port serving the island or on the island itself. The maritime heritage of these island people means that the restaurants are able to offer seafood dishes of incomparable freshness.

BREHAT
6 km north-east
of Paimpol
Pop 450
🛈 Mairie
☎ 96.20.00.36
🛈 ☎ 96.20.04.15
in season

Access *Several times a day from Pointe de l'Arcouest, near Paimpol (10 mins) all year*
A pretty flowery island (or rather two little ones joined by a narrow causeway), there is an almost Mediterranean air to the south while the north is wilder and more reminiscent of Ireland. With no cars allowed on the island, it is ideal for a pleasant walk or cycle tour.
Leisure
Cycling Cycles for hire from Mme Dalibot, le Port-Clos
☎ *96.20.03.51*
Sailing Ecole de Voile 'Les Albatros'
☎ *96.20.00.95*

Hotels
Hôtel le Bellevue **
le Port-Clos
☎ *96.20.00.05*
Hôtel la Vieille Auberge **
☎ *96.20.00.24*
Camping
Municipal de Goareva **
☎ *96.20.00.36*
open all year
Restaurants
Le Chardon Bleu
le Bourg
☎ *96.20.00.08*
Ti Jeannette (crêperie)
route du Bourg
☎ *96.20.00.53*

BATZ
1,5 km off the
coast opposite
Roscoff
Pop 750
🛈 ☎ 98.61.77.76

Access *Several times a day from the port at Roscoff (15 mins) all year*
Small island 4 km long by 1 km wide, the islanders earn a living from market gardening, fishing and the collection of wrack. Pronounced 'Ba', the island is lonely and windswept with some little sandy beaches and wonderful coast walks. The Jardin Colonial is a haven for exotic plants flourishing in the warmth of the Gulf Stream.
Leisure
Cycling Cycles can be hired from Mme Moncus, le Bourg ☎ *98.61.78.92*
Lighthouse The Phare Ile de Batz can be visited by making contact with the keeper.
Watersports In association with the Auberge de Jeunesse Internationale Maritime ☎ *98.61.77.69, sailing, windsurfing and diving tuition Apr-Oct.*

Hotels
Grand Hôtel Morvan
Pors-Kernoc
☎ *98.61.78.06*
Hôtel Roch Ar Mor
la Débarcadère
☎ *98.61.78.28*
Camping
Terrain Municipal
☎ *98.61.77.76 (la Mairie)*
50 places
Restaurants
Restaurant du Port
Pors-Kernoc
☎ *98.61.76.69*
Ti Yann
☎ *98.61.78.66*
On the eastern point of the island

OUESSANT
20 km off the
westernmost point
of Brittany
Pop 1,200
🛈 ☎ 98.80.24.68

Access *Daily ferry service from Brest via Le Conquet (1hr 30 mins) all year; also daily by air with Compagnie Finist'Air from Brest-Guipavas airport* ☎ *98.84.64.87 (15 mins), reservations required*
This remote island, known in English as Ushant, is the ideal place for those seeking solitude, with spacious, wild and beautiful scenery to discover by cycle or on horseback. The islanders – *les Ouessantins* – live chiefly off the sea. Together with the neighbouring islands of

Hotels
Hôtel le Fromveur
Lampaul
☎ *98.48.81.30*
(and restaurant)
Hôtel l'Océan
Lampaul
☎ *98.48.80.03*
(and restaurant)
Hôtel Roch Ar Mor
Lampaul
☎ *98.48.80.19*

Molène and Sein, the island forms part of the Parc Régional d'Armorique. The Centre for Ornithological Research and Island Study is situated here and welcomes students of birds and nature, and the harbour has berths for 25 pleasure boats.

Leisure

Cycling Cycles and mountain bikes for hire from M. Malgorn, place de l'Eglise
☎ 98.48.83.44

Lighthouses Four lighthouses can be visited: La Jument, Kéréon, Le Créac'h and La Stiff and enquiries should be made at the Tourist Office. At the Phare du Créac'h there is a museum devoted to the history of the lighthouse.

Museum Charming reconstructions of typical island homes from over a century ago at the Ecomusée du Niou Huella
☎ 98.48.86.37

Nature Study Centre d'Etude du Milieu (Centre Ornithologique)
☎ 98.48.82.65 welcomes naturalists (groups and individuals) to its study centre here (with accommodation).

Riding Ty Crenn Equitation, Stang ar Glann
☎ 98.48.83.58

Taxis A taxi service connecting aerodrome with town is offered by M. Etienne, Ouessant Presse, Lampaul
☎ 98.48.84.90

MOLENE
Between Pointe Saint Mathieu and the isle of Ouessant
Pop 300
🛈☎ 98.80.24.68

Access Daily service from Brest via le Conquet (1hr 30 mins) except Tues off-season

This flat little island 1.2 km long by 800 m wide belongs to an archipelago of some dozen tiny islets and reefs. With little more than a small collection of houses around the port, the inhabitants earn a living from fishing and the collection of seaweed. A display of objects washed up after the numerous shipwrecks off the coast is housed in the old presbytery.

Camping
Municipal Pen Ar Bed ✶✶
☎ 98.48.84.65 (la Mairie)
120 places

LE CREAC'H, OUESSANT

Hotel
Hôtel Kastell An Daol ✶✶
☎ 98.07.39.11 (and restaurant)
Camping
Municipal
☎ 98.80.24.68 (la Mairie)
40 places
Restaurant
L'Archipel
le Quai
☎ 98.07.38.56

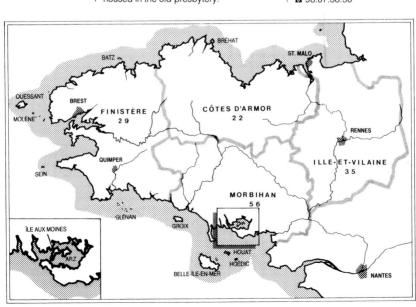

SEIN
8 km off the Pointe
du Raz
Pop 500
▪ Audierne
☎ 98.70.02.38

Access Daily service from Audierne
except Wed off-season
Flat island shaped like a jigsaw puzzle
piece, 2 km long by 800 m or at some
points only 50 m wide; the few islanders
are principally fishermen. A Druid burial
site chosen no doubt for its remoteness,
the island is rocky, windswept and
treeless. In June 1940 the entire male
population answered de Gaulle's call and
left for England to join the Free French
there and continue the fight against
Germany. Many never returned and there
is a monument to the memory of these
patriots, the *Senans Libres*. The small
harbour has berths for 60 craft.

Leisure
Lighthouse The Phare de Sein lighthouse
can be visited by making contact with the
keeper.

Hotel
Hôtel les Trois Dauphins
☎ 98.70.92.09
(and restaurant)
Camping
Municipal
☎ 98.70.90.35 (la Mairie)
Restaurants
Chez Brigitte
quai des Paimpolais
☎ 98.70.91.83
L'Hippocampe
quai des Français Libres
☎ 98.70.91.87
L'Iroise
rue Abbé le Borne
☎ 98.70.90.12
Chez Mamie (crêperie)
rue d'Estienne d'Orves
☎ 98.70.90.19

ARCHIPEL DES GLENAN
18 km south of
Concarneau
▪ Fouesnant
☎ 98.56.00.93
and Concarneau
☎ 98.97.01.44

Access Regular seasonal services only
from Concarneau, Fouesnant, Bénodet
and Loctudy
The archipelago consists of eight tiny
islands, a dozen islets and numerous
outlying rocks which render navigation
hazardous but also provide a popular
challenge for those learning sailing skills.
The islands are uninhabited for most of
the year but are noted for their deep-sea
diving school activities. There is no
campsite or other accommodation
available for anyone other than those
attending such courses.

Leisure
Diving Centre Internationale de Plongée
des Glénans ☎ 98.97.21.19
Watersports Centre Nautique des
Glénans, quai Louis Blériot, 75781 Paris,
☎ (1)45.20.01.40 arranges sailing,
windsurfing and catamaran courses.

ILE DE GLENAN

Hotels
Hôtel de la Marine **
rue du Général de Gaulle
☎ 97.05.80.05
(and restaurant)
Hôtel Ty Mad **
Port-Tudy
☎ 97.05.80.19
(and restaurant)
Camping
Les Sables Rouges ***
☎ 97.05.81.32
125 places 3 Jun–10 Sep
Municipal **
Fort du Méné
☎ 97.86.80.15 (la Mairie)
Youth Hostel
Le Méné
☎ 97.05.81.38
1 Jul–30 Sep
Restaurants
Chez Paul (crêperie)
rue de Port Melite
☎ 97.86.89.72
Les Courreaux
avenue du Général de Gaulle
☎ 97.86.82.66

GROIX
7 km distant from
Lorient harbour
Pop 2,500
▪ Mairie
☎ 97.86.80.15

Access From the port at Lorient (45 mins)
A larger island 8 km long by 3 km wide,
edged by magnificent cliffs which plunge
into the sea and shelter lovely little
beaches, the finest being that of Grands
Sables. At the beginning of the century
Groix was France's chief tuna fishing port
and the majority of today's inhabitants –
les Groisillons – continue to live
principally from the sea. The centre of the
island is farming land with several small
villages where traditional rural life is still
continued. Rich too in megaliths, the
island is popular with day visitors.

Leisure
Car Hire Also taxi service, available from
M Gattefosse, le café du port, Port-Tudy
☎ 97.86.81.57
Cycling Cycles for hire from Loca-Loisirs,
quai de Port-Tudy ☎ 97.86.80.03
Fishing 4 hour sea-fishing trips with
Navette et Taxi Groisillons, résidence des
Grenats ☎ 97.86.54.44
Museum The Ecomusée de l'Ile de Groix,
Port-Tudy retraces the island's history
☎ 97.86.84.60
Riding Centre Equestre du Haut Grognon,,

LOW TIDE ON THE ISLAND OF SEIN

Quelhuit ☎ 97.86.81.34
Sailing Club Nautique de Groix, route des Plages ☎ 97.86.82.84

ARZ
Situated in the middle of the Golfe du Morbihan with its neighbour the Ile aux Moines
Pop 250
🅗 Vannes
☎ 97.47.24.34
🅗 Mairie
☎ 97.44.31.14

Access Daily services from Conleau, near Vannes (15 mins), all year
The island stretches for 3.5 km and was clearly at one time joined to its neighbour the Ile aux Moines. Essentially a quiet agricultural island, it concentrates on cattle rearing but is also popular with sailing enthusiasts who use the year-round school based here.
Leisure
Cycling Cycles for hire from M Guillot ☎ 97.44.31.83. Also taxi service.
Sailing Centre Nautique des Glénans ☎ 97.44.31.16 runs sailing and catamaran courses throughout the year, bookable through the Paris office, quai Louis Blériot, 75781 Paris ☎ (1)45.20.01.40

ILE AUX MOINES
In the middle of the Golfe du Morbihan
Pop 600
🅗 Vannes
☎ 97.47.24.34
🅗☎ 97.26.32.45

Access Daily services from Port-Blanc, Baden (5 mins), all year; and from Vannes, Port-Navalo and Locmariaquer in season
Known as the 'Perle du Golfe', this island has a varied and attractive landscape. The islanders have traditionally lived from the sea and from rearing oysters, but now as its popularity as a resort increases, tourism is a major source of income. There is a permanent Jeunesse et Marine school which introduces youngsters to the sea and its related activities. The Phare de l'Ile aux Moines-en-Sept Iles is open to visitors in summer.
Leisure
Cycling Cycles for hire from M. Labousse, Restaurant le Cap Horn ☎ 97.26.31.12
Sailing The Jeunesse et Marine sailing school takes reservations through its Paris office ☎ (1)45.48.43.70

Le Thonier
rue du Général de Gaulle
☎ 97.86.54.54

Hotel
Hôtel l'Escale ✳
☎ 97.44.32.15
(sea view and restaurant)
Camping
Municipal les Tamaris✳✳
☎ 97.44.30.35 (la Mairie)
70 places 1 Jun-30 Sep

Hotels
Hôtel San Francisco
le Port
☎ 97.26.31.52
Hôtel des Iles
rue du Commerce
☎ 97.26.32.50
(and restaurant)
Camping
Municipal Le Vieux Moulin ✳✳
☎ 97.26.32.61
44 places 15 Jun-15 Sep

HOUAT
Off the Quiberon
peninsula
Pop 400
🛈 Quiberon
☎ 97.50.07.84

Access Daily service from Quiberon (1hr), all year and from Vannes, La Trinité-sur-Mer, Port-Navalo, La Turballe and Le Croisic in season. Out of season it is advisable to check on availability of return trips for the same day!

Pretty sandy beaches and coves and the white-washed houses of the fishing village of Port St-Gildas attract the visitor to this sunny little island. Its southerly coast, a protected dune area, is rich in flora.

Hotel
Hôtel des Iles *
☎ 97.30.68.02
Camping
Municipal
☎ 97.30.68.04 (la Mairie)
Restaurant
Le Vieux Port
route du Vieux Port
☎ 97.30.68.94

HOEDIC
Off the Quiberon
peninsula
Pop 126
🛈 Quiberon
☎ 97.50.07.84
🛈 Mairie
☎ 97.30.68.32

Access Daily services from Quiberon (1hr 30 mins), all year, and additionally from La Turballe and Le Croisic in season. Out of season it is advisable to check on availablity of return trips for the same day!

Surrounded by smaller islets and reefs, this is a low-lying island 2.5 km long by 1 km wide lying at the extreme point of a chain clearly joined at one time to the Quiberon peninsula. Good opportunities for fishing exist, the area being particularly rich in mullet and bass. Fishing and pleasure harbour at Port d'Argol.

Hotel
Hôtel les Cardinaux
☎ 97.52.37.27
(and restaurant)
Camping
Municipal
☎ 97.30.68.32 (la Mairie)
150 places May-Sep

BELLE-ILE-EN-MER
15 km off the
Quiberon
peninsula
Pop 4,200
🛈 quai Bonnelle,
Le Palais
☎ 97.31.81.93

Access Regular services from Quiberon (45 mins), all year. Also from Port-Navalo, La Trinité-sur-Mer, Pornichet, La Turballe and Le Croisic in season. Car transport must be pre-booked: Compagnie Morbihannaise de Navigation ☎ 97.31.80.01. Flights also operate from Quiberon and Lorient.

This is the largest of Brittany's offshore islands, 17 km long by 9 km wide, where fishing, farming and tourism are the chief sources of income. There are four main towns: Le Palais with fishing and pleasure harbour protected by Vauban citadelle and extensive views from Taillefer and Ramonette Heads; Sauzon with hillside houses rising from fishing and pleasure harbour; Bangor and Locmaria.

The island has traditionally been popular with artists and writers as a working retreat. Dumas, Flaubert, Proust and

Hotels
Castel Clara ****
Goulphar, Bangor
☎ 97.31.84.21 (sea view and restaurant)
Le Cardinal ***
Sauzon
☎ 97.31.61.60 (sea view and restaurant)
Le Manoir ***
Goulphar
☎ 97.31.80.10 (sea view and restaurant)
L'Atlantique ***
quai de l'Acadie
Le Palais
☎ 97.31.80.11 (sea view)
Hôtel la Désirade ***
route de Goulphar
☎ 97.31.70.70
Le Bretagne **

THE TOWN OF SAUZON
ON BELLE-ILE-EN-MER

WINDSURFERS OFF ILE DE BATZ

Colette; Matisse, Derain and Monet all stayed here at times, and for a period it was home to Sarah Bernhardt who owned a fort here. A variety of landscapes make this an attractive island with a new 18-hole golf course (the second hole having an exceptional water hazard!), 'thalassotherapy' centre, tennis courts, cycling routes, riding and sailing among the sporting activities offered.

Leisure

Adventure sports Sea-kayaking and mountain biking offered by Vitamine Oxygène, Mairie de Locmaria ☎ 97.31.70.92

Car Hire Cars can be hired from Locatourisle, quai Bonnelle, Le Palais ☎ 97.31.83.56

Cycling Cycles for hire from Cyclotour, 3 quai Bonnelle, Le Palais ☎ 97.31.80.68

Golf 18-hole public course at Golf de Sauzon, 56360 Belle-Ile-en-Mer ☎ 97.31.64.65

Lighthouse Phare de Belle-Ile at Bangor can be visited. This is the most powerful in all France open Easter-Sep.

Riding Centre Equestre La Licorne, Lande de Borgroix, Sauzon ☎ 97.31.71.89

Sailing Bleu-Océan, avenue de Carnot, Le Palais ☎ 97.31.89.11 has hire and tuition facilities as does Guédel Nautisme, Bordardoué, Le Palais ☎ 97.31.52.06 and Yachting Club de Belle-Ile, quai Bonnelle, Le Palais ☎ 97.31.55.85

Thalassotherapy Castel-Thalassa, Institut de Thalassothérapie, Port-Goulphar, Bangor ☎ 97.31.80.15

Le Palais
☎ 97.31.80.14 (sea view and restaurant)
Hôtel les Tamaris **
Sauzon
☎ 97.31.65.09
Camping
Bordeneo ***
Le Palais
☎ 97.31.88.96
165 places 1 Jun-20 Sep
Les Glacis **
le Port, Le Palais
☎ 97.31.41.76
100 places 1 Apr-15 Oct
Municipal Pen Prad **
Sauzon
☎ 97.31.64.82
100 places 1 Apr-30 Sep
Lannivrec **
Locmaria
☎ 97.31.70.92
135 places 15 Jun-15 Sep
Municipal Bangor **
Bangor
☎ 97.31.84.06
60 places 1 Jun-30 Sep
Youth Hostel
Haute Boulogne
Le Palais
☎ 97.31.81.33
open all year
Restaurants
Le Goéland
quai Vauban
Le Palais
☎ 97.31.81.26
La Saline
route du Phare
Le Palais
☎ 97.31.84.70
Le Contre-Quai
rue Saint-Nicholas
Sauzon
☎ 97.31.60.60
L'Escale
Pen Prad
☎ 97.31.62.70
Relais de la Roche Percée
l'Apothicairerie
Sauzon
☎ 97.31.62.14
La Forge
le Petit Cosquet
Bangor
☎ 97.31.51.76

ISLAND BREAKS
Cath Voyages, 11 rue Saint-Guénaël, BP47, 56002 Vannes ☎ 97.42.51.82 specialize in island breaks and offer return boat trip, half-board accommodation in a ** hotel on the island of Bréhat and cycle hire package. They also offer a weekend's hunting on the isle of Ouessant with flight, *** hotel accommodation and accompanied shoot. On the isle of Groix, they offer return boat trip, half-board accommodation in a ** hotel and oilskins and boots for fishing outings. Belle-Ile is also offered in various packages with or without car hire.

ARCHITECTURE

Like antique furniture, seldom dusted

Anyone who wanders through the centre of Brittany's larger cities such as Quimper or Vannes, or who explores smaller towns like Tréguier or Dinan, Roscoff or Dol, is bound to be struck by the extent to which the past lives on in their buildings. More than a century ago an English writer described Brittany as the west wing of an old country house, whose 'furniture is antique, and has seldom been dusted or put in order'; and in spite of the modern suburbs that have grown up around its historic towns and the traffic which clogs many of them throughout the summer, this impression of antiquity is as powerful today as it was in the 19th century.

Brittany is more remarkable for its concentrations of fine old buildings than it is for any individual cathedral, church or castle. Dinan, on the Rance some 30 km or 20 miles inland from the Emerald Coast, is typical of them all. With its narrow medieval streets and gateways, tree-shaded public gardens, ramparts, towers and churches, it fully deserves its popularity as one of the most visited towns in Brittany. Equally popular, though in complete contrast, is the seaport town of St-Malo. Its massive granite walls, encircling streets of tall houses built by shipowners and corsairs grown rich from trade and plunder, make an ideal rampart walk.

Half-timbering in Dinan and granite in St-Malo – these building materials sum up the traditional architecture of Brittany. The sombre grey stone from which Breton towns are built gives them an overall impression of dourness; but old timber-framed buildings often have their own decoration, in the form of beam-ends carved with animal or human figures.

No fewer than seventeen Breton towns have banded together in a group that calls itself *Petites Cités de Caractère* or 'Little Cities of Character'. Scattered over the countryside, they share a combination of small size, under 3,000 inhabitants, picturesque sites and places of historical interest. Among them are two with splendid châteaux open to the public, Josselin

A TRADITIONAL HALF-TIMBERED HOUSE IN RENNES

and Combourg; the hill fortress of Moncontour; and Tréguier, a medieval gem. Locronan, another *petite cité*, is very much on the popular holiday circuit. A virtually complete Renaissance town, its granite houses, built by merchants in the 16th and 17th centuries, have been painstakingly restored and turned into craftsmen's workshops and sale rooms.

Tréguier is the local capital of the northern corner of Brittany once known as Trégor, and its tall-spired cathedral, built mainly in the 13th to 15th centuries, is grand enough for any regional capital. Other notable medieval churches in Brittany are the twin-spired cathedral at Quimper, the extraordinary basilica at Guingamp, divided equally between the Gothic and Renaissance styles, and Redon's basilica whose low arcaded tower, built in the 12th century in a mixture of grey granite and dark red sandstone, is one of Brittany's few examples of Romanesque architecture. Redon's basilica has a free-standing Gothic bell nearby, as does the former cathedral in the market town of St-Pol-de-Léon, south of Roscoff. Known as the Kreisker, St-Pol's splendid spire rises to a height of 78 m or 250 ft.

Mont-St-Michel, standing high on a rocky outcrop and reached via a causeway, was built mainly between the 13th and 16th centuries, and in the full flowering of the Gothic style. Its finest architectural ensemble is built on three levels with the Abbey church itself, built on the summit of the rock, with its Romanesque nave and transepts, Flamboyant Gothic choir and spire, and rather incongruous 18th-century west façade, towering above the whole.

Brittany has no other abbeys to compare with Mont-St-Michel, though it has a handful of impressive monastic ruins. Best of them is Beauport, surrounded by trees near the coast south of Paimpol. The ruins of St-Guénolé, outside Landévennec, stand on a picturesque peninsula looking across the estuary of the Aulne; while Bon-Repos, near the Lac de Guerlédan, is a remote and peaceful spot.

As with Brittany's abbeys, so with its castles. Throughout the centuries of castle-building Brittany was poor in comparison with the rest of France. As a result, few of its many castles, apart from Josselin, headquarters of the powerful Rohan family, can be mentioned in the same breath as the great châteaux found elsewhere; the castle of the Dukes of Brittany in Nantes, the centre of Breton feudal power throughout the Middle Ages, is equally fine, but no longer officially in Brittany. Most warlike of them all is the imposing castle of Fougères, on the Normandy/Brittany border, whose magnificent outer wall has no fewer than thirteen towers round its circuit.

Elsewhere there are plenty of lesser castles, many of them well maintained and often housing small museums. For the drama of its situation, few castles in Europe can match Fort La Latte, built high above the sea on the cliffs of

THE PARISH CLOSE AT GUIMILIAU

Cap Fréhel. Among those castles still in good condition, or partially restored, are Kerjean, in remote countryside south-west of Roscoff; Tonquédec, in wooded country south of Lannion; and Suscinio, near the Gulf of Morbihan. The harbours of St-Malo, Brest and Camaret are guarded by fortified towers; and there are powerful 17th-century fortifications too at Port-Louis, headquarters of the merchants of the Compagnie des Indes.

Brittany is far better supplied with small manor houses, often fortified, than it is with major castles. Among the most attractive of them is is the toylike château of Bienassis, just inland from the Côte d'Emeraude. Other châteaux, such as La Bourbonsais and Caradeuc, between Rennes and St-Malo, are typical of the modest prosperity of Brittany in the 17th and 18th centuries.

Far and away the most characteristic buildings of the whole of Brittany are its numerous small churches and chapels. Dedicated to one or more of Brittany's thousands of saints, they recall a vanished world of deep religious faith given visual reality by armies of long-forgotten builders, stonemasons, carpenters and artists in paint and glass. From simple beginnings, the chapels reached the height of complexity in the 15th and 16th centuries during the Flamboyant Gothic period. In Brittany the Gothic style lingered on long after it had died out in most of the rest of Europe.

Among the finest of them is the church at Les Iffs, half-way between St-Malo and Rennes, which has nine superb windows of Breton-made stained glass. At Kernascléden, in the heart of the Morbihan, the church has delicate stone tracery while its interior walls are covered in 15th-century fresco paintings, which include scenes from the life of Christ and a sinister Dance of Death. Among smaller chapels worth searching out are Notre-Dame-du-Haut, outside the little medieval town of Moncontour, which contains statues of seven saints connected with healing; the chapel of St-Gonéry with its twisted spire in the far north beyond Tréguier; and Notre-Dame-de-la-Joie, standing above the waves near Penmarc'h at the south-easternmost point of Finistère. Outside all these churches and chapels, at crossroads and on roadsides, you will see the stone *calvaires* or wayside

calvaries, ranging from simple crosses to elaborate crucifixion scenes. These reach their height in the huge calvaries of Finistère, where realistic depictions of the Passion rise high above carvings of episodes in the life of Christ. Unique to Brittany – and indeed to the whole of Europe – are the *enclos paroissiaux* or parish closes, consisting of the church and calvary, reached through a triumphal arch and flanked by an ossuary or charnel house.

The finest closes lie along and around the River Elorn and were built mainly in the 16th and 17th centuries by farmers and merchants rich from trading in flax, but who ploughed back their profits into these extraordinary religious complexes. Three of the main ones, signposted for motorists as the *Circuit des Trois Enclos,* form an easily visited group about 32 km south of Roscoff. They are just as accessible to walkers too, lying as they do on the long-distance footpath, the GR380.

Guimiliau, the central close of the three, has the finest of the calvaries, carved in the 16th century with over 200 figures taken from the Bible and Breton legend. Among them is Brittany's classic 'Scarlet Woman', Katell-Gollet or Catherine the Damned, shown being driven into the gaping mouth of hell. The church at Lampaul-Guimiliau contains many brightly coloured carvings of saints, and its rood-beam is carved with a painted frieze depicting the Passion. St-Thégonnec's close is the largest and latest in date, with an enormous triumphal arch, an ossuary built in the 1670s in classical style and an interior with richly carved pulpit and altar.

There are other notable closes at Sizun and at Pleyben, the grandest of them all. One of the most elaborate of all the calvaries is in the village of Plougastel-Daoulas outside Brest, though it does not form part of a parish close.

Equally unique to Brittany are the religious complexes that grew up in the 19th century to hold the vast congregations attending the annual *pardons*, or religious festivals. The largest is at Ste-Anne-d'Auray, in the Morbihan. Dedicated to Ste-Anne, mother of the Virgin Mary and patron saint of the whole of Brittany, it has a gigantic basilica, a huge open space where crowds can gather, and a memorial to the 250,000 Bretons killed in World War I.

HISTORY AND CULTURE

Land of enchantment and independence

Just as Brittany is distinct from the rest of France geographically, so it is in its history, language and every aspect of its culture, from religious gatherings, folk festivals, music and dance, to clothes and household furniture. Its similarity of name to that of its close sea neighbour is most striking however. First known as 'Petite' Bretagne, Brittany's name echoes that of Great Britain or 'Grande' Bretagne, revealing a shared Celtic ancestry parallelled in this as in other features.

Like the rest of western Europe, for tens of thousands of years Brittany was sporadically inhabited by wandering tribes of hunter-gatherers, whose flint weapons can be seen in archeological collections in the museums at Carnac, Vannes and elsewhere. But the first substantial remains of prehistoric man are far later, dating from around 2000 BC. Hundreds of standing stones are scattered across the country, isolated in open fields, half-buried in woodland or engulfed in the housing of today. Most awe-inspiring of all are the vast *alignements* at Carnac, striding across the heathland like an army of stone soldiers.

Stones and Saints

These prehistoric remains fall into two main types: menhirs, or single standing stones – from the Breton *men*, stone and *hir*, long, and dolmens, consisting of uprights with one or more horizontals laid across them – from *dol*, table, and *men*, stone. Dolmens are the remains of burial chambers, originally covered with high mounds of earth to form tumuli, and used as tombs for leaders.

The ten or eleven alignments at Carnac are a colossal concentration of several thousand menhirs, not particularly large individually – there are far bigger ones elsewhere – but staggering by their sheer number. Archeologists have argued for generations about who the megalith-builders were, and why they hauled all these tons of stone across the countryside and laid them out in this particular way. Though the facts will probably never be known, it is now generally thought that they were a caste of priest-kings, who constructed their stone lines as observatories linked to the movement of the sun, moon and stars.

As well as the menhirs, the coastal region round Carnac is full of dolmens, some impressively large, others little more than three stones precariously balanced. Among the finest of them is the so-called *Table des Marchands* or Merchants' Table at Locmariaquer, which has a huge capstone 6 m long by 4 m wide. Across in Ille-et-Vilaine, south-east of Rennes, the *Roche-aux-Fées* or Fairies' Rock is one of the most important megalithic monuments in the whole of France, consisting of an *allée couverte* or covered way built with over forty giant blocks of stone, some weighing over forty tons each.

The megalith-builders will always remain a mystery, but by about the 6th century BC Brittany had emerged on to the fringes of known European history. At this time the Gauls arrived in the Breton peninsula, speaking a Celtic language not far removed from the Breton of today, and, as previously described, calling the coast and hinterland of their new country respectively Armor and Argoat. Their

THE MENHIRS AT CARNAC

main tribes have left their traces in the place-names of today – the Redones in Redon, the Veneti in Vannes, the Curiosolites in Corseul.

The first precise year in Breton history is 56 BC, when the Romans under Julius Caesar won a decisive victory over the fleet of the Veneti. The battle took place in Quiberon Bay, off the Pointe de Kerpenhir, and Caesar is said to have watched it from a mound near Port-Navalo, still known as the Butte de César. From the point of view of later Roman emperors, Gallia Armorica, as the Romans called Brittany, was a remote and impoverished province, and few traces remain of their four centuries of occupation. Brittany's best-preserved Gallo-Roman remains are the walls of the so-called Temple de Mars outside Corseul in the Côtes-d'Armor, probably built at the end of the first century AD.

After the gradual disintegration of the Roman Empire from the 3rd century on, Brittany relapsed into a state of near chaos, continually harried by Norse sea-raiders. During this period of turmoil the first Christian missionaries arrived in the country, along with Celtic refugees from Wales and Cornwall, driven out by invading Angles and Saxons. They ousted the established Druid priesthood, and brought with them their own Celtic church organization, which was a loose federation of monastic settlements and their offshoots, quite different from the rigid territorial divisions of the Roman Catholic church which operated in the rest of France.

Hundreds of surviving Breton placenames date from this early Christian period. Towns and villages with *Lan-* or *Lam-* as their first syllable – Lambader and Landivisiau, for example – were originally monastic settlements, while the prefix *Plou-*, as in Ploumanac'h and Plouezoc'h, means 'parish'. Virtually every early religious leader, however minor, was later revered as a saint, which accounts for Brittany's record number of saints – reputedly 7,847. This odd-looking number is in fact the sum total of seven thousand, seven hundred, seven score (140) and seven. Supreme among them were the *Sept Saints Fondateurs* or 'Seven Founding Saints', among whom SS Malo, Maclou in Breton, and Brieuc (Brioc) are perpetuated in the names of leading Breton towns.

The golden age of the Duchy
Far more shadowy than the army of saints are the figures of King Arthur and his knights, whose legends date from much the same period. Arthur, Guinevere, Merlin and Lancelot haunt the remnants of the ancient and excep-tionally beautiful forest of Brocéliande and live on in Breton placenames, many of them round the little town of Paimpont in the heart of Brittany. Among them the Pont du Secret, where Guinevere confessed her love for Lancelot, and the Forteresse de Merlin, Merlin's Castle which is said to lie hidden below the placid surface of a nearby lake. Traces of the legendary love affair that inspired Wagner's *Tristan and Isolde* linger on round Douarnenez, where the little off-shore Ile Tristan is named after the hero of the story, while King Mark, Isolde's husband, is said to have had a palace in the town.

For several centuries after the departure of the Romans, Brittany was ruled by a succes-sion of squabbling warlords. It emerged from the Dark Ages in the 9th century – to be precise, in 845, when Nominoë, a Breton nobleman, defeated the Frankish army of Charles the Bald and declared Brittany an independent kingdom. The monarchy lasted little more than sixty years, brought to an end by Norman invasions in the early 10th century. Then, in 937, Alain Barbe-Torte 'Alan of the Curly Beard', grandson of the last Breton king, Alain the Great, defeated the Normans outside Nantes. Making Nantes his capital, he estab-lished the Duchy of Brittany, which lasted for almost 600 years.

During the period of the Duchy, Brittany played a major role among the warring states of western Europe, and reached the height of its cultural and architectural splendour, with castles like the ducal château at Nantes and the frontier fortresses of Fougères and Vitré, the cathedrals at Quimper and Vannes, and the first of the great parish closes. Though the dukes wielded nothing like the power of the neighbouring rulers of France and England, the most successful of them played one of these two 'super powers' off against the other with political shrewdness and diplomatic skill.

The golden age of the Duchy came towards its end during the 15th century, when Brittany was ruled by successive dukes of the Montfort family. The last of them, François II, began his reign peacefully enough, but later on made the mistake of engaging in a full-scale battle with the French army. The battle, which took place in 1488 at Aubin-du-Cormier, east of Rennes, ended in an overwhelming defeat for the Bretons. François died soon aftrwards, leaving the Duchy to his eleven-year-old daughter Anne – the famous Duchess Anne, commemorated in street and restaurant names all over Brittany. Besides being the last ruler of an independent Brittany, Anne was married to two French kings; but she left no sons to carry on the ducal line. Her daughter Claude married the French king, François I, and in 1532 the Breton parliament handed over the Duchy's autonomy to France. Six centuries of hard-won independence had finally come to an end.

All the same, Brittany kept a certain amount of self-determination right up to the French Revolution. It had its own parliament, the *Etats* or States of Brittany, which met periodically until 1788 to decide on local administrative matters. Though the Bretons looked back nostalgically to the days of an independent Duchy, they settled down, more or less, under France's centralizing control, apart from an anti-taxation revolt in 1675. Known as the '*Révolte du Papier Timbré*', from the stamped paper on which official documents were written, it was savagely suppressed by the troops of Louis XIV.

During the 1790s, some Bretons joined the Chouans – pro-royalist and anti-revolutionary forces, allied with the English. However, after being defeated by General Hoche on the Quiberon peninsula, the Chouans surrendered. Many of them were shot in a field outside Auray, known today as the Champ des Martyrs.

After the Revolution, Brittany, along with the

TRADITIONAL BRETON COSTUMES

rest of France, was reorganized into today's *départements*. Throughout the 19th century it stagnated as just another poor agricultural province on the outer perimeter of France. In the interests of standardization, the Breton language was discouraged in schools, though it was kept alive by enthusiasts such as Hersart de la Villemarqué, who in 1838 published the *Barzaz-Breiz*, a large collection of Breton ballad-poems. Among Breton-born writers who wrote in French the most influential were François-René de Chateaubriand (1768-1848), the high-priest of Romanticism, who wrote a classic autobiography *Mémoires d'Outre-Tombe*, and Ernest Renan (1823-92), the philosopher and free-thinker whose *Life of Jesus* scandalized the orthodox Roman Catholicism of his day.

During the First World War a quarter of a million Bretons were killed – an enormous loss of life for so small a region; and during the Second World War Breton Resistance fighters were some of the most dedicated and effective in the whole of France. Relics of the last war can be found all round the coast in the form of massive concrete gun emplacements and defence works, the 'Atlantic wall', built by German-controlled slave labour. A number of Breton towns, notably St-Malo, St-Nazaire, Lorient and Brest, were severely damaged towards the end of the war as the Germans fought savage rearguard actions against the allied armies of liberation.

A nation's revival

The latter part of the 20th century has seen a dramatic upsurge in all aspects of Breton life. There has been a great agricultural revival, concentrated in the north-west round the port of Roscoff; while industrial firms have been encouraged to move to Rennes and other major centres. Prosperity has also created an enormous number of new houses, many of

them dotted haphazardly around the countryside, but looking less conspicuous because built in the traditional Breton way with white-painted walls and slate roofs.

There has also been a major renaissance in all aspects of popular culture, especially music and dance, with a growth in museums concentrating on Breton everyday life. This culture can be enjoyed to the full at major annual celebrations, of which the most important is the week-long Festival de Cornouaille, held every July in Quimper. Performers come together from all over Brittany to vie with one another in the virtuosity of their music, the agility and grace of their dancing, and the colour and complexity of their regional costumes.

Such costumes vary enormously from region to region, even from village to village. On the whole, the more mountainous and remote the region, the more sober the costume; while the brightest colours come from the areas where the living is easiest. Typically, the men wear felt hats with ribbons, embroidered waistcoats and baggy trousers, often almost Russian in appearance. The women wear brilliantly decorated aprons, elaborately brocaded and often edged with lace. But the main article of clothing that distinguishes one place from another is the white lace *coiffe* or head-dress, ranging from simple caps to the tower-like structures worn by women from the Pays Bigouden in western Finistère.

Traditional Breton music is normally played on a pair of wind instruments, known as a *couple* because they are invariably found together. They are the *biniou*, or bagpipe, and the *bombarde*, a treble shawm or early form of oboe with a carrying sound suitable for playing out of doors. *Bombardes* and *binious* combine with drums to form a *bagad*, the typical band that accompanied Breton regiments on the march in 1914-18, and accompanies open-air dancing today; or they may be used in conjunction with accordions, hurdy-gurdies and occasionally violins. Nowadays the bands may be brought up to date by electric guitars and keyboards imported from the pop world; but the wind *couple* is still the mainstay of Breton music. The small Celtic harp, more intimate than the orchestral harp, is also enjoying a revival.

The usual Breton dance is a variant of the gavotte, familiar to lovers of classical music as a stately dance-measure from the suites by Bach and other 18th-century composers. But the Breton gavotte is anything but stately: on the contrary, it is extremely lively, with chains of dancers swinging their linked hands and lifting and stamping their feet. The gavotte may be danced by a small group, or by the whole able-bodied population of a village, as happens at the dozens of *fest-noz* or night festivals held throughout the summer.

Almost as common as the secular festivals are the religious *pardons* or processions, usually linked to the local patron saint. Some of the *pardons* are enormous affairs, drawing thousands of people to pilgrimage centres, like the one held at Ste-Anne-d'Auray each July, or the great September gathering at Le Folgoët. But most of them are unpretentious ceremonies, in which the statue of the saint is carried round the town or village at the head of a procession of locals and visitors. Once the saint is safely back in church, religion is forgotten, the music begins, and the day ends with a cheerful country *fest-noz*.

Though many Breton households lovingly preserve their traditional costumes, handing them down from father to son and mother to daughter, this is no longer true of old-style Breton furniture, which can now be seen only in museums at Quimper, Rennes and elsewhere. The most prominent article of furniture was the *lit clos* or box-bed, with sliding doors, often intricately carved and pierced, which gave privacy and protection from draughts. Access to the bed was over the top of a *coffre* or chest, used for storing blankets and linen, while massive cupboards and sometimes a grandfather clock were placed alongside. The baby's carved wooden cradle might be hung from the ceiling by four cords, and food was kept in wicker baskets, slung high out of reach of children and animals.

Fortunately for the Breton language, it is not yet in the position of Breton furniture, as it is still spoken by 600,000 Bretons, or one-fifth of the population, though the number of *bretonnants* is said to be steadily declining. As with Welsh and other minority languages, it is kept alive largely by young enthusiasts in universities and schools and other centres of Breton nationalism.

In former times, French was spoken in the eastern half of the country known as *Haute-Bretagne* or Upper Brittany, *Breizh Uhel* in Breton, while Breton was the language of the western half, *Basse-Bretagne*, Lower Brittany or *Breizh Izel*, so called not because of their respective heights above sea-level, but because of their distances from Paris. The dividing line between the two languages ran roughly from St-Brieuc in the north to Vannes in the south. In spite of the blurring of populations,

the distinction still holds, and you are unlikely to hear Breton being spoken except in Finistère, parts of the Côtes-d'Armor and Morbihan.

The abbreviation BZH for *Breizh*, found on holiday car stickers, is familiar to every motorist who comes to Brittany. The most frequent everyday examples of the Breton language occur as parts of placenames. *Lan-* for monastery and *Plou-* for parish have been mentioned already. Other common components are *Aber* for estuary, *Enes* island, *Ker* town or village, *Pont* bridge, *Porz* harbour, *Sant* saint and *Ti* house. A few useful everyday expressions are: *Demat* good morning, *Kenavo* goodbye and *Yec'hed Mad* cheers.

Apart from the letters BZH, the Breton stickers usually include the *triskell* or triskelion, literally 'Three Legs', which looks something like a three-bladed aircraft propeller. This ancient Celtic emblem, first used as long ago as the 5th century BC and familiar in Britain from the arms of the Isle of Man, has been revived in Brittany, Ireland and other Celtic countries in recent years. Another common emblem is the *hermine*

BRETON BAGPIPES

or ermine adopted by the Dukes of Brittany – a highly stylized representation of the stoat, whose furry coat turns white with black tail-tip in winter, in the form of a triangle surmounted by three small lozenges.

The ermine is an important element in Brittany's national flag, designed in the 1920s by a prominent Breton nationalist. Known from its stark colouring simply as the *Gwenn ha Du* or White and Black, it resembles the American Stars and Stripes, with ermines taking the place of the stars. It has five black stripes symbolizing the five ancient bishoprics of Upper Brittany – Dol, Nantes, Rennes, St-Brieuc and St-Malo; these alternate with four white stripes for those of Lower Brittany – Cornouaille, Léon, Trégor and Vannetais.

Today, wherever Bretons see the Gwenn ha Du fluttering above the turrets of a castle, or brandished proudly at the head of a procession, they are reminded of Brittany's glorious past, and encouraged to look hopefully towards its future.

FOOD AND DRINK

Cuisine marine

The fruits of the sea and the fruits of the land; Brittany is renowned for the richness of its raw materials, whether for its *fruits de mer*, excellent all round the coast; for its young lamb fed on the tender grass of saltings freshened by wind from the sea, or for its globe artichokes, strawberries, chestnuts and other vegetables and fruit of the highest quality.

RAGOUT DE COQUILLAGES

Seafood

First place in the wide range of Brittany's seafood must go to its oysters, found at their best at Cancale in the Baie du Mont-St-Michel, and round the Bélon river on the south Finistère coast near Pont-Aven. Cancale has been an oyster centre for centuries; 300 years ago its oysters were already so highly esteemed that Louis XIV had regular supplies of them sent to him at Versailles. Today's visitors to the town can sample oysters from quayside stalls, eating them in the open air, or sit down in a restaurant to a gourmet feast of a dozen or more, eaten with brown bread and washed down with a chilled white wine.

Oysters come in three main types: the rare *pieds de cheval* or 'horses' hooves', which may weigh half a kilo each and are correspondingly expensive; the *plates* or flat oysters known as *Bélons*, which are a good deal smaller and are reared mainly in the Bélon river; and the *creuses* or hollow oysters, the cheapest and commonest kind, also called *Portugaises*, which originated in Portugal but are now largely bred from Japanese stock. The oysters grow to maturity on the rich silt of the offshore beds or *parcs*, a kilometre or so out in the bay. When they reach edible size they are transferred to stone-built storage tanks, visible at low tide, where they are kept in clear water to get rid of any impurities. The rule that they should only be eaten when there is an 'R' in the month stems

from their breeding season, which lasts roughly from May to August, and because they are likely to be 'milky'.

Mussels are another speciality from the Baie du Mont-St-Michel and the Baie de St-Brienc. Like oysters, they may be grown in *parcs*, but they taste just as good – though they tend to be a good deal smaller – if you gather them yourself from the rocks along the tideline. In Brittany, as elsewhere in France, they are eaten as *moules marinières*, simmered in white wine and their own juices, with plenty of onions and herbs. Other typical shellfish are *coquilles Saint-Jacques* or scallops and *palourdes* (and the smaller *praires*) or clams, normally baked or boiled. *Bigorneaux* or winkles are first boiled for about 15 minutes and then skewered out of their shells and eaten.

Lobsters, crayfish, crabs, *langoustines* or giant prawns, and all the other crustaceans are highly prized. The lobster dish *homard à l'Armoricaine*, in which the lobster is sautéd in oil and served with a sauce which includes brandy, garlic and white wine among its ingredients, is said by food experts to have been invented in Brittany, the Roman Armorica; though other authorities say it is a mis-spelling for '*à l'Américaine*'. Whatever its origins, it is a favourite in top-class Breton restaurants.

Among the fresh fish found on Breton menus are salmon caught in the Trieux, the Scorff and the Aulne, trout from the Ellé, and conger eels from Belle-Ile, Though no longer officially in Brittany, the Loire is a great supplier of fish to Breton tables including *mulet* or mullet, *lamproie* or lamprey, and *brochet*, pike. *Anguilles* or eels and *civelles*, young eels, are eaten in stews called *matelotes*, or as delicacies smoked over peat (*fumées à la tourbe*).

Perhaps the most typical Breton fish dish is the soup called *cotriade*. This northern version of *bouillabaisse*, originally cooked by fishermen aboard their boats, consists of chunks of white fish boiled with potatoes and seasoned with onions, bay and thyme.

Breton pancakes

Just as typical of Breton food as its fish dishes are its *crêpes* or pancakes, called *krampouez* in Breton, and *galettes* or flat scones, sold in the *crêperies* that are to be found even in the smallest hamlets. Cheap to buy, quickly pre-pared and eternally popular with children, they are eaten with every variety of filling, from sugar or jam to fish, eggs or sausage. While more commonly known as a desert, it is possible to have a complete meal or *repas de crêpes*.They are usually made of ordinary wheat called *froment* if they are sweet, or from buckwheat or *blé noir* if savoury. Buckwheat is also known as *sarrasin*, meaning Saracen, as it was brought back from the Near East by Bretons returning from the Crusades. *Kouign aman*, literally 'butter cake' is a rich dough-cake, made with plenty of butter and sugar, preferably eaten slightly warm.

Salt-meadow lamb

Like other relatively poor regions, Brittany has never produced or eaten much meat, apart from lamb fed on the *prés-salés* or salt-marshes round the Baie du Mont-St-Michel, on the island of Ouessant and elsewhere. The Bretons have tended instead to eat pig-meat, served up straight as bacon, pork or ham, or turned into the *andouilles* or sausages, *boudins noirs* or black puddings and *rillettes* or meat spread found in any Breton *charcuterie*.

Traditional Breton meat dishes tend to be on the solid side, from recipes handed down from the days when meals had to provide ample energy for days of hard work in the fields. A typical dish is *kig ha farz*, literally 'meat and flour', an immensely filling stew of ham, dumplings and vegetables. *Kuign-pot* or 'boiled pudding' is another solid dumpling dish in which a dough of milk, eggs, flour and sugar is boiled for about an hour together with pieces of pork. Like the Scots, the Bretons have a tradition of eating *bouillie d'avoine* or porridge, boiling up a cauldron of oatmeal with a large lump of butter in the middle.

The 'golden' belt

In recent years, Brittany-grown vegetables have won a European reputation for quality, notably the globe artichokes and cauliflowers grown in the 'golden' belt of rich agricultural land inland from Roscoff known as the *Ceinture Dorée* or *Doréale*. Early potatoes, lettuce, shallots and winter carrots are also excellent. For years after the war, 'Onion Johnnies' on their bicycles were a familiar sight in England, selling Breton

PANCAKES WITH CRAYFISH

onions festooned around their handlebars. Though they have been superseded by motor transport, Brittany still produces splendid onions for home consumption and export. Haricot beans, peas and spinach are also grown.

Local fruit is just as good. You will see orchards of apples, including cider apples, and pears all over the region, while certain areas tend to specialize – for example, cherries are grown round Fouesnant, strawberries round Plougastel and chestnuts round Redon. Chest-

nuts are used in local dishes with turkey and chicken, or simmered in buttermilk.

Unlike Normandy, and until the agricultural revolution of the 60s, Brittany was not a cattle-rearing country, and so has no great cheese-making tradition. The only home-grown cheese is the mild-flavoured Saint-Paulin.

Cider and wine

Being so far north, Brittany has no local wines, apart from the wine produced round Nantes in the Loire valley; though Loire wines, like Loire fish, are no longer officially Breton. There are

BRETON ARTICHOKES

two sorts of Loire wine which match particularly well the eating of oysters: Muscadet, a fairly dry white wine and Gros Plant, which is slightly drier. Brittany's only home-produced drink is *cidre bouché* or flat cider, which makes the ideal accompaniment to a solid meal of Breton pancakes.

The Bretons have adopted one excellent Norman custom, the *Trou Normand*. Literally 'Norman Hole', it is a glass of apple brandy (*calvados*) drunk between courses, which supposedly burns a hole through the food so far eaten, thus making room for more! A local cure for a cold is to drink a litre of hot cider with *eau-de-vie* (brandy) and sugar.

A Breton drink which you can find if you look around for it is *hydromel* or mead, made from honey and something of an acquired taste. Known as *Chouchen*, it is a sweet and rather heavy apéritif. The ancient Gauls are said to have derived much of their courage in battle from draughts of *hydromel* taken beforehand!

Round Douarnenez in Finistère, the old-style Breton communal feast has been revived in the past few years. As many as 500 people may sit down to this *Koan Vraz* or 'Great Meal', where they eat their way through salt bacon or black bread, grilled sardines and tuna and Breton cakes and pastry, washed down with cider and Muscadet. Hardly *nouvelle cuisine* perhaps, but then the Bretons have never been slaves to fashion, in food or any other aspect of life.

LEISURE ACTIVITIES

The following pages cover the prime holiday pursuits
visitors to the region might like to enjoy, at whatever time
of year; cruising the canals and rivers, playing golf
against an ocean backdrop, restoring the body to a
state of trim fitness at a thalassotherapy centre and, of
course, enjoying the landscape through walking
and motoring tours.

LEFT THE NANTES-BREST CANAL AT JOSSELIN

LOISIRS ACCUEIL

For the holidaymaker who is seeking something
different, the Loisirs Accueil organization offers
unusual and interesting short break ideas with
accommodation arranged in local *gîtes*, hotels
or camp sites. What is offered varies from one
département to another, but the main themes of
leisure and sporting activities are covered.
Thus there are, for example, fishing and
waterway holidays, canoeing and sea-kayaking
courses and trips, cycling and riding holidays,
language study courses, craft and gastronomy
weekends, corsair weekends, golf tuition
breaks, holidays in horse-drawn caravans.

It should be noted that most of the brochures
describing these holidays are in French and,
where tuition may be involved in the holiday,
this too is likely to be given in French. Your
enjoyment of this type of holiday is therefore
dependent on having a reasonable command
of the French language.

Depending on your area of interest, contact
one of the following four offices for further
information:

Loisirs Accueil Côtes-d'Armor
29 rue des Promenades,
22000 Saint-Brieuc
☎ 96.62.72.11

Loisirs Accueil Ille-et-Vilaine
1 rue Martenot,
35000 Rennes
☎ 99.02.97.43

Loisirs Accueil Morbihan
Hôtel du Département,
56009 Vannes
☎ 97.54.06.56

Loisirs Accueil Loire-Atlantique
Maison du Tourisme,
place du Commerce,
44000 Nantes
☎ 40.89.50.77

SPORTS

Further practical information on the following
popular sports and activities can be obtained
direct from the addresses given below.

Cruising
Comité des Canaux Bretons,
Comité Régional du Tourisme de Bretagne,
3 rue d'Espagne, BP 4175,
35041 Rennes
Fishing
Conseil Supérieure de la Pêche,
134 avenue de Malakoff, 75016 Paris
For fishing purposes, French waters are
classified into category 1 (for salmon and trout),
and category 2 (for all other fish). Local
regulations from the Tourist Offices.
Golf
Fédération Française de Golf,
69 avenue Victor Hugo, 75116 Paris
Rambling (and cycling)
Association Bretonne des Relais et Itinéraires
(ABRI),
3 rue des Portes Mordelaises,
35000 Rennes
Riding
Association Régionale du Tourisme
Equestre en Bretagne (ARTEB),
1 rue Gambetta,
56300 Pontivy
Sailing (schools)
Comité Régional du Tourisme de Bretagne,
3 rue d'Espagne, BP 4175,
35041 Rennes
Sand yachting
Ligue Régionale de Char à Voile,
26 bis, rue Belle Fontaine,
56100 Lorient
Underwater diving and spear fishing
Comité Régional Bretagne-Normandie de la
Fédération Française des Sports Sous-marin,
78 rue Ferdinand Buisson,
44600 St-Nazaire
Water skiing and motor boating
Ligue de Bretagne de Ski Nautique,
BP 99, 49300 Cholet

CRUISING

Inland waterways of great beauty

THE NANTES-BREST CANAL AT ROHAN

The 640 km or 400 miles that make up the canals and navigable waterways of Brittany represent one of the most beautiful cruising regions available to tourists. Unlike other areas of France, here there is no commercial traffic, making these waterways a pleasure to cruise. For the traveller with time to spare, this is the perfect way to discover the unspoilt and peaceful interior of Brittany, as its varying landscapes of meadows, hills, river valleys, forests and moorland drift past. This is a placid, unhurried world for the photographer or painter to revel in – and ideal too for someone who just wants to catch up on some reading, for at maximum speeds of 6 kmh or 3 mph on the canals and 8-10 kmh or 4-6 mph on the rivers, this means of travel imposes a calming, leisurely influence all of its own. About 32 km or 20 miles a day is a reasonable target, and, since many of the Breton waterways are canals, or sections of canalized rivers, the preponderance of locks will in any case limit your advance. Most cruise companies operate between March and October, so if the peak holiday months of July and August should prove too expensive, consider instead the spring or autumn, when the rates are cheaper and the countryside still as lovely. By arrangement with the operator, you can choose to travel one-way or return; some also hire out boats for a *mini-semaine* or long weekend, or, just for a taster, by the day.

Types of boat vary between fully-equipped hire cruisers for two to eight people and the traditional *péniches* – narrowboats or barges. You may think it worth hiring a cruiser with cabin capacity greater than your actual number to allow for extra comfort, particularly on wet days. A couple of bicycles on board are also a recommended extra, essential for shopping and touring excursions, and most hire companies will provide them. No previous experience is necessary to handle one of these craft. With one forward gear and one backward gear it is simplicity itself, and the operator will familiarize you with water refilling and other requirements. What he will not be able to prepare you for, however, is your first lock, and this is when the funniest thing happens: perfectly civilized people somehow manage to fall out in a matter of minutes when it comes to organizing the manoeuvring and negotiating of a small boat through a small space! Suddenly there are as many people with ideas on how it should best be done as there are days in the week. It's all good fun though and soon forgotten, but your early efforts invariably attract an audience!

A memorable and relaxing holiday it certainly will be, but add a bicycle or two and carry some energetic children on board, and the holiday can be as active as you want to make it! Deliberate stops can be made en route at locations where there are optional extras to be enjoyed: your cruise hirer will supply you with detailed itinerary maps and guides. The country is dotted with beautiful churches and manor houses; every town and village is waiting to be explored, restaurants tried, fresh food bought. Many places offer such additional leisure pursuits as horse-riding, canoeing and tennis, and there's always the towpath for walks and cycle rides. At some points, Dinan and La Roche-Bernard for example, the local bus will transport you to the nearest seaside resorts for a day of beach fun. Above all though, perhaps, are the pleasures to be had in meeting the local people, attempting or perfecting their language and enjoying their countryside, food and wine.

Further information and cruising literature is available from:
Comité de Promotion Touristique des Canaux Bretons, ABRI, 9 rue des Portes-Mordelaises, 35000 Rennes
☎ 99.31.59.44

A list of French boat hire companies belonging to the Syndicat National des Loueurs de Bateaux de Plaisance is available from:
French Government Tourist Office (FGTO), 178 Piccadilly, London W1V 0AI
☎ 071-491 7622

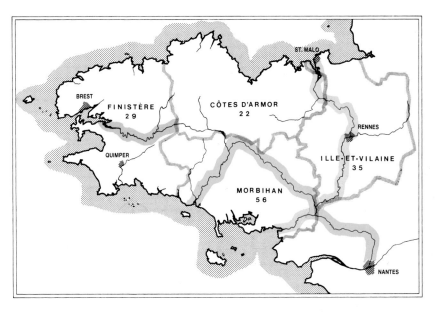

The Waterways

The navigable waterway system of Brittany consists of three main sections, each of which comprises a canal-river mix. Looking on the map like a ragged cross they are:
The major part of the Nantes-Brest canal. Nantes to Redon by way of the River Erdre, Redon to Pontivy along the Nantes-Brest canal, and continuing to Lorient along the canalized section of the River Blavet.
The north-south waterway known as 'la liaison Manche-Océan'. Much used by sailing craft cutting across between the Channel and the Atlantic, the waterway runs from St-Malo to Arzal by way of the Ille-et-Rance canal and the River Vilaine.
The western, Finistère, section of the Nantes-Brest canal and the River Aulne from Port-Carhaix to Port-Launay.

Route suggestions

The following table gives an idea of the sort of journeys which are achievable in a given length of time:

FROM	1 WEEK	10 DAYS	2 WEEKS
ARZAL	To Josselin and back To Nantes and back To Rennes and back		To Dinan and back To Pontivy and back
GUIPRY-MESSAC	To Josselin and back To Nantes and back To Tinténiac and back To Dinan or vice-versa one-way		
REDON	To Josselin and back To Rennes and back To Nantes and back	To Rohan one-way To Pontivy one-way	To Dinan and back

The Loisirs Accueil organization in Morbihan also offers cruising holiday options in its brochure based on Josselin (address on page 25).

For those who prefer to book with a UK hire company, the following operate in Brittany:

Bases Arzal, Guipry-Messac and Dinan
Contact Blakes Holidays
Wroxham, Norwich NR12 8DH
☎ 0603 784131

Bases Dinan and Guipry-Messac
Contact Blue Line Cruisers
PO Box 9, Hayling Island, Hampshire
PO11 0NL ☎ 0705 468011
Base Port de Redon
Contact French Country Cruises
Andrew Brock Travel Ltd, 10 Barley Mow Passage, Chiswick, London W4 4PH
☎ 081-995 3642
Bases Arzal and Guipry-Messac
Contact Hoseasons Holidays Abroad
Sunway House, Lowestoft, Suffolk NR32 3LT ☎ 0502 500555

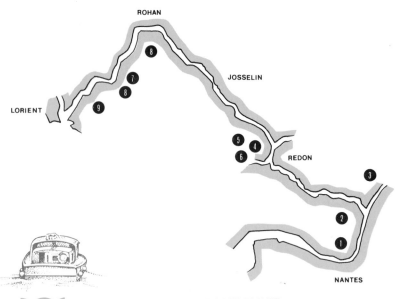

NANTES-BREST CANAL AND RIVER BLAVET

Constructed between 1824-38, this canal once linked the city of Nantes to the Channel port of Brest, allowing free inland transport between the two coasts. Running from the tip of Finistère down to the Loire, it is today only navigable in parts. The through route was closed in 1920 to allow for the creation of a hydro-electric power plant at Guerlédan which in turn has resulted in a huge reservoir very popular for all sorts of watersports. Its reconnection is, however, being considered for the future.

From Nantes to Pontivy is 206 km or 125 miles and includes 107 locks. The section covering the first 18 locks is forested and very pretty. Places worth visiting on this stretch are Nantes itself and Blain. The River Erdre runs north from Nantes through Sucé-sur-Erdre and then across the Nantes-Brest canal and on to Nort-sur-Erdre. You will find yourself sharing these waters with the elegant dine-and-cruise boats from Nantes. Exploring this section of the Erdre is worth the short detour involved before rejoining the canal and heading on towards Redon.

Redon is very much the crossroads of the Breton waterway system and travel can either continue west on the Nantes-Brest canal towards Pontivy with 90 locks, or turn off north or south onto the River Vilaine. This is probably the most popular stretch scenically of them all and recommended stops on the Redon-Pontivy section are Redon, La Gacilly, well worth the 9 km diversion up the River Aff, Malestroit, Josselin, Rohan and finally Pontivy.

Navigation now continues by means of the canalized River Blavet. From Pontivy to Hennebont is 60 km or 37 miles and includes 28 locks. This is a lovely waterway and pleasant stops en route can be made at St-Nicholas-des-Eaux for Plumeliau, Pont-Augan for Baud and Hennebont. Sea-going vessels will continue along the River Blavet, via Hennebont and on to the seaport of Lorient, a further 14 km or 9 miles.

Hire operators on the Erdre, the Nantes-Brest canal and the Blavet

1 Base Nantes
Contact Cro-Agera
1 bis rue du Capitaine, Corhumel, 44000 Nantes
☎ 40.20.57.25

2 Base Sucé-sur-Erdre
Contact Bretagne Fluviale
quai de l'Erdre, 44240 Sucé-sur-Erdre
☎ 40.77.79.51

3 Base Nort-sur-Erdre
Contact Air et Soleil Mutualité
2 quai St-Georges, 44390 Nort-sur-Erdre
☎ 40.29.56.29

4 Base Port de Redon
Contact Comptoir Nautique de Redon
2 quai Surcouf, 35600 Redon
☎ 99.71.46.03

5 Base Port de Redon
Contact Bretagne Plaisance
quai Jean-Bart, 35600 Redon
☎ 99.72.15.80

6 Base Port de Redon
Contact Locaboat Plaisance,
quai du Port-au-Bois, 89300 Joigny
☎ 86.91.72.72

7 Bases Port de Josselin and Nantes
Contact Le Ray Loisirs
14 rue Caradec, 56120 Josselin
☎ 97.75.60.98

8 Bases Rohan and Pontivy
Contact Rohan Plaisance
BP 19, 56580 Rohan
☎ 97.38.98.66

9 Base St-Nicolas-des-Eaux
Contact Breiz Marine
St-Nicolas-des-Eaux, 56150 Plumeliau
☎ 97.45.03.54

A SLUICE GATE ON THE NANTES-BREST CANAL

LIAISON MANCHE-OCEAN (ILLE-RANCE CANAL AND THE RIVER VILAINE)

Much used by yachtsmen travelling between the Channel and the Atlantic who gain access via the tidal River Rance from St-Malo. The section between Le Châtelier and Rennes is 85 km or 53 miles long and includes 48 locks, 11 of which form the spectacular staircase at Hédé and will take two hours to pass through. Very rural in character and with a number of châteaux to visit en route, this is most pleasant cruising country with stops recommended at Dinan from where day trips can be made to the seaside, Léhon, Tinténiac, Rennes, Redon – the crossroads – and La Roche-Bernard, again day excursions can be made to the seaside from here. From Rennes as far as Arzal navigation is via the River Vilaine for 136 km or 85 miles with just 15 locks. South of Redon is the lock-free, dammed-off estuary of the Vilaine.

Hire operators on the Ille-Rance canal and the River Vilaine

1 *Base* Port de Lyvet, la Vicomté-sur-Rance
Contact Chemins Nautiques Bretons 22690 Pleudihen-sur-Rance
☎ 96.83.28.71
2 *Bases* Dinan and Guipry-Messac
Contact Blue Line Bretagne Port de Plaisance de Messac, 35480 Messac
☎ 99.34.60.11
3 *Base* Port de Betton
Contact Argoat Nautique Port de Betton, 35830 Betton
☎ 99.55.70.36
4 *Base* Port de Redon
Several operators are based here, see opposite page
5 *Base* Arzal
Contact Breiz Marine Zone Portuaire, 56190 Arzal
☎ 97.45.03.54

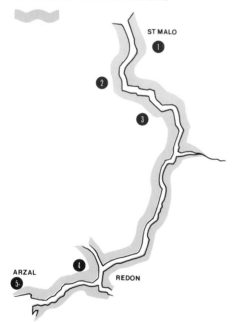

NANTES-BREST CANAL AND SECTION OF THE RIVER AULNE

This route consists of part of the Nantes-Brest canal and then canalized sections of the rivers Aulne and Hyères. This is again a very quiet and lovely cruising area, with little traffic and consequently no supervision at the locks, and one that is particularly renowned for its salmon and pike fishing. From Port-Carhaix to Châteaulin is 76 km or 47 miles long with 35 locks. Travel is via Châteauneuf and then on the River Aulne as far as Port-Launay before running out at the presqu'île de Crozon, the distance between Châteaulin and Landévennec being 33 km or 21 miles. Recommended stops for exploring are at Port Carhaix for Carhaix-Plouguer, Penn-ar-Pont for Châteauneuf-du-Faou, Pont Coblant for Pleyben-Gouezec, and Châteaulin.

Hire operators on the Aulne

1 *Base* Pont Coblant
Contact Crabing Loisirs 20 rue du Frout, 29000 Quimper
☎ 98.95.14.02
2 *Base* Port de Penn-ar-Pont
Contact SBDM Nautique BP 1, 29119 Châteauneuf-du-Faou
☎ 98.73.25.34

Golf de Baden-Kernic (New)
Tel 97 57 22 05. [18. 9 Hol

GOLF

Cross-Channel links

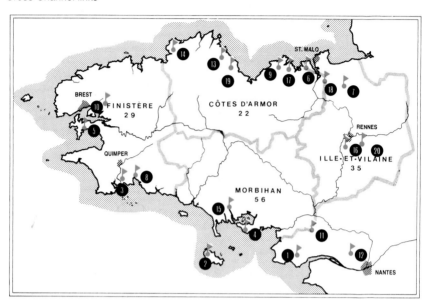

Golf was first played in France in the Pyrenees, on the Basque coast and in Brittany, all places which, over the past hundred years, have been favoured holiday and retirement retreats of wealthy English families. Did two Scots officers of Wellington's army 'design' a course at Pau when quartered there in 1814 during the Peninsular War? Perhaps. What is certain is that the first club in France opened in Pau in 1856, and that almost eighty years later, membership was still almost exclusively British.

Brittany has always been a great favourite for holidays, and Dinard golf course opened in 1887 to meet the needs of British residents there. A year later Biarritz, fashionable resort of royalty and high society, had its own course, and Compiègne in Picardy followed seven years later.

However, there was never the same surge in golf-course construction in France as there was in Great Britain, and never the same passion for the game. Holiday golf for the tourist and 'society' golfer was well catered for by Spanish and Portuguese clubs and by the travel organizations and hotels linked with them. Then, it seemed, as home interest grew, there was a sudden explosion of golf planning in France. New courses were designed and constructed: sports complexes around 18- and 9-hole courses and, in many cases, courses with a clutch of three interchangeable 9-holers. What had long been chic at St-Cloud, Cannes-Mougins and St-Nom-la-Bretèche was now being played not only by tourists but by a swelling number of French family groups.

In 1981 there were only 43,000 members of French golf clubs. Six years later the figure had trebled. In every corner of the country there was an annual increase in membership of over twenty-five per cent, the interest being shown by women as well as men. To keep up with this growth there was a flowering of new clubs throughout the country. There are over 200 clubs today and the number increases by the month.

What then does golf in Brittany have to offer the visitor? There are championship courses, courses built round or dominated by magnificent châteaux, and, naturally, seaside courses where conditions are similar to such courses in Scotland. Some courses are real tests of skill, others more suitable for a friendly family round. Some are privately owned, others are public municipal courses and while visitors are welcome at both, the private clubs may have certain facilities exclusively reserved for the use of golfers whereas at public courses non-golfers are welcome. Those with handicaps should take a handicap certificate, as weekend competitions are regularly held and open to visitors. The green fee rates vary and are generally quoted by the day rather than the round. They are, as a rule, higher than those in Britain, about 150FF being an average midweek charge, while at some clubs weekend rates can rise to 300FF and more. Equipment too is more expensive; balls tend to cost twice as much as in the UK. Most clubs, like most shops, close for one day a week. It is wise to reserve a tee at least a day in advance and certainly at weekends. Weekend golf in France tends to take place largely in the afternoon and the attitude to the game is far less serious than in Britain. It is quite often a game for the whole family and tends, therefore, to be slow in playing; five hours a round is not exceptional. But the enthusiasm is there, if not always the strictest observance of the rules of etiquette!

Golf in France can be said to have taken off in fine style. Now is the time to try the flavour of some of its courses and their locations. As the French learn to love the sport more and more we can expect also to see the emergence of their own Ballesteros and the full flowering of the country as a golfing nation.

The following is a list of the principal Breton courses, together with details of the hotels which offer set price short breaks inclusive of green fees. Some also offer green fee discounts to off-season visitors.

❶ La Baule
Golf de La Baule
Domaine de Saint-Dénac
44117 St-André-des-Eaux
☎ 40.60.46.18
10 mins from La Baule on the D47.
18-hole private course, par 72. Min handicap 24 in summer, 35 out of season. Green fees 150-300FF according to season. Instruction courses twice a month over three to five days. Competitions Mar-Dec. This is a championship course designed by Peter Alliss and Dave Thomas in a park and woodland mix and with very fine greens. Closed Tues in winter. Bar and restaurant.
Hotels
L'Hermitage ★★★★
☎ 40.60.37.00
Castel Marie-Louise ★★★★
☎ 40.60.20.60
Le Royal ★★★★
☎ 40.60.33.06

BELLE-ILE-EN-MER

❷ Belle-Ile-en-Mer
Golf de Sauzon
56360 Belle-Ile-en-Mer
☎ 97.31.64.65
Boats for the island leave from Quiberon, then shuttle service.
New 18-hole public course. Min handicap 30 men, 36 ladies. Green fees 130-200FF according to season. Instruction courses, Sunday competitions. Restaurant in summer.
Hotels
Hôtel Castel Clara ★★★★
Bangor
☎ 97.31.84.21
Manoir de Goulphar ★★★
Bangor
☎ 97.31.80.10

❸ Clohars Fouesnant
Golf de l'Odet Quimper
Clohars Fouesnant
29118 Bénodet
☎ 98.54.87.88
12 km from Quimper on D34.
Fairly new 18-hole public course, par 72, plus 9-hole course for beginners. Green fees 130-200FF. Sunday competitions held Apr-Oct. Open all year, closed Thurs in winter. Bar and restaurant.
Hotels
Hostellerie de l'Abbatiale ★★★
Le Port, Bénodet
☎ 98.57.05.11
Hôtel Eurogreen (on site) ★★★
☎ 98.82.84.86

❹ Le Crouesty
Golf du Kerver
56730 St-Gildas-du-Rhuys
☎ 97.45.30.09
Near Crouesty, on the road to St-Gildas.
New 18-hole course, par 72. Min handicap 36. Green fees 130-200FF according to season. Bar and restaurant.

❺ Crozon
Golf de Crozon
29160 Crozon
☎ 98.27.10.28
3 km from Crozon on D791.
Driving range and putting green.

❻ Dinard
Golf de Dinard
35800 St-Briac-sur-Mer
☎ 99.88.32.07
6 km west of Dinard on D786, 6 km from the airport.
18-hole private links course, par 69, the second oldest course in France founded in 1887 and with some spectacular views over the bay. Min handicap 35. Green fees 180FF. Open throughout the year. Restaurant.
Hotel
Hôtel des Dunes ★★
rue Clémenceau
Dinard
☎ 99.46.12.72

7 Dol-de-Bretagne
Golf des Ormes
35120 Dol-de-Bretagne
☎ 99.48.10.19
8 km from Dol-de-Bretagne and 10 km from Combourg.
18-hole private course, par 72, within the château grounds. Green fees 180FF weekdays, 240FF weekends. Restaurant.
Hotel
Château des Ormes 4 rooms, camping.

8 La Forêt Fouesnant
Golf de Quimper et de Cornouaille
Manoir de Mesmeur
29133 La Forêt Fouesnant
☎ 98.56.97.09
10 km from Concarneau on D44.
Mature and well maintained 9-hole private course with 18 tees. Players without a handicap admitted before 9 a.m. and after 5 p.m. during the summer. Green fees 100-140FF weekdays, 120-170FF weekends. Open daily in summer, closed Tues in winter. Restaurant.
Hotels
see Clohars Fouesnant.

BELLE-ILE-EN-MER

9 Fréhel
Golf des Sables-d'Or-Les-Pins
22240 Fréhel
☎ 96.41.91.20
At Sables-d'Or on D34.
9-hole private course with 18 tees, par 68, half woodland, half links. Min handicap 32. Green fees 128-152FF according to season. Bar snacks.
Hotels
Enquire about discounts offered at hotels in Sables-d'Or.

10 Landerneau
Golf de Brest-Iroise
Parc des Loisirs de Lann Rohou
29220 Landerneau
☎ 98.85.16.17
5 km south of Landerneau.
18-hole public course, par 72, set within the grounds of a country park. Green fees 130-185FF weekdays, 170-210FF

weekends. Open all year. Bar snacks and restaurant.
Hotel
Océania ★★★
Brest
☎ 98.80.66.66

11 Missillac
Golf de la Bretesche Missillac
44780 Pontchâteau
☎ 40.88.30.03
Nantes-Vannes RN165, exit Missillac.
18-hole private course, par 72, set within the grounds of the Château de la Bretesche. Min handicap 35. Green fees 130-250FF according to season. Instruction courses. Competitions held Jun-Sep. Bar, café and restaurant. Tennis courts and swimming pool.
Hotels
Hôtel Restaurant du Golf (on site) ★★★
☎ 40.88.30.05
Maeva Loisirs
☎ 40.88.31.18
Self-catering cottages (on site)

12 Nantes
Golf de Nantes
44360 Vigneux-de-Bretagne
☎ 40.63.25.82
15 km from Nantes on the Vannes road.
18-hole private course, par 72. Min handicap 35. Green fees 150-240FF. Summer instruction courses, competitions every weekend except during July and August. Bar and restaurant closed Tues.
Hotel
Hôtel Mercure ★★★
Sautron
☎ 40.57.10.80

13 Pléhédel
Golf du Boisgélen
Pléhédel
22290 Lanvollon
☎ 96.22.31.24
10 km from Paimpol on D7.
18-hole private course, par 72, set within the château grounds. Green fees 100FF weekdays, 150FF weekends. Restaurant.
Hotel
Château de Coatguélen (on site) ★★★
☎ 96.22.31.24
The château also arranges golf instruction courses Mar-Dec, and runs cookery courses.

14 Pleumeur-Bodou
Golf de Saint-Samson
route de Kérenoc
22560 Pleumeur-Bodou
☎ 96.23.87.34
4 km from Trégastel on D788.
18-hole private heathland course, par 72, with marvellous coastal views. Green fees 160-180FF. Instruction courses, Sunday competitions. Bar and two restaurants.
Hotel
Golf Hôtel de Saint-Samson (on site) ★★
☎ 96.23.87.34

⑮ Ploëmel
Golf de Saint-Laurent Ploëmel Carnac
56400 Auray
☎ 97.56.85.18
11 km south-west of Auray, on D22.
Pleasant and busy 18-hole public course, par 72, set within the forested St-Laurent leisure park. Min handicap 35. Green fees 150-180FF according to season. Open all year. Instruction courses and Sunday competitions. Bar and restaurant.
Hotel
Hôtel Fairway (on site) ★★★
☎ 97.56.88.88

⑯ Rennes
Golf de Rennes
35000 St-Jacques-de-la-Lande
☎ 99.64.24.18
8 km south-west of Rennes on Redon road.
9-hole private course with 18 tees, par 70. Min handicap 36. Green fees 100FF weekdays, 150FF weekends. Tuition and weekend competitions. Open all year, closed Tues. Bar and restaurant. 18-hole course opens Sep 1990.
Hotel
Novotel ★★★
avenue du Canada
Rennes
☎ 99.50.61.32

Golf de la Freslonnière
35650 Le Rheu
☎ 99.60.84.09
3 km from Rennes on RN24 in the direction of Lorient exiting at La Freslonnière, then signposted.
New 18-hole course, par 71. Green fees 180FF weekdays, 220FF weekends. Driving range and putting green. Restaurant, closed Tues. No handicap restrictions.

⑰ St-Cast-le-Guildo
Golf de Pen Guen
22380 St-Cast-le-Guildo
☎ 96.41.91.20
1 km from St-Cast on the road from Dinard.
9-hole private course with 18 tees, par 68, suitable for beginners and juniors in a beautiful position facing the sea. Players without a handicap admitted after 5.30 p.m. in high season. Green fees 120FF for 9 holes in season, 120FF for 18 holes off season. Sunday competitions. Bar snacks.
Hotel
Hôtel des Dunes ★★
St-Cast-le-Guildo
☎ 96.41.80.31

⑱ St-Malo
Golf de St-Malo Le Tronchet
35540 Miniac Morvan
☎ 99.58.96.69
12 km from Dinan on N176.
Well designed par 72, 18-hole

championship course with many water hazards, plus 9-hole, par 36 course for beginners. Green fees 180FF. Tuition. Closed Tues in winter. Bar and restaurant.
Hotels
Hostellerie de l'Abbatiale (on site) ★★★
☎ 99.58.93.21
Hôtel le Mascotte ★★
La Chaussée du Sillon
St-Malo
☎ 99.40.36.36
Hôtel le Mercure ★★★
St-Malo
☎ 99.56.84.84

⑲ St-Quay-Portrieux
Golf des Ajoncs d'Or
Kergrain-Lantic
22410 St-Quay-Portrieux
☎ 96.71.90.74
Take the D786 out of St-Brieuc and leave it at Binic. Proceed to Chatelaudren then Pléguien.
18-hole public course, par 72, interestingly laid out with a lake and raised greens. Much in evidence is the gorse! Min handicap 35 in summer. Green fees 170-185FF according to season. Instruction courses and Sunday competitions. Bar snacks.
Hotel
Hôtel le Ker Moor ★★★
St-Quay-Portrieux
☎ 96.70.52.22

⑳ Vitré
Golf des Rochers-Sévigné
Route d'Argentré du Plessis
35500 Vitré
☎ 99.96.52.52
South of Vitré on D88.
18-hole private course, par 72. Green fees 150FF weekdays, 200FF weekends. Bar and restaurant.

GOLF WEEKENDS
Based at the Hôtel Fairway and using the facilities of the lovely parkland golf course at St-Laurent near Carnac and Quiberon, this break is offered by the Loisirs Accueil organization. The price of 580FF-730FF according to season, includes two nights' accommodation in a double room, breakfasts and green fees, with use of hotel facilities (swimming pool, sauna and gym) and meals at the clubhouse or hotel.

Week-long coaching holidays are also offered based on a stay of six days and eighteen hours' tuition, priced at 3,454FF-3,730FF with full board and accommodation. Both holidays are bookable through Loisirs Accueil Morbihan, Hôtel du Département, 56009 Vannes
☎ 97.54.06.56

HEALTH AND THE SEA

Reaping the benefits, naturally

For those needing to relax and recover from the strains of modern-day living, the idea of a break combining complete relaxation with time to devote to taking care of yourself could prove the ideal holiday option.

SEA SPRAY

THALASSOTHERAPY

'The sea cures man's ills' wrote the Greek tragedian Euripides over 2,000 years ago. In Brittany, it seems, tourism was born when hydrotherapy became popular in the reign of Louis-Philippe (1830-48). People began to look upon sea bathing as a means of regaining their health, and then, as swimming rapidly became a leisure activity in its own right, so the bathers became tourists.

Over the past few years progress in the field of medicine has confirmed the benefits of the sea and a maritime climate, and the use of thalassotherapy has spread. Today, with over 1,500 million days a year being spent at such centres, sea water therapy and what it has to offer is becoming more fully appreciated. Thus tourism seems to have turned full circle. The term 'thalassotherapy', derived from the Greek *thalassa* meaning the sea, was coined in 1867 by a doctor Bonnardière in Arcachon, and the first thalassotherapy institute was founded thirty years later in Roscoff by a Breton, Louis Bagot. Bagot's training as a biologist led him to the belief that our 'bodies are no more than aquariums swum in by billions of cells'. What then could be closer to nature than the sea for healthy, natural living? The only ingredients for thalassotherapy treatment are seaweed and sea water, their special properties bringing the body all the minerals and trace elements it needs. The all-important first consultation with one of the specialist doctors at the

institute will establish where weaknesses exist and propose an individual programme of *soins* or treatments to rectify them. Carried out under the constant supervision of medical practitioners and professionals, these are employed imaginatively and vary from being deliciously relaxing, such as the almond oil massage beneath a hot sea-water shower, to invigorating, such as the pressurized underwater jets and bubbling algae baths designed to help the circulation. Though you may not appreciate the smell, hot seaweed, in the form of paste, is also applied directly to various parts of the body beneath a layer of silver foil, a technique of controlled weight loss.

Courses of treatment last anything from one to three weeks and are designed primarily to tone the muscles. As such they are particularly recommended for rheumatism sufferers and as post-operative therapy. Physiotherapy, of course, both in and out of the water, has long been advocated, and exercises in heated sea-water pools are most effective, the body weighing fourteen times less when immersed in water. Underwater or overhead jets are used to help those with back or neck pain. Though the centres originally specialized in this form of treatment for those with recognized complaints, they are equally recommended and enjoyed today as general health and fitness packages whereby the body is given head-to-toe attention through facials, pedicures, saunas, yoga and aerobics classes, early morning runs along the beach and sessions in the fully-equipped work-out gyms. They will concentrate too on aspects to benefit the 'patient's' general well-being, such as restoring good posture, teaching relaxation techniques for repairing stressed and fatigued minds, prescribing anti-smoking regimes and imposing suitable diets for those needing to lose or gain weight.

Brittany is the main area for this kind of treatment in France and all the establishments listed are located in top seaside resorts. Further information can be obtained by writing direct to the individual thalassotherapy establishment, or to the Tourist Office at the resort itself.

Carnac
Centre de Thalassothérapie de Carnac
avenue de l'Atlantique
BP 100, 56341 Carnac
☎ 97.52.53.54
Situated between the sea and the salt marshes, this centre is only a short

distance from the ancient Roman spas. Treatment is by means of jacuzzi, jet showers, underwater jets, massages and algo-therapy – whatever has been individually prescribed by the resident physicians. Cures last one or two weeks and allow for the combined benefits of air, sea and sun along with fitness and beauty programmes designed to instil a feeling of well-being and relaxation.

*Open 1 Jan-20 Nov, accommodation is in either the linked *** Novotel or in a wide range of nearby hotels.*

Dinard
Thalassa Dinard
Institut de Thalassothérapie
avenue du Château Hébert
BP 70, 35802 Dinard
☎ 99.82.78.10
A brand-new centre situated in a beautiful site overlooking the sea. Equipped with heated sea-water pool, sauna, spa, Turkish bath and gym, individual treatments are prescribed after medical consultation. The well-being of the body as a whole is achieved through a range of health and beauty treatments complemented by exercise.

*Open throughout the year, accommodation can be arranged in the linked ***Novotel where each bedroom has a sea view, or in any of the many alternative hotels nearby.*

Douarnenez
Centre de Cure Marine
de la Baie de Tréboul-Douarnenez
42 bis rue des Professeurs-Curie
BP 4, 29100 Douarnenez
☎ 98.74.09.59
At the innermost point of the Baie de Douarnenez, the centre overlooks the sea and benefits from a temperate climate. The equipment used includes heated sea-water pools, showers, massage and algae baths and provides for specialized treatment of sports injuries.

Open throughout the year, accommodation is either in the centre itself or in one of the nearby hotels.

THALASSOTHERAPY AT ST-MALO

Quiberon
Institut de Thalassothérapie de Quiberon
BP 170, 56170 Quiberon
☎ 97.50.20.00
At the southernmost point of the Quiberon peninsula, bordering the Goviro beach, the institute's ultra-modern architecture gains maximum sea frontage. Equipment ranges from the bubbling pools and underwater sea jets, foot and hand baths, physiotherapy and gymnastics to algae and mud baths and specially prescribed diets.

*Open between Feb and Dec, accommodation is in either of the two **** luxury linked hotels, Sofitel Thalassa or Sofitel Diététique.*

Roscoff
Clinique de Rééducation Fonctionelle Ker-Léna
BP 13, 29211 Roscoff
☎ 98.24.33.33
This institute has recently been completely renovated and enlarged to receive those requiring physiotherapy and thalassotherapy treatments while continuing the orthopaedic care for which it was originally established. Three heated sea-water pools, underwater jet baths, bubbling sea-water baths, massage and electrotherapy are all included in the treatment courses.

Accommodation is offered within the centre, which is open all year, or in the range of hotels in this small holiday port.

Institut Marin Rockroum Centre de Thalassothérapie
BP 28, 29211 Roscoff
☎ 98.29.20.00
By the sea and facing the Ile de Batz, the institute was founded in 1899 in a resort already renowned for the tonic effects of its climate and the charm of its setting. Two heated sea-water pools, underwater jets, algo-therapy, bubbling baths and massage are amongst the treatments employed in both relaxation and health courses.

Accommodation in nearby hotels.

St-Malo
Les Thermes Marins
Grande Plage
100 boulevard Hébert
BP 32, 35401 St-Malo
☎ 99.56.75.75
The centre is situated on the sea front and overlooks the fine sandy beach which stretches from St-Malo to Rothéneuf. Courses of treatment run through the year from February to mid-December and cater for those with rheumatic complaints, post-traumatic disorders and more generally for those wishing to get back into top condition.

*Accommodation is in either the hotel *** which adjoins the centre, or in any of the wide range of nearby hotels.*

MOTORING TOURS

This section outlines seven itineraries to help you explore the very diverse regions of Brittany by road. Minor roads have been chosen in many cases, to make the journey more pleasant for drivers and less arduous for cyclists. The routes connect up the more important places of historical, architectural and ecological interest, including several of the *enclos paroissiaux* or parish closes unique to Brittany and some of its most spectacular scenery and viewpoints. They also take you to a number of smaller castles and châteaux, and fascinating village churches dedicated to some of the many hundreds of local Breton saints, as well as to typical fishing villages along the coast.

Each itinerary is, in fact, a circular tour, or, in the case of the Pink Granite Coast, a drive which can, if you prefer, be treated as one, two or three separate round trips. For each of the tours we have indicated a number of staging points along the route where you can break your journey for the night, or at least for a meal; towns where you will find good restaurants and a choice of hotel accommodation, most of which are described in the alphabetical Gazetteer section.

Ranging from 115 km to 203 km in length, the drives can be varied to suit individual taste. You can go at your own pace – making a whistle-stop tour in a single day with just a glance at each point of interest, or taking three or four leisurely days to cover the same ground, stopping whenever you wish for a stroll, a swim or a shopping trip, and deviating from the suggested route if you feel like it.

The maps (scale 1:250,000) show you the places of special interest in each area, and the starting point of each drive is cross-referenced to the atlas at the back of the book, enabling you to plan your own drives if you wish.

A TOUR OF BRITTANY'S BORDERLANDS

198 Km
Map ref.
127 E5

'Digemer mat': this 'Welcome' sign in the Breton language greets visitors arriving in Vitré by the motorway from Paris. Until recently however, before the fast road was opened and when most of the traffic to and from the capital went through lower Normandy, it was Fougères that acted as frontier post.

So from Fougères we shall set out on our exploration of this beautiful region of France, a region that has great character and takes special care to preserve its individuality.

In any case the likeness between these two neighbouring cities in Brittany's border country or 'Marches' is such that each possesses a magnificent fortified castle, on the strength of which each has built up a solid tourist trade. Each has, over the centuries, served as a stronghold, though with differing fortunes. And in the shelter of their towers each has achieved an enviable prosperity, based largely on the manufacture and sale of linen and hempen fabrics.

Other recommended staging posts on the route are St-Aubin-du-Cormier and Bazouges-la-Pérouse.

Fougères boasts one of the best-preserved examples of medieval military architecture – an 'impregnable' fortress (captured time and again by French, Spanish, Catholic League and Vendéen assailants!). **Vitré** for its part vies with Dinan and Vannes for the title of best-preserved old town in Brittany, and a visit is highly recommended.

La Guerche, also a border town, cannot be compared to the two already described, but some of its old houses and their porches may catch the eye. And La Guerche is an excellent departure point from which to explore the **Roche-aux-Fées**, one of the most impressive megalithic edifices in Armorica. A covered alley 19 metres long and 3-5 metres wide, it is constructed of schist, the eight roofing slabs each weighing from 40-45 tons. The fairies, who according to legend built this monument by transporting the stones in their aprons, are still, we are assured, continuing their good offices on behalf of engaged young couples who come here to beg their favours.

By way of **Châteaugiron** we now head for **Champeaux** where the village square and the stalls with their Renaissance canopy and stained glass windows of the church are certainly worth the detour. **St-Aubin-du-Cormier** unfortunately has only the ruins left of a fortress that in the Middle Ages matched those of Fougères and Vitré. Just beyond the village of **Bazouges-la-Pérouse**, the château of **La Ballue** comes into view, a sombre building of schist. This leads us on to another château belonging to Gilles Ruellan, a supporter of Henry IV, at **Le Rocher-Portail**, a fine 17th-century building. Finally, in the neighbourhood of **Coglès**, we pass through an area of quarries and stone-built houses, some of them still with outside bread-ovens, and so return to Fougères and the thirteen towers of its feudal castle.

CHATEAUBRIAND TOUR

178 Km
Map ref.
125 6B

Born in St-Malo, François-René de Chateaubriand lies at rest at the foot of its celebrated ramparts, on the little island of Grand-Bé in the harbour. So a 'Chateaubriand Tour' naturally starts there, from the 'Quic-en-Groigne' tower, a stone's throw from where this most famous of all Breton writers first saw the light of day. Staging posts are Combourg, Tinténiac, and Cancale near the start and St-Briac near the end, both on the Emerald Coast.

The road leading to **Cancale** keeps as close as it can to the rocky and jagged line of the Emerald Coast, where the waves of the Channel break in festoons of foam. After the unforgettable panorama of the **Pointe du Grouin**, Cancale offers a gastronomic treat for those who like oysters, gathered here from their beds opposite the port landing stages.

Next you follow the low-lying coast of Mont-St-Michel Bay as far as **Vivier-sur-Mer**, where you fork right towards **Dol-de-Bretagne** and its cathedral of St-Samson, formerly the seat of a rich bishopric. Don't miss the drive by the circular road around Mont-Dol, an inland replica of Mont-St-Michel, and perhaps a premonitory picture of what may happen there too, if invading sands are not kept at bay.

At the château-fortress of **Combourg** one can visit the room where the author of the *Mémoires d'outre-tombe*, or 'Memories from Beyond the Grave', spent two years in his youth.

At **Tinténiac** the Folk Museum of Tools and Trades alongside the Ille-et-Rance canal is worth a stop; and so is the 'ladder' of 11 locks at **Hédé** by means of which the waterway makes a 27-metre shift of altitude. The Flamboyant Gothic church at **Les Iffs** merits attention, as its windows are the work of Michel Bayonne; and the past prosperity of **Bécherel** is evidenced by some fine merchants' houses built of granite, standing out from

FRESH OYSTERS

a maze of alleyways that belong to another century. **La Chapelle-aux-Fitzméens** attracts visitors to view its pigeon-loft, still in its original condition, with 5,000 nesting-holes, but it also offers a church with the original bell tower and a 17th-century château, both of which are full of interest.

Another more imposing château is at **La Bourbansais**, a superb residence, built in the 16th and 18th centuries, at the centre of a formal park which now includes a small zoo. There are formal gardens also at the Montmarin château near **Plouër-sur-Rance**.

At **St-Briac** we happily find ourselves back on the Emerald Coast, and shall not leave it again till we reach **Dinard**, the haughty rival of St-Malo which we shall have in view from the Pointe du Moulinet, and then from the Pointe de la Vicomté, on the road along the dam of the tidal power-station on the Rance. At last we return to **St-Malo** and its stronghold, with a passing glance at **St-Servan** and the Tour Solidor, an ancient watch-tower built by Duke Jean IV of Brittany to subdue the troublesome 'Malouins' and control the river shipping.

THE EMERALD COAST

THE PINK GRANITE COAST

184 or
230 Km
Map ref.
122 B3

An absolute 'must' for all visitors to Brittany, the dream landscape of pink rocks at Ploumanac'h alone is worth the journey of exploration.
This tour of 184 or 230 km can, if you wish, be divided into two loops, both centred on Tréguier, or for those who have the time be extended to include Guingamp. Possible staging posts are Paimpol, Pontrieux, Guingamp, Trébeurden and Perros-Guirec. Whichever you decide to do, the tour starts out from **Tréguier**, the seat of an ancient bishopric, built on the banks of

THE COAST NEAR PLOUMANAC'H

the River Jaudy, and sacred to the memory both of St-Yves, protector of the poor, and of his compatriot the agnostic Ernest Renan, author of the *Prayer on the Acropolis*. The cathedral of St-Tugdual, flanked by its cloister, is claimed to be one of the finest examples of church architecture in Brittany. A very well attended *pardon* takes place on 19 May (or the Sunday following).
We now head towards **Pleubian**, and from there on to a natural curiosity, the **Sillon de Talbert**, a small tongue of land, or spit, covered in shingle (like the Chesil bank) but constantly menaced by the sea. At **Lézardrieux** we cross the broad estuary of the Trieux, and passing through Paimpol reach **Loguivy-de-la-Mer**, immortalized in a famous melody, and then the **Pointe de l'Arcouest**, where boats leave for the island of Bréhat. **Paimpol**, celebrated in prose by Loti and in song by Botrel, and now a country market town again since the cod-fishing came to an end, carefully preserves the impressive ruins of the abbey at Beauport. The next stop, after passing through Lézardrieux again, is at **La Roche-Jagu**, a large 15th-century

château whose imposing silhouette dominates the Trieux valley. Then, via **Pontrieux**, we come to the little town of **Runan**, whose richly decorated church of the 14th and 15th centuries was built by the Templars. At this point, either return to Tréguier or continue the drive to **Guingamp** and its half Gothic, half Renaissance basilica; then via the picturesque little town of **Belle-Isle-en-Terre** to visit the chapel of Sept-Saints which is partially built on a dolmen. The route continues on to Tréguier via **La Roche-Derrien** then west to **Lannion** which has some unspoilt ancient houses in the older part of the town. To get to the

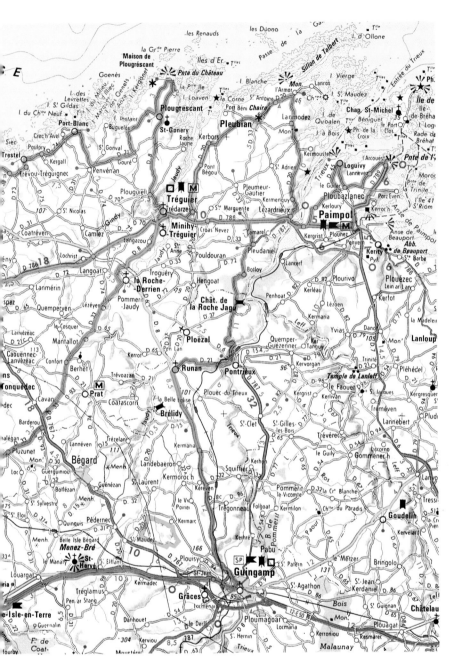

Romanesque church of Brélevenez, you have to climb a stairway of 142 steps, a spot popular with artists and craftsmen. At **Trébeurden** you come out on the Pink Granite Coast. This pretty seaside resort is, alas, in the process of being disfigured by the construction of a pier which is quite unworthy of the place. Here you will have to make a detour via the 'Radôme', or radar station at **Pleumeur-Bodou**, a satellite communications centre, before reaching the rose-coloured rocks at **L'Ile-Grande**, and then, at **Ploumanac'h**, one of the most stunning stretches of rocky coast in France.

Perros-Guirec, the leading resort in the Côtes-d'Armor, built in a horse-shoe curve above the splendid Trestraou beach, is only a little farther on. It is also the port for boats to the Sept Iles and specifically to Rouzic, the island where gannets nest in their thousands.

Continuing along the coast you come to **Trestel**, then the tiny fishing village of **Port-Blanc**, and eventually the 'gulf' or chasm at the very end of the **Plougrescant** peninsula. You may choose to stop at the **St-Gonéry** chapel with its crooked spire and its primitive frescos. The tour is completed as you head south for Tréguier's tall pierced spire.

TOUR OF THE PARISH CLOSES IN LEON

203 Km
Map ref.
120 3B

This tour can start from Roscoff, but also from Morlaix or even from Huelgoat or Landivisiau – which are the recommended staging points along the route.

We suggest you start or end this tour at **Roscoff**, and preferably on foot. Look upwards so as not to miss any of the carved window frames and dormers testifying to the past glory of this city of corsairs. Notice, too, the ancient cannon, ready loaded and pointed towards the English 'enemy', and which are set in the lantern-windows of the Renaissance bell tower of the church of Notre-Dame-de-Kroaz-Baz. Splendid 15th-century

incredible stone edifices as proof to posterity of their faith and enterprise. A further halt at **Commana** will complete the orgy of statuary carved out of hard Kersanton granite, decorated rood-beams and gilded altar-pieces.

Huelgoat and its great rocky outcrop, set in peaceful rural surroundings, will appeal to visitors (as will the combined inn-cum-museum at **Locmaria**, 3.5 km away, with a remarkable collection of old Breton furniture), before you reach **St-Herbot**. Here again, in the midst of this doll's-house hamlet, you will come on a Gothic church which possesses an extraordinary carved oak rood screen. From **Brasparts** the road climbs towards another **Mont-St-**

VIEW OF THE PARC REGIONAL D'ARMORIQUE

alabasters are also to be seen inside. After **St-Pol-de-Léon** (where you can climb the Kreisker, at 77 metres high the tallest bell tower in Brittany), the road crosses the peaceful estuary of the River Penzé. Then, just past **Carantec**, city of hydrangeas, it follows the left bank of the romantic River Dossen, at the head of which an impressive two-level railway viaduct overlooks the busy municipality of **Morlaix**, a town built within the ria, a river valley flooded by the sea. Picturesque old houses with projecting upper storeys point to the town's past wealth, derived from trade in linen cloth woven in the parish villages round about.

Today those parishes are noted for their 'closes', found nowhere else in the world; and in particular those of **St-Thégonnec**, **Guimiliau** and **Lampaul**. Nearly 400 years ago the three villages, near neighbours and rivals, began to vie with each other in constructing these

Michel, at 384m altitude one of the highest points in Brittany, and boasting incomparable views over the austere line of the **Monts d'Arrée** and the lake of Brennilis.

St-Rivoal, where the 'House of Rural Trades and Traditions' offers an instructive exhibition run by the Armorique Regional Park, marks the start of a typical Breton road, as whimsical as you could wish for, leading on to the triumphal arch at **Sizun**, and then to the oldest of Léon's parish closes, at **La Martyre.**

Then, after Ploudiry and Landivisiau we reach **Lambader**, with a granite spire rivalling the Kreisker, and carved wooden rood screen. Make a detour via the 16th century château at **Kerjean**, often called the 'Breton Versailles', and there, beyond the fields of artichokes and cauliflowers, the elegant silhouette of Notre-Dame-de-Kroaz-Baz at Roscoff comes into view once more.

TWO TOURS IN CORNOUAILLE

'Vast' is the word for Brittany's 'Cornwall'. Vast, varied, and rich in natural beauty, ancient monuments, and local activities based mainly on fisheries, agriculture and tourism (yachting and cruising). You can't hope to see it all in a single day, so we have split the journey of discovery in two, both tours based on Quimper.

AUDIERNE

THE AULNE, PORZAY AND CAP SIZUN

142 Km
Map ref.
130 D1

Suggested staging points on this northern part of the exploration are Châteaulin, Locronan, Douarnenez and Audierne. **Quimper**, capital of one of the most typically 'French' *départements* and certainly the most maritime with its 600-kilometre coastline, is a pleasant, neat town, perfect for long or short stays. The town is an almost obligatory departure point for countless excursions and rambles on foot, or by car or bicycle, into the charming and picturesque Cornouaille region of which it is both head and heart. But it also offers interesting features of its own: a Gothic cathedral with fine 15th-century windows, an art gallery and a Breton museum displaying Finistère's artistic riches and traditional folklore. The ideal time for a visit is during the third week of July when the Festival de Cornouaille fills the town with colourful and noisy celebrations.

If you take the old road, the D770, towards Brest, you can photograph the triangular-based rural calvary at **Quilinen**, a little-known masterpiece of Breton sculpture, though admittedly not on the same scale as its grander brother at **Pleyben**.

Following the now-canalized valley of the Aulne we come next to **Châteaulin**, a salmon-fishing centre and gateway to the wild countryside of the Crozon Peninsula. Gateway too to **Menez-Hom**, dominating the nearby Bay of Douarnenez from its altitude of 330m. In fine weather it offers

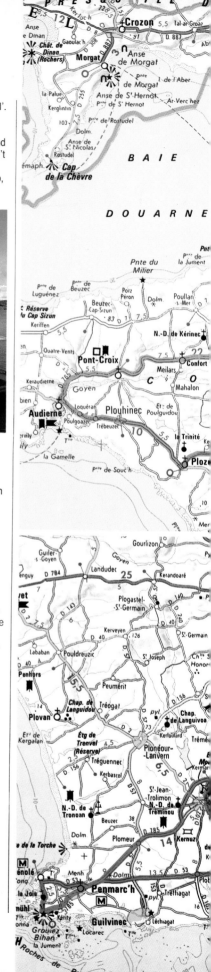

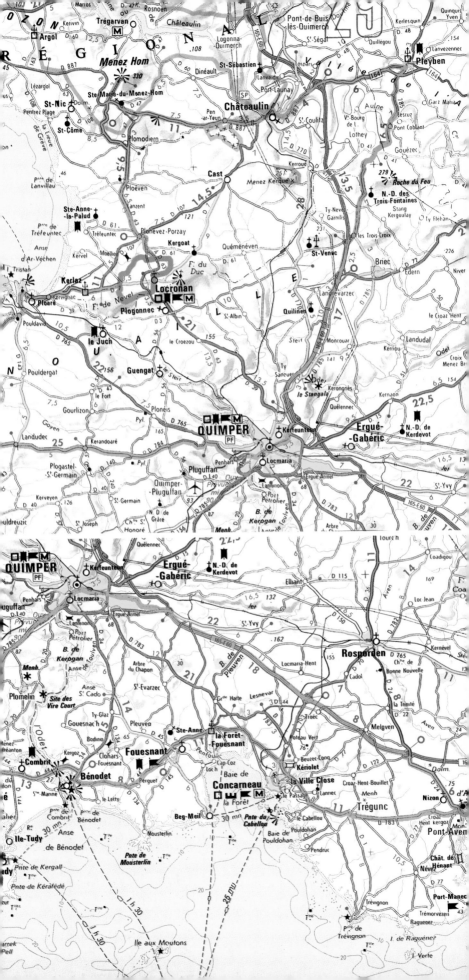

the most wonderful panoramic views of Brittany: the whole western coastline, the shipping in the rade de Brest, the peninsula and the green valley of the River Aulne running between the Monts d'Arrée and the Montagnes Noires.
In the midst of the rich Porzay farmland, not far from Ste-Anne-la-Palud where one of the great Breton *pardons* is held, **Locronan** must not be missed. This ancient weavers' city, run by people of foresight who repaired its cobbled streets when so many other towns were spreading bitumen on theirs, now counts its daily visitors by the thousand at peak holiday times; visitors who never tire of

coming to see its town square, granite houses and ancient well. **Douarnenez**, where you should ask for *Kouign aman* for tea, still manages to live as best it can from the sea, though its heyday when the sardine was king is over, recalled now only in its charming maritime museum.
At **Audierne**, in the centre of Cap Sizun, when the tide is high you get the extraordinary impression that the boats in the harbour are on top of the harbour walls, an image of the merging of sea and land, in the true Cornouaille style.
The road back to Quimper takes you through **Plozévet** and **Landudec**, following the D784.

THE ODET RIVER NEAR BENODET

ARTISTS AND FISH AUCTIONS

145 Km
Map ref.
131 4F

This second tour in Cornouaille starts by heading south-east in search of art, before turning back west along the coastline where hard-working fishing ports alternate with leisure resorts. Suggested staging points are Pont-Aven, Concarneau, Bénodet and Pont-l'Abbé.
Among other praiseworthy enterprises launched in the marvellous summer of 1990, which broke all Brittany's weather records, was the setting up of a *Route des Peintres*, centred of course on **Pont-Aven**, for people wishing to visit the places where Gauguin and other painters stayed and worked a century ago. The great man himself was always hard-up, and paid for his board and lodging in kind, giving his landlady the occasional canvas which she hid away in the attic. It was Gauguin's posthumous reputation

that gave Pont-Aven its name as 'City of Painters'. And this in turn made it the cradle of a 'Pont-Aven School', whose members were mostly daubers of dubious talent hoping a spark or two of his skill and fame might attach itself to their mediocre paintings. So the art you find at Pont-Aven will be bad as well as good. The 'good', naturally, are the works of Gauguin and his disciples – the true ones – to which the municipal museum gives pride of place.
Next we come to **Concarneau**, the first and largest link in the chain of fishing ports on which a substantial part of the region's economy is based. Concarneau's Moros quay where the fish auction is held, and its 'Ville Close' or walled town with fortifications built by Vauban, are the two faces of this remarkable town.
Then, as you travel west, the twin resorts of **Fouesnant** and **Bénodet** vie for leadership in the field of tourism with competing leisure centres, 4-star camp sites and cider-drinking by the bowlful!
Then, almost at once, driving across the Odet, perhaps the prettiest river in France, you arrive in a different world altogether, that of the 'Pays Bigouden'. Part of its claim to fame derives from the beautiful work of its lace-makers; more is due to the courage and toil of its fishing-fleet and men who, all along the coast from **Loctudy** to **St-Guénolé** (known as 'St-Gué') by way of **Lesconil** and **Guilvinec**, haul up from the deep the best fresh fish in all France. In the late afternoons of summer these men can hardly push their way through the crowds of inquisitive tourists as they carry their catch to the auctioneers on the quays, where within the hour it will have been sold to the highest bidders.
The flat Bigouden country contrasts with the rocky headland of St-Guénolé (not shown on map), where in heavy weather the Atlantic waves break with special fury. The calvary at Tronoan, a few kilometres away to the north is the oldest in Brittany and much venerated by sailors and fishermen. From there you head back, via **Pont-l'Abbé**, to Quimper.

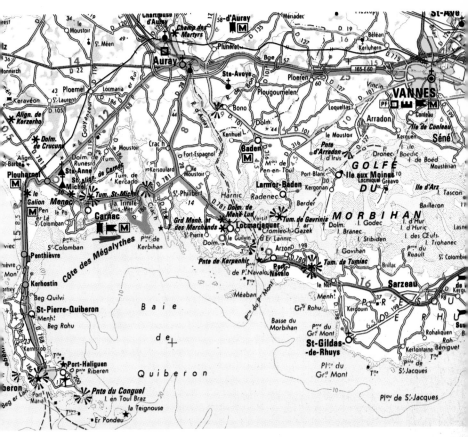

TOUR OF THE MEGALITHS

115 Km
Map ref.
139 B6

On this journey of discovery, at least, drivers should have no difficulty in persuading their small children to go with them. Just think of a drive into Asterix's home country! The prospect of exploring the stamping ground of the Gallic 'Superman' must surely be an exciting one. The suggested staging points are Auray, Quiberon and Carnac.

The starting point is **Vannes**, gateway to the Gulf of Morbihan, a lovely old city where you will enjoy a stroll through the lanes leading to the ramparts, and to the picturesque gardens of the lower town. Continue in the direction of **Auray**. Here you must not miss the medieval quarter of St-Goustan, a marvel of freshness and authenticity straight out of the 15th century, on the river's east bank. The tour leads straight to the little town of **Plouharnel**, with a Benedictine abbey nearby where they maintain the tradition of Gregorian chant as at Solesmes; and thence on along the isthmus joining **Quiberon** to the rest of the continent. At **Kerhostin** you take the road to the right, along the 'Côte Sauvage' or Wild Coast, which has the peninsula's finest scenery of cliffs, caves and little sandy beaches pounded by swelling seas. Near Quiberon, on the rocky Pointe du Conguel opposite Belle-Ile, is the thalassotherapy institute founded by Louison Bobet, one of the most famous champions of the 'Tour de France' cycling race.

But we shall spend the greater part of our time among the fields of standing stones at **Carnac**: row upon row of them as far as you can see. At first you will hardly believe your eyes. How on earth did 'they', whoever they were, manage to transport these 'pebbles', each weighing several tons, and then set them upright in such regular order? So far no archaeologist has discovered a sure answer to the enigma of this amazing human feat. That infernal Asterix has certainly hidden the rules of the game! The wealth of stones continues as far as **Locmariaquer**, where the largest-known menhir in Armorica awaits you – 20-30 metres high but alas broken into three pieces. Close by is the so-called 'Merchants' Table', a dolmen with passage-way, under whose lintel stone one can make out the lines of a plough, carved in the hard stone. Without doubt we are faced here with the work of a very ancient and well-developed civilization. On the return journey we pass through Auray once more, perhaps pushing on from there for a visit to the basilica at Ste-Anne (6 km north-east on the D17), where the most popular of all the Breton *pardons* is held on 26 July. From here we return to Vannes.

WALKS

All the walks described in this section have been supplied by ABRI, the Association Bretonne de Randonnées et Itinéraires, the regional ramblers' association. Further information on the walking guides (*topoguides*) they produce is available from: ABRI, 9 rue des Portes-Mordelaises, 35000 Rennes ☎ 99.31.59.44

This chapter offers a large and varied selection of itineraries that will help you get to know Brittany and its people by exploring its different regions on foot. The fifteen walks range from 4.5 km to 19 km in length, with some of the longer routes divided into shorter circuits or sections which can be combined or undertaken separately in whatever way you please or have time for. The great majority of them are fully waymarked, in many cases following the established *Grande Randonnée* footpaths for most or all of the way.

In the order presented the routes take you all round Brittany's fantastically beautiful and exciting rocky coastline, starting from Cancale in the north-east along the English Channel to the westernmost point of Finistère, and then southward around the bays and headlands of the Atlantic coast, with their splendid leisure resorts, to the fishing ports of Morbihan, with excursions to two of the offshore islands as you go.

Then turning inland they explore this country of legend and ancient monuments, with its incredible array of prehistoric megaliths, its wilder heaths, moors and marshland around the lakes of Guerlédan and St-Michel, and its medieval military and religious architecture in many out of the way places, of which the parish closes south-west of Morlaix are a prime example.

All maps in this section are 1:25,000 unless otherwise stated. In order to pinpoint the location of these walks, each is provided with a map reference relating to the regional atlas.

ROCKY CLIFFS ON THE EMERALD COAST

16 Km
Map ref.
127 6B

Centred on Cancale, this walk follows the GR34 footpath for 11.5 km along the coast from the port of la Houle and the Pointe de Crolles to the spectacular viewpoint of the Pointe du Grouin, then on to the beautiful beach of the Anse du Verger cove. Then 4.5 km by minor roads takes you back to your starting point. Other access points on the D201 coast road from St-Malo are Port-Mer and Port-Briac.

The picturesque resort and fishing port of **Cancale** itself still retains some of its local colour, even though the characteristic '*bisquine*' fishing boats are gone. For a long time it has been the oyster which has reigned supreme here.

All along this route rocky cliffs, in places as high as 40 metres and covered with gorse and whin, alternate with pleasant beaches and pretty little ports.

From the **Pointe du Hock** you can look out over the oyster-beds which make Cancale a place of pilgrimage for gourmets, and a little farther on the **Pointe de la Chaine** gives you a view of the **Rocher de Cancale** islet and the little **Ile de Cancale** with its ancient fortress. Towards **Port-Briac** you will need to take care, as the cliffs become more precipitous and the path is steep. After the next little headland, the **Pointe du Chatry**, you come to **Port-Mer**, and then, rounding another point, to the **Pointe du Grouin** itself. From the rocky end of the point the panoramic view is stupendous, with sea on every side, running from the looming saddle of Cap Fréhel 35 km away to the west; to the north the faint outline of the Channel Islands, with Jersey and Guernsey rising like blurred shadows from the deep; and away to the east the jutting headlands of Granville, Carolles, and then Avranches. Finally, farther round still across its wide bay, you may be able to make out the often misty silhouette of Mont-St-Michel.

Doubling back south-westwards the route runs along the coast road for a time before bending right, to follow the coastline around the **Pointe de la Moulière** where again it becomes precipitous, and great care is needed. From this stretch of the route, or from **Le Verger** a little farther on, a number of different minor roads will take you the 4.5 km back to Cancale or La Houle.

SEA SPRAY AND ROCKS

RED SANDSTONE AND SEA BIRDS

6 Km
Map ref.
124 B3

Whichever end you start from, access to this stretch of the GR34 coastal path is via Plévénon, and then either the D16 road to the Cap Fréhel lighthouse or the D16A to the Fort de la Latte.

Cap Fréhel itself is one of the most impressive sites on the northern coast of Brittany. Its red, grey and black cliffs look down on the sea from a height of more than 60 metres, while a heavy surf lashes the rocks at their feet. On the cliff top a new lighthouse built in 1948 has replaced an old one destroyed by the Germans. The particular rock formation here, in a series of folds like a staircase, provides favourable nesting sites for sea birds. **La Fauconnière**, a designated reserve of the Society for the Study and Protection of Nature in Brittany, is home to colonies of cormorants, gulls and kittiwakes.

Leaving Cap Fréhel with its splendid views over the rugged cliffs and rough sandy moorland of the bird sanctuary, the path curves south and east around the whole length of the bay, the **Anse des Sévignés**, past **Les Fontaines** and the **Pointe de la Pie** to the **Fort de la Latte**. Built in the 13th and 14th centuries, the ancient fortress stands on a rocky outcrop in what must be Brittany's most extraordinarily dramatic location. Linked to the mainland only by a pair of drawbridges built in 1806 across deep sea-filled ravines, it is open to visitors.

A NESTING GANNET

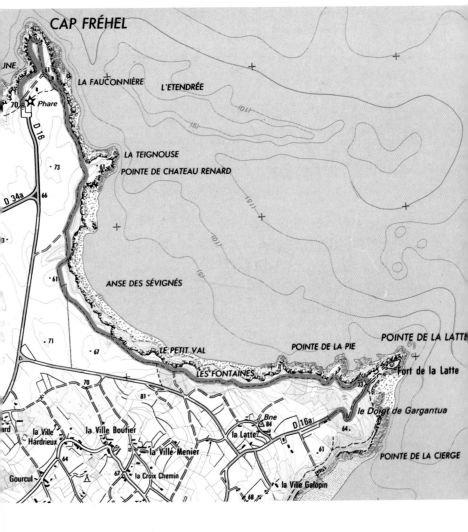

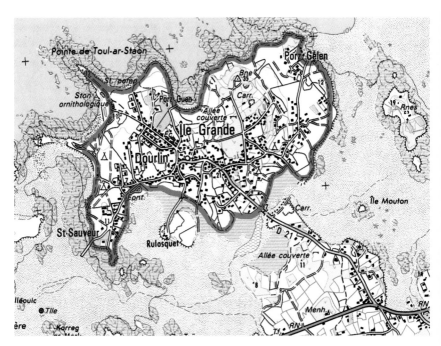

THE ILE GRANDE, A HAVEN OF PEACE

4.5 Km
Map ref.
121 B6

Access to this short island tour is via the D21, either from Pleumeur-Bodou (where you can leave the car) or by turning off the D788 coast road at Penvern, between Trébeurden and Trégastel.

The **Ile Grande** is full of charm and interest, its picturesque houses huddled together along the narrow lanes, its little port where fishing boats lie at anchor, and its pretty beaches for summer visitors. The footpath – once again the GR34 – takes you all around its coastline, by contrast, as you will discover, a coast of jagged rocks, steep ups and downs and windswept moorland.

Going in an anti-clockwise direction you come first to **Porz Gélen** at the north-east corner of the island, then, to the north-west, the Sept Iles Ornithological Station has an exhibition showing how sea birds have been acclimatized here, with information panels and books available. Close by, there are ancient granite quarries. Offshore to the west is the Ile Aganton, where pilgrims used to go and offer a loaf of bread and say prayers at the foot of three low crosses, hoping to be cured of whooping-cough. From **St-Sauveur** there are fine views back to the mainland coastline and the little islets scattered between. Follow the road along the coast to return to Penvern.

THE COAST AT LOCQUEMEAU NEAR ILE GRANDE

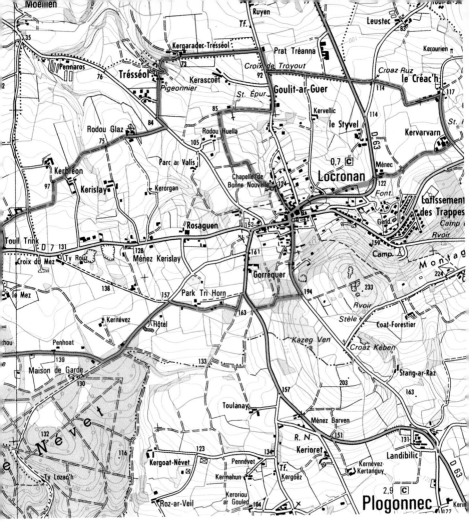

WOODS AND FIELDS OF LOCRONAN

12 Km
Map ref.
130 C1

This circular tour is centred on the prosperous little town of Locronan, which lies on the north-west slopes of a hill on the southern edge of the Porzay. Easily reached from the triangle of roads linking Quimper (21 km away) with Châteaulin (16 km) and Douarnenez (9 km). Waymarked in yellow.

Starting from the church in **Locronan** you take the rue St Maurice in the direction of **Plogonnec** – a minor road so steep that in the old days stage-coach passengers were made to get out and walk to the top of the hill. From there the road goes down again through mixed woodland where some of the trees are labelled: maritime pines, Norway pines, beeches, oaks. After following the Quimper road for a little way the path runs between steep slopes planted with young chestnuts. Then, leaving the main road at a fork it opens up, and near the houses at **Parc Tri-Horn** the woodland gives way to cultivated fields of rich black soil.

Some 1.5 km farther on you turn on to a track running behind residential gardens, and on reaching the farm of Le Mez, red and white waymarks appear alongside the yellow ones of the

woodland tour, which shares the GR38 route from Redon to Douarnenez for some distance.

As you start to descend towards **Kermenguy** you get a better and better view of the Crozon Peninsula, with the bell tower of Plonevez Porzay to the north and farther away, at the foot of Ménez Hom, the village of Plomodiern. Now turning your back on the sea you plunge into the woodland again along a winding footpath, as far as the farm of Rodou Glaz. From there the path leads towards Trésséol, of whose ancient manor nothing is left but a pigeon-cote – and of the mill which once adorned this valley, nothing but the memory. Climbing up the slope again you will see Locronon nestling at the foot of its hill.

On reaching a calvary, you can return to the road by way of the Bonne Nouvelle Chapel, with notable stained glass windows by A. Manessier, or you can extend the journey a little by taking a broad shady path from the calvary (the important local *pardon* of La Troménie follows this route), and then a winding path to the hamlet of **Le Créac'h**.

Finally you return to Locronan by turning down a steep path just beyond the farm buildings at **Kervarvarn**.

CLIFFS AND CAVES OF CAP DE LA CHEVRE

4.5 or 5 Km
Map ref.
119 F5

Access to the Cap de la Chèvre is via the little fishing port that has given its name to the whole Crozon peninsula – one of the most striking stretches of Brittany's seaboard, whose deeply indented coastline of rocky cliffs, reefs, and marvellous sandy beaches, some sheltered some lashed by ocean winds and waves, attracts many visitors each year.

From **Crozon** you go on to the port of **Morgat**, where you cannot fail to be impressed by the awesome cliff walls along the shoreline; and which offers several ways of reaching the **Cap de la Chèvre**. At the foot of the last sea wall a stairway leads to the coastal footpath along the eastern edge of the peninsula overlooking the bay. Or you can take a shorter route farther to the west, through **Montourgar** and **St-Hernot**, or even go by boat and visit the caves along the shore.

To get to the footpath along the cliffs from the far end of the port, you start by climbing up through a pinewood and pass close to a lighthouse. Soon afterwards you can see the gaping mouth of the *Cheminée du Diable* or 'Devil's Chimney' down by the sea, and there are fine views from the **Pointe de Morgat**. Between this point and the **Grande Roche** the path is often very steep and in places runs along the very edge of the cliff before reaching the **Coz Semellec**

CROZON

rock. Next you come to the **Pointe de St-Hernot**, where again there is a viewpoint, and then pass the **Ile de la Vierge**. And at last you reach the Cap de la Chèvre, standing a sheer 100 metres above the sea, like a gigantic breakwater protecting Douarnenez Bay.

From the Cape itself there are panoramic views out to sea and towards the jutting headlands of Finistère. From right to left you can see the Pointe de Pen Hir and the Tas des Pois, the Ile de Sein, and Cap Sizun with its two 'finistères' or 'land's-ends': the Pointe du Van and Pointe du Raz, at the southernmost end of Douarnenez Bay. You can choose among several 'inland' routes leading back to Morgat.

The map below is scale 1:100,000.

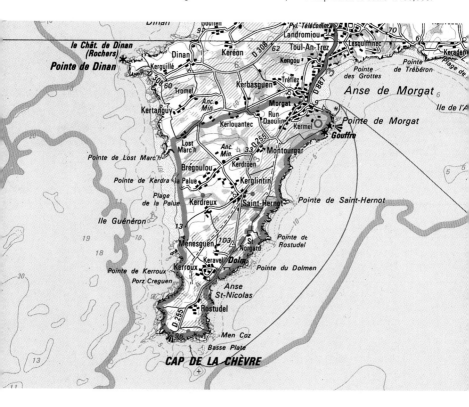

A STROLL IN PONT-AVEN'S BOIS D'AMOUR

4 Km
Map ref.
131 E4

This brief tour along the banks of the salmon-rich River Aven and into the wooded hillside above the town gives an impression of the landscapes that have been the inspiration of so many painters. Pont-Aven is situated on the D783

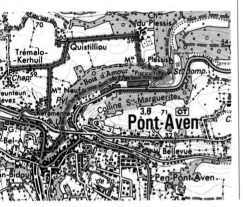

between Quimperlé and Concarneau and further information on fishing possibilities is available from the Tourist Office.
Start from the **Pont-Aven** town centre – where there is plenty of parking space – and the river banks are a favourite place for a stroll. To reach the **Bois d'Amour** or Lover's Wood, cross over by one of the foot-bridges and follow the mysterious '*chaos*' of rocks along the bank. You can imagine the artists at work here: splashes of yellow, green and blue in a seductive landscape. Sadly, the Bois d'Amour was badly damaged in the 1987 hurricane. Leave the riverside and take a 'hollow' path up the hill, with rocks on either side. An avenue of beeches leads you to the 16th-century chapel at **Trémalo**, and an imposing chestnut avenue then leads you gently back towards Pont-Aven. The banks of the Aven that inspired the painters may be fine for walks, but this little coastal river is also famed throughout the *département* for its abundance of salmon and trout.

CLIFFS AND DUNES OF KERBIHAN

6.5 Km
Map ref.
139 C4

The coastal footpath around the Pointe de Kerbihan starts near the southern end of the port of La Trinité, 11 km south of Auray via the D28. La Trinité is not only a beautiful seaside resort and busy fishing port, it is also a major yachting centre frequented by many well-known yachtsmen of the region, foremost among them being Eric Tabarly, a native of the place, whose reputation enhances the enthusiasm of both locals and visitors for sailing.
Once beyond the bathing beaches and

the port, you will find that **La Trinité** is a mosaic of interesting natural features. There are the rocky cliffs of the **Pointe de Kerbihan** all along the estuary of the Crac'h, with views over the river, the dunes at **Kervillen** and the salt marshes of **Men Du**, now mostly abandoned but where you may still find a few salt-pans and storehouses. From the dunes at **Kervourden** you can return by road to where you started. But if you should wish to extend your walk there is a *Petite Randonnée* local route, waymarked in blue, which follows a series of sunken roadways back to the port.

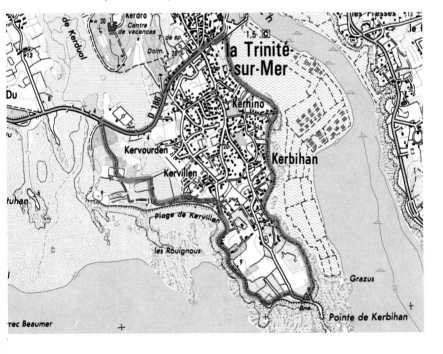

AN ISLAND 'WILD AND FAIR'

6 Km
Map ref.
138 3E

Having crossed over from the mainland, this walk can easily be made in a day. Belle-Ile is the biggest of the Iles de Ponant and, according to the locals, the *Bellilois*, the most beautiful. You will be able to see the famous 'Aiguilles' or 'Needles' which Claude Monet painted thirty-eight times!

You can get to Belle-Ile-en-Mer by boat from Quiberon's Port Maria to the island port of Le Palais, 2 to 10 daily crossings according to season ☎ 97.30.80.01 and SNCF stations). Onward transport to Bangor on the south-west coast, and the

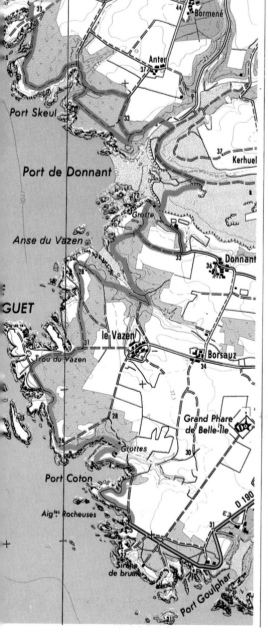

CYCLING ON BELLE-ILE

footpath from Port Coton to Port Donnant, is by bus – or cycle hire ☎ 97.31.81.93, with parking at Port Goulphar.

The southern coastline beyond **Bangor** is wild and rugged with strangely-shaped rocks continually battered by the Atlantic swell. Its irregular cliff-line, riddled with caves and grottoes, has a violent and ever-changing beauty.

But this same coast also offers the gentler aspect of its valleys, its fine sandy beaches, the green waters of its creeks, its dunes, and the majestic ocean rollers crowned with foam. This is what you will find at **Port Donnant**; and this is also the coast that helps to safeguard the lives of sailors, with its great lighthouse, the *Grande Phare*, whose beams light up the seas to a distance of 32 miles.

Stretching along the coast from **Port Coton** to Port Donnant the footpath presents no difficulties for walkers, as it runs across open moorland ablaze with the colours of whin and heather, with splendid views from the headlands at either end.

THE NEEDLES, PORT COTON

ENCIRCLING ROCHEFORT-EN-TERRE

19 Km
Map ref.
134 F2

As both are centred on the little town of Rochefort, situated between Redon (25 km away) and Vannes (35 km), and reached via the D774 or D771, these two tours can if you wish be combined and undertaken as one full day's outing.

The first walk, (12 km) and waymarked in yellow, starts off northward on the D774 along the Gueuzon valley giving fine views over the River Arz, where there are menhirs and a dolmen to see as well as slate quarries.
After passing the Moulin d'Arz, follow a cutting through woodland to **Brambien**, from where the road opens out on to the Lanvaux moors, a mysterious area with a number of fallen menhirs. The path leads over a footbridge to Brécéhan and then heads on towards the village of **Beauchat** beyond which, in the wood on your right, stands the Dolmen des Follets. The route again follows tracks through woodland

before going back down into the Arz valley – only to climb up again towards the schist hills known as the '*grées*', where old slate quarries, now unworked, are set amidst lovely scenery. At Guenfol, notice the pit known as the 'Blue Lake', and before starting back down the hillside, take time to enjoy the view over Rochefort.

The second walk, (7 km) and waymarked in blue, starts from the fairground and encircles Rochefort itself.
From the fairground the path takes you up and along the rocky hills north of the town known as the '*grées*'; then brings you down again, past the stretch of water at the **Moulin Neuf** which has been developed as a centre for tourists, and along in front of the hostel, an old farmhouse that has been renovated. Farther on you come to the manor of St-Fiacre. This tour has the advantage of enabling you to explore the town from within the two valleys which surround it.

TWO SHORT WALKS FROM LIZIO

*10 Km
in all
Map ref.
134 D1*

Lizio lies just off the road from Malestroit (17 km away) to Josselin (18 km); soon after Le Roc-St-André fork left towards Lizio, as far as the Val Jouin Ramblers' Centre. Both these walks are waymarked with arrows.

The first walk (5 km), is of botanical interest. Although it is an all-year round walk, it is most interesting when the autumn colours show or alternatively at the height of spring.
Starting from the **Val Jouin** Ramblers' Centre the path runs south-east along old shady sunken tracks and narrow little valleys where trout streams flow.
All along the route there are more than forty varieties of trees and shrubs labelled with the French, Latin and local names of each species. Some of the panels also have questions which enable you to verify your own botanical knowledge: if you don't know the right answer, look at the back of the label. After the walk you will at last be able to identify the oaks, beeches, aspens, poplars, birches, ashes, and the various conifers that make up this landscape.
On your way you can also visit a bee-keeping centre at the manor of **Tromeur**, and spend an hour seeing the hives, the extraction of honey, and an interesting exhibition on the subject. The path then continues north-west and back to the starting point.

The second walk (5 km) also starts from the Val Jouin centre. The path takes you through a landscape that is typical of the Breton moorlands, where gorse and broom abound.
You set off northwards from the Val Jouin centre. After the first kilometre or so, the path turns sharply southwards again to bring you back to the little town of **Lizio**. Here you can pause to admire the beautiful old granite buildings, before continuing back to the Val Jouin centre.

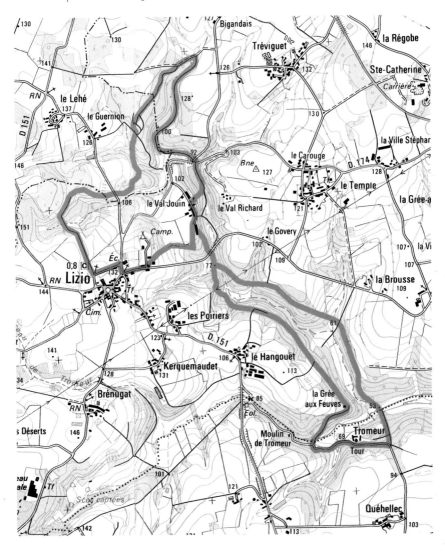

IN THE REGION OF LAKE GUERLEDAN

15 Km
Map ref.
132 B3

The walk is based on St-Aignan, 3 km from Mur-de-Bretagne on the road to Guémené-sur-Scorff, with two link paths enabling you to plan shorter circuits if you wish. Waymarks are red and white on the GR34 alongside Lake Guerlédan, then yellow on the local PR routes. A magnificent lake, some 400 ha in extent, whose waters stretch for 13 km along the winding gorges of the River Blavet, drowning 18 erstwhile locks on the Nantes-Brest canal. This immense reservoir was created in 1923-25 by the building of the Guerlédan dam, 206 m wide at the top, 45 m high and 35 m thick at the base. The power station on the left bank has three sets of turbo-alternators, with a capacity of 15,000 to 45,000 kilowatt hours. Because of seasonal variations in the water-level of the Blavet, a second dam, of earth, has been built 600 m downstream, to even out the flow.

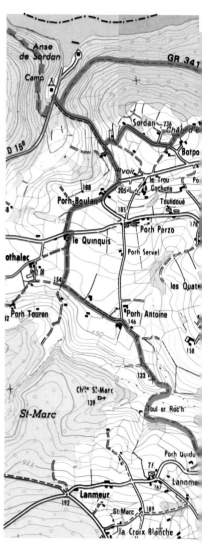

A FORGOTTEN BOAT

You start from **St-Aignan**'s *mairie* or from its 16th-century church, restored in the 18th and 19th centuries and worth visiting for its Flamboyant doorways, carved wooden altarpieces depicting the Tree of Jesse and the Holy Trinity, and pietà. Head north to **Guerlédan**. On the way you will pass the secondary dam on the Blavet, and a farm built entirely of schist. At the Guerlédan sluice the path joins the GR34 and will follow it all the way to the **Anse de Sordan**. At the foot of the dam fork left along a steep path up the hillside, which soon brings you to the Guerlédan car park, a viewpoint overlooking the dam and across to the communes on the northern bank of the lake: Mur-de-Bretagne to the right and Caurel straight ahead. The GR34 then runs through brushwood, where you should stop at the chapel of Ste-Tréphine. Continue on the GR34 to the Anse de Sordan, here and there catching glimpses of the lake. **Sordan** itself is a yatching centre, with camp site, restaurant and boat trips. From

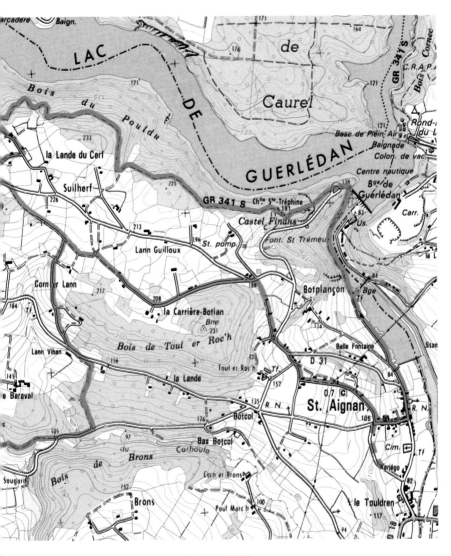

BROOM NEAR LES FORGES, MORBIHAN

Sordan onwards you will be following the yellow PR waymarks south towards **Porh Boulan**, **Quinquis** and **Porh Antoine**. A track through a deep cutting (wet and muddy in winter) leads down into the Corboulo valley, then climbs up again towards **Toul-er-Roc'h** and **Porh-Quidu**. To the left of Porh-Quidu another sunken road, on your right, with a steep bank on one side and an electric fence on the other, takes you down into the Corboulo valley again and beside a series of private lakes.

A pleasant path through brushwood leads north again, to **Lann Vihan**. Then you follow the field track to **Corn-er-Lann** and bear slightly left on a sunken track. On reaching a crossroads, where one of the link paths comes in from the left, turn right along a pleasant track to **La Carrière-Botlan**. At the crossing with the road from Sordan take a minor road leading down to St-Aignan.

FOUR WALKS IN THE MONTS D'ARREE

15 Km
Map ref.
121 F4

These four short walks on the southern side of the St-Michel reservoir take you from the heights of Brittany's highest 'mountains' to the lonely marshlands of the Yeun Ellez. Access is via Brasparts on the D785 Quimper-Morlaix road, and then from the car park at Mont-St-Michel-de-Brasparts just south of Ménez-Mikel. Despite their modest height (384m at most), the Monts d'Arrée offer panoramic views and the mists which often shroud their summits give the impression of greater altitude. Mont-St-Michel has

always been a 'holy' hill; first a Druid shrine dedicated to the Celtic sun-god, Bénélos, and then taken over by the Christians, St Michael the Archangel ousting the pagan deity. At the heart of the massif is a vast lake surrounded by peat bogs – an area full of mystery and the scene of some of Brittany's most renowned and fearful Breton legends. The map below is at the scale 1:50,000.

Waymarked in light green, this 4 km walk starts from the old St-Michel farm (with car park) where there is a permanent exhibition of the work of more than 200

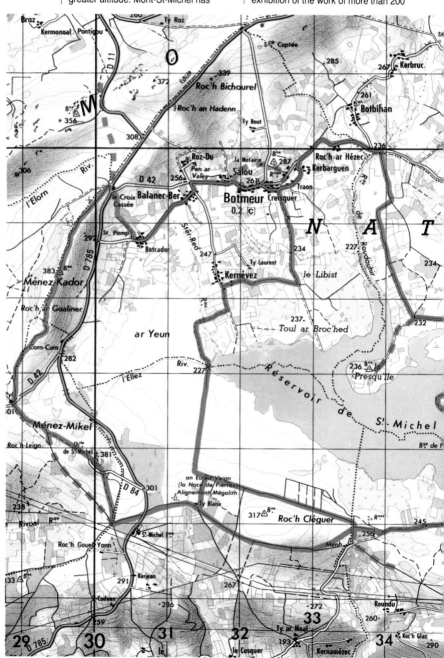

Breton craftsmen, all hand-made originals which make popular souvenirs.

Starting therefore from the St-Michel car park and not far from the now abandoned farm at **Ty-Blaise** you will find an alignment of megaliths known as the 'Stone Wedding' (in Breton, An Eured Veign), hidden away in the moorland. The legend is that some wedding guests, engaged in a wild and frenzied dance, prevented the parish priest of Brasparts from taking extreme unction to a dying man, and as the *biniou* (the Breton bagpipe) played its final note, the revellers were turned to stone.

Finally from the summit of the high quartzite rocks of **Roc'h Cléguer** you can get a panoramic view out over the Yeun Ellez marshland.

This *Petite Randonnée* route, (4 km) and waymarked in violet, starts from Roc'h Cléguer and is the best way of approaching the Yeun Ellez marshes, along a gravel road.

From the foot of **Roc'h Cléguer**, you turn north to the marshy area stretching along the south-western bank of the lake. Regarded in ancient times as the gateway to Hades (**Le Youdic**), it is the subject of many legends.

This area is also interesting from the natural history angle, whole stretches of the damp marshland glowing with bog-myrtle, a low-growing bush of the willow family, and the peat bogs pale with the spongy cushions of sphagnum mosses that gradually turn into peat, used in past times by the local people as fuel. Bird-watchers, too, will be able to observe migratory Montagu's harriers, as well as the native hen-harriers, that are native to the region, curlews, cuckoos and ring-ouzels. You can then carry on to the **Yeun Forc'han** marshes in **Loqueffret**, which stretch as far as the nuclear power station.

Starting from the Forc'han Belvedere, this short loop (1 km), waymarked in dark blue, gives you an unprecedented view of the St-Michel reservoir, 800 hectares in extent, retained by a dam built in 1930, and now enclosed within the perimeter of the Monts d'Arrée nuclear power station developed between 1966 and 1985.

Until the belvedere is reopened, a pleasant road between high banks enables you to visit the picturesque village of **Forc'han**. From there you should go on to visit the church (a designated site) at **Brennilis**, and then to the dolmen at **Bellevue** known as the 'House of the Dwarfs' (in Breton, Ty ar Boudiked). Returning to the lake, at **Nestavel-Bihan** there is a shady walkway along the bank, which continues along an old tree-lined road.

Waymarked in white, this walk near the banks of the Roudoudhir (6 km) is full of interest for nature-lovers, in spite of its proximity to the nuclear power station now in the process of being shut down. Along the lake shore many species of water birds can be seen. As you climb northwards you will see the enormous bulging peat-bog of Vénec – a very dangerous area, *not* to be ventured upon. And on the banks of the Roudoudhir stream the Armorique Nature Park has reintroduced some families of beavers. Guided visits are organized by the Armorique Nature Park, to allow visitors to explore the wildlife here more fully.

RIVERS AND ROCKS OF HUELGOAT

12 Km
Map ref.
121 F5

This tour, centred on the town of Huelgoat, runs through one of the most beautiful forests of inland Brittany, unfortunately damaged by the 1987 hurricane. It is waymarked in yellow and white.

From **Huelgoat**'s main square, turn left down the rue du Docteur Jacq to the Promenade du Canal. To develop the silver-bearing lead mines here, already known to the Romans, a dam was built in the 19th century creating a lake and two canals. By following the upper canal which serves a small hydro-electric station, you finally reach the mine, and on your left, the River d'Argent. Cross the footbridge and take the path to the left into an area of brushwood. Quite soon you reach the Mare des Fées or Fairies' Mere. The river then runs under the rocks, and you come to the '*Gouffre*' where it plunges down 8 metres into a chasm and disappears again under the great blocks of granite. Here a stairway takes you up to the road again. After reaching the Pont Rouge turn right, along the Promenade du Fer à Cheval at the end of which you reach the Pont Rouge car park.

From here the Clair Ruisseau path leads into the woodland, and a little stairway leads down to the **Mare aux Sangliers**, a small lake of clear water in an attractive rocky setting where you can imagine you see the heads of lurking boars, and a rustic bridge spans the stream. Follow the Allée de la Mare on your left. After an impressive stairway of more than 200 steps that offers a short cut up to the **Camp d'Artus**, or Arthur's Camp, you will see above you the **Grotte d'Artus** – a cave where King Arthur of the Round Table is said to have dug himself a bed in the rock, perched high as a precaution against prowling animals of the night. The path leads you up to the camp, a defensive earthwork of Celtic or Gallo-Roman origin, with two encircling banks and a mound at the entrance (as a descriptive panel explains).

The **Louarn** footpath continues the journey through the forest, with outcrops of rock appearing at intervals, till it reaches the 'Lovers' Walk' leading to the Chaos Rocheux or 'Rocky Wilderness' exhibition park by the River d'Argent. Here you can visit the Home of the Virgin, the Greenwood Theatre, the Logan Stone, the Devil's Cave and the mill among the rocks. Especially interesting is the clog-maker's hut, a faithful replica of the huts which the clog-makers regularly built in the forest, where they and their families could stay while cutting the wood necessary for their trade. At the exit from the mill, follow the lakeside road back to the main square of Huelgoat which is now close at hand.

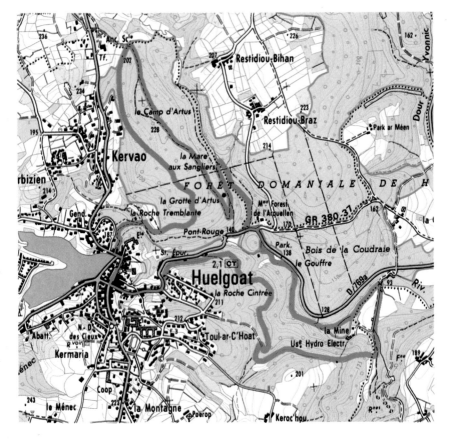

AN ANCIENT CHURCH IN A WOODED VALLEY

8 Km
Map ref.
120 E3

To reach Le Cloître-St-Thégonnec, 15 km south of Morlaix in the Queffleuth valley, you take the D111 from the Plessis crossroads on the Morlaix-Huelgoat road – or the GR380 from Kermorgant.

After a look round **Le Cloître-St-Thégonnec**'s little 12th to 18th-century church, you take the **Quillien** road out of the village, beyond the D111. At the top of the slope there is a radio antenna, broken down by a storm. From this high point – 256m altitude – you get a superb view over **Morlaix** to the north and the **Monts d'Arrée** to the south.

Before reaching the hamlet of Quillien fork left on a gravel road which becomes an earth track, and continue across the moorland to the Caon farm. After crossing the D111 follow a sunken track (wet in winter) which crosses another road, and then another earth track leading to **Kermorgant**, a pretty village where the houses mingle harmoniously with the rocks. You should notice a splendid house with an exterior staircase dating from 1830 – and don't miss the public wash-place and drinking-trough for animals (fairly recent) as you climb up again on the GR380, waymarked in red and white. On reaching **Kergollon**, follow the road to the left for 150 metres. Then, near the houses at **Roz-ar-Han**, turn right on to a small earth track that runs through the fields, and eventually comes out at a camping site. From there you take the road back to Le Cloître-St-Thégonnec.

ST-THEGONNEC

GAZETTEER

The A-Z gazetteer section which follows features a selection of the region's top seaside resorts, small fishing harbours, sleepy, rural villages of great charm and major centres for shopping and cultural excursions.
Each entry contains details about the organizations to contact for sports and activity pursuits such as riding, golf or cycling and numerous other leisure activities are listed to add to the enjoyment of your stay.
Selected hotels, camp sites and restaurants are included, with a host of facts of historical, architectural and general interest to complete your appreciation of this great holiday region.

In fact, all your questions are answered on what to do, what to see and where to go.

Although Brittany is divided administratively into four *départements* or regions: Côtes-d'Armor, Finistère, Ille-et-Vilaine and Morbihan, historically and culturally the *département* of Loire-Atlantique has more associations with Brittany than with the Pays de la Loire within whose boundaries it now technically falls. For the purposes of this guide, therefore, it is also included here.

LEFT FISHING BOATS AT ROSCOFF
ABOVE THATCH IN LA GRANDE BRIERE

AUDIERNE
Map ref 129 D4
Pop 3,000
Quimper 36 km
Brest 91 km
Rennes 242 km
Nantes 264 km
Paris 591 km
🅱 place de la
Liberté
☎ 98.70.12.20

Towards the westernmost tip of Europe, Audierne is essentially a lobster and cray-fishing port situated at the mouth of the Goyen estuary. An attractive small town where pleasure trips are catered for with daily sailings lasting about an hour out to the **Ile de Sein**, a rocky, windswept island formerly a Druid burial site. For ornithologists there is an important bird reserve nearby at **Cap Sizun**, where colonies of nesting and migratory sea birds can be observed.

One cannot fail to be impressed by the wild and rocky **Pointe du Raz** for this is Brittany's own 'Land's End' – *finis terrae* – where the land falls away to a highly dramatic buffeting and crashing as the Atlantic roars round the finger tips of rock far below, every movement perilously threatening for the tiny fishing boats circling the headland.

The large sweep of sandy beach, the **Baie des Trépassés** or Bay of Dead Souls, beyond Plogoff, is surprisingly sheltered and pleasant despite its morbid name. It was from here that the dead priests were transported out to the Ile de Sein. This bay vies with that of Douarnenez as the location of the 5th-century sunken city of Ys, and there are tales of ghostly riders emerging from the sea and of the sound of church bells ringing out from the deep.

Leisure
Beach Good beach nearby.
Bird reserve Accompanied walks are offered by the Réserve de Cap Sizun at Goulien on Mon and Thurs between 10 a.m. and 6 p.m. during July and Aug, by prior booking ☎ 98.70.13.53
Canoeing Lessons from Club Nautique du Goyen. ☎ 98.70.86.27
Diving Deep-sea diving tuition ☎ 98.70.03.90
Tradition Pardon, last Sun in Aug.
Windsurfing CNBA offers lessons ☎ 98.70.21.69

Hotels
Hôtel Le Goyen ★★★
place Jean Simon
☎ 98.70.08.88 (sea view and restaurant)
Hôtel au Roi Gradlon ★★
3 boulevard Manu-Brusq
☎ 98.70.04.51 (sea view and restaurant)
Hôtel Les Dunes ★★
3 rue Ampère
☎ 98.70.01.19 (sea view)
Hôtel Le Cornouaille ★★
le Port
6 place de la Liberté
☎ 98.70.09.13 (sea view)
Camping
Kerhuon ★★
50 places 1 Apr-30 Sep
☎ 98.70.10.91
Kerivois ★★
30 places 15 Jun-15 Sep
☎ 98.70.26.86
Restaurant
L'Horizon ★
40 rue Jean-Jacques Rousseau
☎ 98.70.09.91

AUDIERNE

AURAY
Map ref 139 B4
Pop 10,000
Vannes 19 km
Rennes 128 km
Nantes 129 km
Brest 164 km
Paris 478 km
🅱 place de la
République
☎ 97.24.09.75

Situated on the Auray river, this is an attractive small town of historical and artistic interest with an old quarter containing houses of the 15th to 17th centuries and an ancient stone bridge contrasting with the bustling pleasure harbour of St-Goustan. The very pretty countryside surrounding this river valley attracts both the walker and bird-watcher while the numerous creeks leading into the Golfe du Morbihan have become popular with amateur sailors.

Leisure
Boat Trips Up the Auray river and around the Golfe du Morbihan.
Cycling Cycles can be hired from the SNCF station.
Golf See Carnac and Vannes.
Tradition Just north of Auray is one of Brittany's most important shrines.
The pilgrimage of the Grand Pardon of Ste-Anne-d'Auray on 25-26 July attracts large crowds.

Hotels
Hôtel de la Mairie ★★
place de la Mairie
☎ 97.24.04.65
Hôtel du Loch ★★
quartier Petite Forêt
☎ 97.56.48.33
(and restaurant La Sterne)
Hôtel le Branhoc ★★
route du Bono
☎ 97.56.41.55
Camping
Les Pommiers ★★
Branhoc
☎ 97.24.01.48
150 places open all year
Restaurant
L'Abbaye
Pont de St-Goustan
☎ 97.24.10.85

SLIPPING OVER THE BORDER   *into Pays de la Loire*

LA BAULE
Map ref 140 F2
Pop 15,000
Vannes 71 km
Nantes 75 km
Rennes 122 km
Brest 249 km
Paris 437 km
🛈 8 place Victoire
☎ 40.24.34.44

A smart and colourful seaside town on the Côte d'Amour, with the lively fishing port of **Le Pouliguen** sharing the long, sweeping bay. Pavement cafés, tree-lined avenues, chic shops, extensive watersports facilities, a championship golf course, and nearby horse racing at **Pornichet** give this resort international appeal and attract around 100,000 visitors each summer.

A charming way to escape the beating sun and crowds for a while is provided by the nearby regional park, the **Parc Naturel de la Brière**. An unusual region of quiet marshy landscapes, peat bogs, thatched cottages and abundant wildfowl. Numerous small outlets offer guided trips in their *chalands* or flat-bottomed boats by way of the network of canals and smaller channels. Good places to start from are **St-Joachim** and **St-Lyphard**, small villages typical of the area.

Leisure
Beach Vast curved safe and sandy beach.
Casino ☎ *40.60.20.23*
Cycling Cycles can be hired from the SNCF station.
Golf 18-hole private course at Golf de La Baule, Domaine de St-Dénac, 44117 St-André-des-Eaux ☎ *40.60.46.18. This is a championship course with very fine greens, closed Tues in winter. See also St-Nazaire.*
Regional Park The Parc de la Brière headquarters at 180 Ile de Fédrun, 44720 St-Joachim ☎ *40.88.42.72 will provide details of what to see and where.*
Riding Centre Equestre de La Baule ☎ *40.60.39.29*
Sailing Numerous sailing and water-skiing schools. Club de Voile Jean-Yves Derrien ☎ *40.60.63.76 and Centre de Voile Pajot* ☎ *40.24.34.85*

Hotels
Hôtel Castel
Marie-Louise ****
esplanade F.-André
☎ *40.60.20.60 (sea view and restaurant)*
Hôtel Hermitage ****
esplanade F. André
☎ *40.60.37.00 (sea view and restaurant)*
Hôtel Royal ****
esplanade F. André
☎ *40.60.33.06 (sea view)*
Hôtel Alexandra ***
☎ *40.60.30.06 (sea view)*
Hôtel Bellevue-Plage ***
27 boulevard de l'Océan
☎ *40.60.28.55 (sea view)*
Hôtel le Christina ***
26 boulevard Hennecart
☎ *40.60.22.44 (sea view)*
Hôtel les Alizés ***
10 avenue de Rhuys
☎ *40.60.34.86 (sea view)*
Hôtel Majestic ***
esplanade F. André
☎ *40.60.24.86 (sea view)*
Résidence Orion ***
32 avenue des Lilas
☎ *40.24.39.44*
Hôtel Atlantic **
7 avenue des Flandres
☎ *40.60.25.46 (sea view)*
Camping
La Roseraie ****
120 places Easter-30 Sep
☎ *40.60.46.66*
Les Ajoncs d'Or ***
200 places Easter-15 Oct
☎ *40.60.33.29*
Camping Municipal ***
350 places 24 Mar-30 Sep
☎ *40.60.11.48*

LA BAULE

Tennis 24 courts at Country Club, 113 avenue de Lattre ☎ 40.60.23.44 and 18 courts at Sporting Club, 45 avenue de l'Etoile ☎ 40.60.28.73
Thalassotherapy La Baule les Pins, 28 boulevard de l'Océan ☎ 40.24.30.97
Walking Follow the sentier des douaniers or Customs officers' path along the rocky coastline.

BEG-MEIL
Map ref 130 E2
Pop 1,000
Quimper 20 km
Brest 91 km
Rennes 202 km
Nantes 224 km
Paris 555 km
🅱 Syndicat d'Initiative
☎ 98.94.97.47
Jun-Sep

Modest little harbour resort in unspoilt countryside with a good selection of shops and cafés. Beautiful views over the **Baie de la Forêt** and towards Concarneau, half an hour distant by regular boat service. Sandy bays and little rocky coves alternate for bathing.
Leisure
Boat Trips To the Iles de Glénan and up the River Odet estuary.
Golf See Concarneau and Bénodet.
Naturism The extreme westerly part of the beach at Mousterlin is given over to naturists.
Riding Pony Club at Ferme de Kérancoréden, 29118 Gouesnac'h ☎ 98.54.67.07; Pony Club also at Renouveau ☎ 98.94.98.47
Sailing UCPA Village de Vacances Renouveau ☎ 98.94.98.47 offer sailing and windsurfing hire and tuition. There are also deep-sea diving schools at Beg-Meil and on the Iles de Glénan.
Tennis 5 hard courts for hire at Kerlosquen ☎ 98.56.00.93 Jun-Sep; and 2 at the Renouveau Village de Vacances ☎ 98.94.98.47
Tradition Pardon, first Sun in Aug.

Hotel
Hôtel Thalamot ✶✶
4 le chemin Creux
Beg-Meil
29170 Fouesnant
☎ *98.94.97.38*
(and restaurant)
Camping
La Piscine ✶✶✶
92 places
Kerleya
Fouesnant
☎ *98.56.56.06*
La Roche Percée ✶✶✶
150 places
Kerveltrec
Fouesnant
☎ *98.94.94.15*
Le Vorlen ✶✶✶
600 places
Kérambigorn
Fouesnant
☎ *98.94.97.36*

BENODET
Map ref 130 E1
Pop 3,000
Fouesnant 8 km
Brest 87 km
Rennes 206 km
Nantes 228 km
Paris 558 km
🅱 51 avenue de la Plage
☎ 98.57.00.14

The traditional charms of promenade cafés and restaurants, sandy beaches, secluded coves and pine forests ensure the continued popularity of this delightfully pretty little town. Today it acts as a magnet, particularly to the British, as a windsurfing and yachting centre with frequent regattas, and there are boat trips across to the **Iles de Glénan** and river trips up the pretty wooded Odet estuary, as well as good river fishing.
A visit to the lighthouse, the Phare Pyramide, makes an interesting diversion and gives sweeping views stretching from Penmarc'h to Trévignon. Be prepared, though, for the 192 steps!
Leisure
Beaches Choice of sandy, supervised beaches plus numerous secluded coves.
Boat Trips Cruises up the River Odet estuary to Quimper operate several times a day, Apr-Oct. These can be combined with a delicious lunchtime or evening meal. Vedettes de l'Odet ☎ 98.57.00.58
Casino Avenue de la Plage ☎ 98.57.04.16
Golf New 18-hole public course at Golf de l'Odet Quimper, Clohars Fouesnant, 29118 Bénodet ☎ 98.54.87.88. See also Concarneau.
Lighthouse Phare Pyramide open daily

Hotels
Hôtel Gwel Kaer ✶✶✶
3 avenue de la Plage
☎ *98.57.04.38 (sea view and restaurant)*
Hôtel Ker Mor ✶✶✶
avenue de la Plage
☎ *98.57.04.48 (sea view)*
Hôtel Kastel Mor ✶✶✶
avenue de la Plage
☎ *98.57.05.01 (sea view)*
Hôtel Menez Frost ✶✶✶
rue Jean Charcot
☎ *98.57.03.09*
Armoric Hôtel ✶✶
rue Penfoul
☎ *98.57.04.03*
Domaine de Kereven ✶✶
Kereven
☎ *98.57.02.46*
(and restaurant)
Hôtel â l'Ancre de Marine ✶✶
5 avenue de l'Odet
☎ *98.57.05.29 (sea view and restaurant)*
Hôtel de la Poste ✶✶
rue de l'Eglise
☎ *98.57.01.09*
(and restaurant)
Hôtel des Bains ✶✶

during the summer. Contact the keeper
☎ 98.57.00.41
Riding Club de Lasso. Enquire at the
Tourist Office.
Watersports Sailing and windsurfing
school at Yacht Club de l'Odet
☎ 98.57.26.09; also UCPA ☎ 98.57.03.26.
Water-skiing at Duck Jibe ☎ 98.57.24.01

THE ODET RIVER

rue de Kerguelen
☎ 98.57.03.41
Hôtel le Cornouaille **
62 avenue de la Plage
☎ 98.57.03.78
Hôtel le Minaret **
corniche de l'Estuaire
☎ 98.57.03.13 (sea view)
Hôtel de l'Arrivée *
avenue de Ker Creven
☎ 98.57.03.75
Hôtel l'Ermitage *
11 rue Laënnec
☎ 98.57.00.37 (sea view)
Camping
Letty ****
511 places 21 Jun-6 Sep
☎ 98.57.04.69
Port de Plaisance ***
242 places 15 May-30 Sep
☎ 98.57.02.38
La Pointe St-Gilles ***
485 places 1 May-30 Sep
☎ 98.57.05.37
De La Mer Blanche **
200 places 1 May-30 Sep
☎ 98.57.00.75
La Plage **
300 places 1 Jun-15 Sep
☎ 98.57.00.55
Le Poulquer**
250 places 1 Jun-30 Sep
☎ 98.57.04.19
Restaurants
La Ferme du Letty
'Le Letty Izella'
☎ 98.57.01.27
Le Jeanne d'Arc
Sainte Marine
☎ 98.56.32.70

BREST
Map ref 119 D5
Pop 150,000
Quimper 71 km
Rennes 240 km
Nantes 292 km
Paris 569 km
🛈 place de la
Liberté
☎ 98.44.24.96

Second only to Toulon as France's
greatest military port, the **Rade de Brest** is
a vast natural harbour, large enough to
provide safe anchorage for all the world's
military shipping; today the location of
France's nuclear submarine base and
naval docks as well as a busy commercial
port and small pleasure boat marina. Boat
excursions operate around the Rade
offering glimpses of this industrial
waterfront with vessels of all kinds and
views of the impressive **Pont de
Recouvrance**, the largest vertical-lift
bridge in Europe.
Heavily bombed during the last war, the
city is predominantly modern in style and
without much to commend it
architecturally. It is however an excellent
base from which to explore the
neighbouring countryside and coastlines –
the **Monts d'Arrée**, highest hills in
Brittany, the **Presqu'île de Crozon** and, by
sea, the wild and beautiful isle of
Ouessant.
Leisure
Art Musée des Beaux Arts at 22 rue
Traverse houses a collection of French
and Italian paintings of the 16th to 18th
centuries as well as works from the Pont-

Hotels
Hôtel Ajoncs d'Or ***
rue Amiral Nicol
☎ 98.45.12.42
Hôtel Continental ***
rue de Lyon
☎ 98.80.50.40
Hôtel de la Paix ***
32 rue d'Algesiras
☎ 98.80.12.97
Hôtel des Voyageurs ***
avenue Clémenceau
☎ 98.80.25.73 (sea view
and restaurant)
Hôtel Océania ***
82 rue de Siam
☎ 98.80.66.66 (and restaurant)
Youth Hostel
rue de Kerbrait
Port de Plaisance du Moulin
Blanc
☎ 98.41.90.41
Restaurants
Le Rossini
16 rue Amiral Linois
☎ 98.80.70.00
Les Antilles *
12 rue de Siam
☎ 98.46.05.52

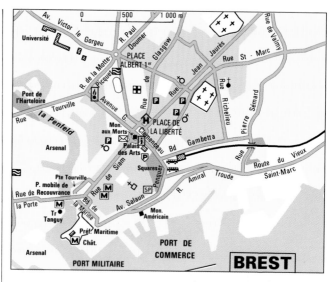

BREST

Aven school of art ☎ 98.44.66.27
Boat Trips Around the enormous harbour and regular daily services out to the isle of Ouessant.
Botanical garden The Conservatoire Botanique de Brest, allée du Bot, is located at the heart of the Stangalarc'h valley, and consists of a huge area of public gardens and greenhouses housing the world's most endangered plant species.
Cycling Cycles can be hired from the SNCF station.
Golf See Landerneau.
Museum Océanopolis, a new scientific and cultural centre, explores the world of the sea: situated at the Port de Plaisance du Moulin Blanc ☎ 98.34.40.40. Also of interest is the naval history museum sited in the 15th-century Tour Tanguy.
Sailing Grand Prix des Multicoques in May, a competition for multi-hulled boats.

LAMPAUL BAY, OUESSANT

CANCALE
Map ref 125 B6
Pop 5,000
Dinan 32 km
Rennes 73 km
Nantes 181 km
Brest 230 km
Paris 357 km
🛈 44 rue du Port
☎ 99.89.63.72

Cancale is an important fish-processing rather than fishing port, specializing in shellfish factories and, of course, ostréiculture, or oyster farming, with vast areas of the bay's seabed devoted to the nurturing of these little bi-valves, the full extent of which becomes visible with the retreating tide.
The port is small and combines great charm with very good restaurant choice. Benefiting from the influence of the Gulf Stream, the climate here has consistently attracted holidaymakers, who enjoy the pine and mimosa-clad coastline of pretty beaches and creeks. Cruises embrace the Baie de Cancale and the Baie du Mont-St-Michel and there are opportunities for fishing, sailing, water-skiing and scuba-diving.
Throughout the 19th century, and until as recently as 1951, fishermen used sailing boats known as bisquines. Faithfully reconstructed with its huge billowing sails, the Cancalaise takes tourists on half-day or full-day trips to experience this

Hotels
Hôtel le Continental ***
4 quai Ad. Thomas
☎ 99.89.60.16 (sea view and restaurant)
Hôtel de la Pointe du Grouin
(5 km north) **
☎ 99.89.60.55 (sea view and restaurant)
Hôtel Emeraude **
7 quai Ad. Thomas
☎ 99.89.61.76 (sea view)
Hôtel le Phare **
6 quai Ad. Thomas
☎ 99.89.60.24 (sea view and restaurant)
Camping
Le Bel Air ***
280 places Easter-30 Sep
☎ 99.89.64.36
Port Mer ***
85 places Easter-30 Sep
☎ 99.89.63.17
Notre-Dame du Verger ***
67 places 25 Mar-30 Sep

traditional form of sailing, with the crew teaching some basic manoeuvres. Splendid walks and panoramic views are possible along the stretch of coast culminating in the **Pointe du Grouin** 5 km to the north. Offshore lies the **Ile des Landes**, a bird sanctuary and, in the distance, hazy Mont-St-Michel.

Leisure

Beaches Pretty beaches and creeks at Port-Briac, Port-Pican, Port-Mer, du Saussaye, du Verger and du Petit-Port.
Boat Trips Circling the Ile des Landes, from the Gare Maritime at Vivier-sur-Mer ☎ *99.48.82.30*
Golf See Dinard and St-Malo.
Museum Set within an old renovated church, this museum explores life and traditions in this region amongst other themes; daily in July ☎ *99.89.79.32*

☎ *99.89.72.84*
*Municipal La Pointe du Grouin ***
166 places 27 Mar-30 Sep
☎ *99.89.63.79*
*Les Genets ***
85 places 25 Mar-30 Sep
☎ *99.89.76.17*
Restaurant
*De Bricourt ****
1 rue du Guesclin
☎ *99.89.64.76*

OYSTER AND MUSSEL FARMING

With the arrival of motorized fishing vessels, the traditional sailing ships called *bisquines* with billowing sails became redundant. In the past, they would congregate in groups to haul up the horse-shoe oysters found on the seabed in the bays or to search for cuttle fish. Today you will be lucky to see one of them at sea, an elegant reminder of the maritime heritage of this coastline.

Oysters were already considered a delicacy in Roman times, and in La Houle harbour in Cancale you will see modern oyster farmers at work, adapting their activities to suit the tide. In the days of intensive trawling the horse-shoe oyster was over-fished, and was replaced by the cultivated European or Portuguese variety that continue to maintain the high reputation enjoyed by Cancale and the bay. Walk across the vast expanses of sand at low tide to see the shellfish farmers at work harvesting their catch. Flat-bottomed *chalands* or punts are used to ferry the loads between beds and shore, with about 25,000 tons harvested in this fashion annually.

The Baie du Mont-St-Michel has become, over the past thirty years, one of the foremost areas for mussel farming. Amphibious craft collect their catch from the miles of *bouchots* or oak posts hammered into the sand, which the mussels cling to, producing an annual yield of between 8,000 and 10,000 tons.

CARNAC

Map ref 139 B4
Pop 4,000
Vannes 32 km
Rennes 137 km
Nantes 142 km
Brest 166 km
Paris 481 km
🛈 74 avenue des Druides
☎ 97.52.13.52

Smart seaside resort set amidst pine forests with wide, sheltered, south-facing beaches, a yacht marina and plenty of watersports. Nightlife is lively in this extremely popular resort.

Within walking distance of the beach and town area are the 3,000 standing stones or menhirs which are as old and mysterious as those at Stonehenge, and equally important as a prehistoric site. Set in 3 distinct alignments, Ménec, Kermario

Hotels
*Hôtel Le Diana ****
21 boulevard de la Plage
☎ *97.52.05.38 (sea view and restaurant)*
*Novotel Carnac Plage ***
avenue Atlantique
☎ *97.52.53.54 (sea view and restaurant)*
*Résidence Orion ***
Port-en-Drô
☎ *97.52.22.68*
*Hôtel Armoric ***
53 avenue de la Poste
☎ *97.52.13.47*
(and restaurant)
*Hôtel Chez Nous ***
place de la Chapelle
☎ *97.52.07.28*
(and restaurant)
*Hôtel la Marine ***
4 place de la Chapelle
☎ *97.52.07.33*
(and restaurant)
*Hôtel le Bateau Ivre ***
boulevard de la Plage
☎ *97.52.19.55 (sea view and restaurant)*

FARMLAND NEAR CARNAC

and Kerlescan, the visitor can only marvel at the effort involved in their positioning and wonder at their ancient significance.

Leisure
Beaches Gently shelving, wide, sandy beaches.
Boat Trips Cruises tour the Golfe du Morbihan and are bookable from Locmariaquer. ☎ 97.57.39.15
Golf Pleasant and busy parkland 18-hole public course at Golf de St-Laurent Ploëmel, 56400 Auray. ☎ 97.56.85.18. Also 9-hole practice course.
See also Vannes.
Museum Prehistoric archaeology theories explored at the Musée Miln-le-Rouzic, closed Tues. ☎ 97.52.22.04
Riding Le Manio. ☎ 97.55.73.45 and Pony Club de la Plage, Kerallan. ☎ 97.52.94.67
Thalassotherapy Open 1 Jan-20 Nov, Centre de Thalassothérapie, avenue de l'Atlantique, BP 100, 56340 Carnac ☎ 97.52.53.54

Camping
La Grande Métairie ★★★★
352 places 27 May-16 Sep
☎ 97.52.24.01
Les Menhirs ★★★★
350 places 1 May-1 Oct
☎ 97.52.94.67
Rosnual ★★★★
160 places 1 May-30 Sep
☎ 97.52.14.57
L'Etang ★★★
165 places 1 Apr-31 Oct
☎ 97.52.14.06
Le Moulin de Kermeaux ★★★
120 places Easter-16 Sep
☎ 97.52.15.90
Les Druides ★★★
90 places Easter-15 Sep
☎ 97.52.08.18
Les Pins ★★★
160 places open all year
☎ 97.52.18.90
Les Saules ★★★
200 places Easter-30 Sep
☎ 97.52.14.98
Moustoir ★★★
165 places 1 Jun-15 Sep
☎ 97.52.16.18
Restaurants
Lann-Roz
36 avenue de la Poste
☎ 97.52.10.48
Kerank
route de Quiberon
Plouharnel
☎ 97.52.35.36

MENHIRS NEAR CARNAC

SLIPPING OVER THE BORDER   *into Pays de la Loire*

CHATEAUBRIANT
Map ref 137 F4
Pop 14,000
Rennes 52 km
Nantes 65 km
Fougères 80 km
Brest 277 km
Paris 342 km
🛈 22 rue de Couéré
☎ 40.28.20.90

One of a line of frontier châteaux which stand between the Channel and the Loire and which marked the ancient division between Brittany and the rest of France, the **Château de Châteaubriant** stands as a reminder of that turbulent period. Part medieval, part elegant Renaissance, it has its share of horror stories to tell: restored in the 16th century for his new wife by the Count of Châteaubriant, he became consumed by jealousy at her infidelity with the king, François I, and locked her and their only child in the castle till their deaths. History both ancient and modern is represented in this little town. A reminder of more recent brutalities is the memorial to those executed in a quarry just east of the town, suspected of being local Resistance workers.

Hotels
Hostellerie de la Ferrière ★★★
route de Nantes
☎ 40.28.00.28 (and restaurant)
Hôtel Armor ★★
place de la Motte
☎ 40.81.11.19
Hôtel au Vieux Château ★
11 place Charles de Gaulle
☎ 40.81.22.27
Hôtel du Pont St-Jean ★
☎ 40.28.04.54
Camping
Municipal les Briotais ★★
35 places 15 Jun-15 Sep
☎ 40.81.05.53

COMBOURG
Map ref 126 E1
Pop 5,000
Rennes 41 km
St-Malo 41 km
Nantes 148 km
Brest 229 km
Paris 345 km
🏛 Maison de la
Lanterne, place
Albert-Parent
☎ 99.73.13.93

'It was in the woods of Combourg that I became what I am today' wrote François René de Chateaubriand, most famous of Romantic writers, immortalizing forever this charming small town. The perfectly preserved and furnished medieval fortress, built between the 11th and 15th centuries, is set in parkland on the edge of a lake. Chateaubriand's childhood home, it is owned and lived in by a descendant of his today.

The **Château de la Bourbonsais** lies 13 km outside Combourg at Pleugeuneuc and was built for domestic rather than military purposes. As such it possesses stylish interiors and formal gardens, with the added attraction today of a small zoo and a pack of fifty hounds.

Leisure
Château Open Apr-Oct except Tues
☎ *99.73.22.95*
Cycling Cycles can be hired from the SNCF station.
Golf See Dol-de-Bretagne.
Zoo In the grounds of the Château de la Bourbonsais.

Hotels
Hôtel du Château ★★
1 place Chateaubriand
☎ *99.73.00.38 (lake view and restaurant)*
Hôtel du Lac ★★
2 place Chateaubriand
☎ *99.73.05.65 (lake view)*
Hôtel de France ★
18 rue des Princes
☎ *99.73.00.01*
Camping
Le Vieux Châtel ★★
70 places Easter-15 Sep
☎ *99.73.07.03*

CONCARNEAU
Map ref 130 E3
Pop 18,000
Quimper 23 km
Brest 90 km
Rennes 190 km
Nantes 212 km
Paris 542 km
🏛 quai d'Aiguillon
☎ 98.97.01.44

An important fishing port, Concarneau is also a pleasant seaside resort with an old walled town, the **Ville Close**, circled by ramparts and entirely surrounded by the waters of the colourful harbour. This is a good shopping centre and a large sailing base. Boat trips by hydro-jet from here to the **Iles de Glénan** take only 25 minutes and there are several safe and sandy beaches, at low tide, however, liable to be very seaweedy.

The economy of the region is primarily drawn from the sea, with catches including *langoustines* or prawns, hake, skate, monkfish, sole, coley, sea bream, mackerel and, between June and September, enormous catches of tuna fish, the largest in France. Between May and October the fleets fish for sardines, sprats and anchovies, and are often away for ten days at a time hauling back their mixed catch weighing anything up to 20 tons. The ice-making factories produce 250 tons per day, an example of the peripheral activities essential for the commercial viability of this major fishing port concerned with delivering its fresh fish to the demanding urban centres throughout France as quickly as possible.

Leisure
Cycling Cycles can be hired from the SNCF station.
Fishing Good river and sea fishing. Fish auction between 7-9 a.m. and 10-11 a.m. the first four days of the week.
Golf Mature and well maintained 9-hole private course at Golf de Quimper et de Cornouaille, Manoir de Mesmeur, 29133 La Forêt-Fouesnant ☎ *98.56.97.09*
Museum History of Brittany's fishing industry in a fascinating museum in the walled town, open all year
☎ *98.97.10.20; and Marinarium, in place*

Hotels
Le Relais Belle Etoile ★★★★
le Cabellou-Plage
☎ *98.97.05.73 (sea view and restaurant)*
Hôtel de l'Océan ★★★
☎ *98.50.53.50 (sea view)*
Hôtel Ty Chupen Gwenn ★★★
plage des Sables-Blancs
☎ *98.97.01.43 (sea view)*
Promotel ★★★
avenue du Cabellou
☎ *98.97.32.18*
Grand Hôtel ★★
1 avenue Pierre Guéguin
☎ *98.97.00.28 (sea view)*
Camping
Camping des Prés-Verts ★★★
route de la Forêt-Fouesnant
150 places 15 Jun-15 Sep
☎ *98.97.09.74*
Camping du Dorlett ★★
150 places 1 Jun-30 Sep
☎ *98.97.16.44*
Kerandon ★★
100 places 15 Jun-15 Sep
☎ *98.97.15.77*
Kerseaux ★★
200 places 15 Jun-10 Sep
☎ *98.97.37.41*
Lanandan ★★
route de la Forêt-Fouesnant
110 places 15 Jun-15 Sep
☎ *98.97.17.78*
Lochrist ★★
100 places open all year
☎ *98.97.25.95*
Youth Hostel
place de la Croix
Open all year
☎ *98.97.03.47*

du Vivier, devoted to the world of the sea,
open Jun-Sep ☎ 98.97.06.59
Sailing Societé Nautique de la Baie
☎ 98.97.34.84
Tennis The sporting complex at Porzou
offers a dozen courts amongst other
facilities ☎ 98.97.01.85
Tradition Festivities are popular here
during the summer and reflect the
maritime heritage. Over 3 days in July,
including the 14th, is the Rassemblement
des Vieilles Coques or Old Boats
Rally; in mid-July the Salon de Livre
Maritime book fair is held; and at the end
of July and early August the Festival
International de Chants et Danses. August
sees the Fête des Filets Bleus or Blue
Nets in the week preceding the
penultimate Sunday.
Watersports Water-skiing at Locabellou
☎ 98.97.41.03 and windsurfing at rue des
Iles ☎ 98.50.67.83

CROZON-MORGAT
Map ref 129 E5
Pop 9,000
Douarnenez 44 km
Brest 57 km
Rennes 237 km
Nantes 278 km
Paris 583 km
🛈 Toul Au Trez,
Morgat
☎ 98.27.07.92

Although the long, splayed Crozon
peninsula is wild, there are sheltered
inlets, and beneath the high rugged cliffs
topped with gorse, thistle and heather,
are tiny beaches fringed in summer by an
azure blue sea.
The port of Morgat once specialized in
sardine fishing, but as the principal resort
of the peninsula and with its marvellous
sandy beach facing into the Baie de
Douarnenez, it caters instead today for
family holidays. The modern yachting
marina has moorings for 600 craft and is
a popular port of call for the British sailing
fraternity. There are sea-fishing trips
along the coast and popular and frequent
exploratory trips round the high cliffs,
allowing the visitor to sail into deep inlets
and· caverns, the 'Chambre du Diable'
for example, only accessible from the sea.
There are wonderful panoramic views
from the **Cap de la Chèvre** and, at the
Pointe de Dinan, a fascinating natural
arrangement of rocks. Other sites of
stunning cliff scenery which should not be
missed include la Pointe de Toulinguet, la
Pointe de Penhir, the Presqu'île de
Roscanvel and the Pointe des Espagnols.
Part of the peninsula is however a
restricted military zone.

Leisure
Boat Trips 45-min sea trips, with
commentary, to visit the deep cliff inlets
and caves. Bookings from Vedettes
Sirènes, at the port entrance, Morgat
☎ 98.27.22.50
Canoeing Lessons available from ULAMIR
☎ 98.27.01.68
Fishing Sea-fishing trips organized by
Vedettes Sirènes ☎ 98.27.22.50
Golf Driving range and putting green at
Golf de Crozon, 29160 Crozon
☎ 98.27.10.28
Riding Centre Equestre de
Trébéron ☎ 98.26.21.15
Sailing Centre Nautique de
Crozon-Morgat school ☎ 98.27.01.98

Restaurants
La Galian
15 rue St-Guénolé,
Ville Close
☎ 98.97.30.16
La Coquille
1 rue du Moros
☎ 98.97.08.52
La Dauarce
71 avenue Alain Le Lay
☎ 98.97.30.17
Chez Armande
15 avenue du Dr. Nicolas
☎ 98.97.00.76
La Gallandière
3 place du Général de Gaulle
☎ 98.97.16.34

Hotels
Hostellerie de la Mer ∗∗
le Port
☎ 98.27.61.90 (sea view)
Hôtel Moderne ∗∗
61 rue Alsace-Lorraine
☎ 98.27.00.10
Hôtel Ville d'Ys ∗∗
quai Kador
☎ 98.27.06.49 (sea view)
Camping
La Plage de Goulien ∗∗∗
90 places 5 Jun-20 Sep
☎ 98.27.17.10
Les Pins ∗∗∗
120 places 5 Jun-20 Sep
☎ 98.27.21.95
Pen ar Menez ∗∗∗
150 places Easter-30 Sep
☎ 98.27.12.36
Les Pieds dans l'Eau ∗∗∗
90 places 15 Jun-15 Sep
☎ 98.27.62.43
Kernaou ∗∗
100 places
☎ 98.27.64.65
Restaurant
Le Roof à Morgat
☎ 98.27.08.40

POINTE DE DINAN

BERTRAND DU GUESCLIN (1320-80)

Born in Dinan, du Guesclin, the eldest son of an obscure Breton nobleman, rose to become Constable of France, then the highest military post in the French army.

Ugly and illiterate, the young du Guesclin started life as a brigand, to the despair of his family, but his prowess as a fighter brought him recognition and honour at jousting tournaments. With the onset of the Hundred Years' War between the English and French crowns, du Guesclin put these skills to military use. Surrounding himself with a band of Breton mercenaries, he adopted the French cause and achieved a series of victories against the English and their allies.

Du Guesclin's genius lay, however, in his recognition of the superiority of English weaponry and tactics. After Crécy and Poitiers, two resounding French defeats, he waged guerrilla warfare and refused pitched battles. Constantly harrying the English army's extended lines of communication and supply, du Guesclin set about the piecemeal recapture of the towns and castles that had fallen into English hands. So successful were these tactics that by the time of his death in 1380 the English had all but been driven out of French territory. Unfortunately, the French subsequently forgot the basis of du Guesclin's success, and in 1415 they again took to the field against the English at Agincourt, with disastrous results.

Although achieving great status as the military commander of France, du Guesclin never forgot his Breton origins. On one occasion he was ordered to march against his fellow countrymen, and when his own Breton mercenaries refused, he offered his resignation to the king. After du Guesclin's death his body was taken to St-Denis in Paris for burial with all the pomp and splendour due to a Constable of France, but his heart was buried in the church of St-Sauveur in Dinan.

DINAN

Map ref 125 D5
Pop 14,000
St-Malo 29 km
Rennes 53 km
Nantes 161 km
Brest 205 km
Paris 363 km
🛈 6 rue de l'Horloge
☎ 96.39.75.40

Lovely medieval town enclosed by ramparts and situated along and above the pretty River Rance. For centuries Dinan's river has provided access inland from the sea and as such it has always been a particular favourite with amateur British sailors. A marina now caters specifically for these water-borne visitors, but the river and the delightful views it offers can also be enjoyed by those taking the regular *vedette* excursions to Dinard and St-Malo.

The elegant half-timbered houses and narrow, cobbled streets invite leisurely strolling, with the old port area especially charming. Guided tours offer a fuller appreciation of the ancient churches and buildings, and will introduce too the character of Bertrand du Guesclin, local hero of the Middle Ages, whose equestrian statue dominates the square. Victor Hugo described Dinan as 'a beautiful old town clinging tight like a swallow's nest to the ledge overhanging a precipice on which it is built'. Its many attractions continue to draw thousands of visitors and the town is also a perfect base for excursions, either towards the coast or further inland into the heart of Brittany. Close by and worth a special detour is St-Juvat, one of France's prettiest small villages. At Pléven, between Dinan and Lamballe, stand the impressive ruins of the medieval Château de la Hunaudaye.

Leisure

Boat Trips Regular services on the River Rance as far as Dinard and St-Malo, Apr- Sep. Journey takes 2 hours 30 min, return by bus, bookable from Émeraude Lines, quai de la Rance.

Cycling Cycles can be hired from the SNCF station and from the Youth Hostel.

Garden The Jardin Anglais is situated behind the church of St-Sauveur and offers good views over the valley.

Hotels

Hôtel d'Avaugour ★★★
place du Champ
☎ 96.39.07.49
(and restaurant)
Hôtel Abbatiale ★★★
le Tronchet
☎ 99.58.93.21
Hôtel le Bretagne ★★
place Duclos
☎ 96.39.46.15
Hôtel de France ★★
place du 11 novembre
☎ 96.39.22.56
(and restaurant)
Hôtel le Marguerite ★★
29 place du Guesclin
☎ 96.39.47.65

Camping

Camping de la Hallerais ★★★★
Taden
230 places Mar-Nov
☎ 96.39.15.93
Municipal Chateaubriand ★★
50 places 15 Apr-31 Oct
☎ 96.39.11.96
Municipal Beauséjour ★★
St-Samson/Rance
120 places Jun-Sep
☎ 96.39.53.27

Youth Hostel

Moulin du Méen
Vallée de la Fontaine des Eaux
Open all year
☎ 96.39.10.83

Restaurants

Chez la Mère Pourcel ★★
place des Merciers
☎ 96.39.03.03
La Caravelle ★
19 place Duclos
☎ 96.39.00.11

Golf See Dinard, Dol-de-Bretagne and St-Malo.
Loisirs Accueil Week-long riding instruction culminating in an exhilarating gallop along the beach! In an approved establishment located close to Dinan, the courses run from Mon-Sat and are either for beginners or improvers. Cost 2,400FF per person, throughout the year, includes accommodation in ** hotel. Contact Loisirs Accueil Côtes-d'Armor (address on page 25).
Riding Centre at Nonchaux ☎ 96.84.46.62
Museum Castle museum ☎ 96.39.45.20
Tennis Courts to hire in Dinan at route de Ploubalay ☎ 96.39.80.80 and elsewhere at Lanvallay, Léhon and Taden.

DINAN

DINARD
Map ref 125 B5
Pop 10,000
Rennes 74 km
Nantes 182 km
Brest 212 km
Paris 367 km
🏛 2 boulevard Féart
☎ 99.46.94.12

Popular for over a century, evidenced by the luxury villas and gardens, the fashionable Côte d'Emeraude resort of Dinard is attractively situated at the mouth of the River Rance opposite St-Malo. Dinard is the largest resort on the north coast with a choice of sandy beaches in attractive rocky coves bathed by the warming currents of the Gulf Stream. The resort has become particularly popular with the British. Indeed its mild climate and fashionable calendar of events with tennis and golf tournaments, show-jumping and sailing and windsurfing regattas, encourage year-round family holidaymakers as well as patronage as a conference venue.

Leisure
Casino Palais d'Emeraude, boulevard Wilson ☎ 99.46.15.71
Cycling Cycles can be hired from the SNCF station.
Dam The first tidal-powered dam in the world, the Barrage de la Rance can be toured with guides. Enquire at Tourist Office.
Fishing For sea and pool fishing enquire at the Tourist Office.
Golf 18-hole private links at Golf de Dinard, 35800 St-Briac-sur-Mer ☎ 99.88.32.07. Founded in 1887, this is the second oldest course in the country. See also St-Malo.
Museum Museum at 17 avenue George V detailing the sea voyages of the explorer Charcot (1867-1936) who had the famous vessel Pourquoi pas? or Why not? built in St-Malo, from which he disappeared during a voyage to Antarctica ☎ 99.46.13.90
Riding Centre Equestre de Dinard Le Val Porée ☎ 99.46.23.57
Thalassotherapy Open all year, Thalassa Dinard, Institut de Thalassothérapie, avenue du Château Hébert, BP 70, 35802 Dinard ☎ 99.82.78.10
Walking For short walks from the town centre and heading west, follow the coastal path to the plage de l'Ecluse, corniche de la Malouine, pointe des Etêtés, plage de St-Enogat, plage du Port-Blanc; alternatively, head to the east by

Hotels
Hôtel Reine Hortense ★★★★
rue de la Malouine
☎ 99.46.54.31 (sea view and restaurant)
Le Grand Hôtel ★★★★
avenue George V
☎ 99.46.10.28 (sea view and restaurant)
Hôtel le Crystal ★★★
15 rue de la Malouine
☎ 99.46.66.71 (sea view)
Hôtel Altair ★★
18 boulevard Féart
☎ 99.46.13.58
(and restaurant)
Hôtel Balmoral★★
26 rue du Maréchal-Leclerc
☎ 99.46.16.97
Hôtel Climat de France ★★
rue des Genêts
☎ 99.46.69.55 (sea view and restaurant)
Hôtel des Bains ★★
38 avenue George V
☎ 99.46.13.71 (sea view and restaurant)
Camping
Le Prieuré ★★★★
100 places 20 Mar-1 Nov
☎ 99.46.20.04
Municipal Port Blanc ★★★
500 places 1 Apr-30 Sep
☎ 99.46.10.74
Manoir de la Vicomté ★★
65 places 1 May-30 Sep
☎ 99.46.12.59
Youth Hostel
Ker Charles
8 boulevard l'Hôtelier
Open all year
☎ 99.46.40.02
Restaurants
La Coquille ★★
4 rue Georges Clémenceau
☎ 99.46.14.47
Le Trezen ★★
3 boulevard Féart
☎ 99.46.14.87

following the path from the plage de l'Ecluse, corniche du Moulinet, along the Clair-de-Lune promenade, plage de la Prieuré, Pointe de la Vicomté giving views across to St-Malo and arriving at the dam.

DOL-DE-BRETAGNE
Map ref 126 C1
Pop 5,000
Dinan 26 km
Rennes 57 km
Nantes 164 km
Brest 231 km
Paris 338 km
🖬 3 Grande-Rue
☎ 99.48.15.37

This small town on the edge of the Dol marshes boasts the striking St-Samson cathedral and some beautiful old houses, and there is evidence too of early Viking presence here. To the south of the town the massively tall **menhir de Champ-Dolent** is numbered amongst the most impressive in Brittany and, just to the north, the granite outcrop of **Mont Dol** offers an exceptional panorama across the marshy plains beyond, which some 7,000 years ago were below water.

Leisure
Cycling Cycles can be hired from the SNCF station.
Golf 18-hole private course in the grounds of the château at Golf des Ormes, 35120 Dol-de-Bretagne ☎ 99.48.10.19. *See also Dinard and St-Malo.*
Museum History museum in the place de la Cathédrale with masterpieces of local sculpture. Open Easter-Sep.

Hotels
Hôtel du Tertre ★★
le bourg, Mt-Dol
☎ 99.48.20.57
Logis de la Bresche Arthur ★★
boulevard Déminiac
☎ 99.48.01.44
(and restaurant)
Grand Hôtel de la Gare ★
avenue Aristide Briand
☎ 99.48.00.44
(and restaurant)
Hôtel de Bretagne ★
place Chateaubriand
☎ 99.48.02.03
(and restaurant)
Camping
Municipal les Tendières ★★
95 places 1 May-30 Sep
☎ 99.48.14.68

DOUARNENEZ
Map ref 129 C5
Pop 18,000
Quimper 24 km
Brest 73 km
Rennes 229 km
Nantes 251 km
Paris 575 km
🖬 2 rue Dr-Mével
☎ 98.92.13.35

Working life here revolves around the sea and its associated industries, while holidaymakers and tourists are attracted by its picturesque setting, the pleasant beach at **Tréboul** close by and the good watersports. They are often to be rewarded too by the sight of Breton women going about their business in traditional dress, and the fish auction held at **Rosmeur** harbour every morning at 6 a.m. is fun.

Leisure
Beach Most facilities offered at the plage des Sables Blancs at Tréboul.
Cycling Cycles can be hired from the SNCF station.
Fishing Sea-fishing trips on the Vedette Rosmeur ☎ 98.27.10.71
Museum Interesting museum devoted to traditional fishing boats at Musée du Bateau, place de l'Enfer, open daily, Jun-Sep ☎ 98.92.65.20
Sailing Also canoeing and windsurfing lessons from Centre Nautique
☎ 98.74.13.79; *also Voile d'Iroise*
☎ 98.92.76.25
Thalassotherapy Open all year, Centre de Cure Marine de la Baie de Tréboul-Douarnenez, 42 bis rue des Professeurs Curie, BP 4, 29100 Douarnenez ☎ 98.74.09.59. *The centre specializes in the treatment of sports injuries.*
Tradition Douarnenez's pardon, held on the last weekend in Aug, culminates in the little chapel of Ste-Anne-la-Palud north along the coast. Folklore festival, 11 Aug.
Walking Short circuits are detailed in leaflets available from the Tourist Office, and cover Tréboul (9 km), Pouldavid (7 km) and Ploaré (8 km).

Hotels
Auberge de Kerveoc'h ★★
route de Kerveoc'h
☎ 98.92.07.58
(and restaurant) ★★★
Grand Hôtel de la Plage des Sables Blancs ★★
Tréboul
☎ 98.74.00.21 *(sea view and restaurant)*
Hôtel le Bretagne ★★
23 rue Duguay-Trouin
☎ 98.92.30.44
Camping
Camping de Kerleyou ★★
100 places 30 Apr-15 Sep
☎ 98.74.03.52 *or* 98.74.13.03
Croas Men ★★
80 places Easter-30 Sep
☎ 98.74.00.18
Camping de Trésulien ★★
200 places Easter-15 Sep
☎ 98.74.12.30
Municipal le Bois d'Isis ★★
150 places 15 Jun-15 Sep
☎ 98.74.05.67
Restaurants
Chez Fanch
rue Anatole-France
☎ 98.92.31.77
L'Océan
rue Anatole-France
☎ 98.92.60.98
La Cotriade
46 rue Anatole-France
☎ 98.92.06.45

ERDEVEN
Map ref 138 B3
Pop 3,000
Carnac 13 km
Rennes 144 km
Nantes 149 km
Brest 156 km
Paris 497 km
🛈 7 bis, rue
Abbé le Barh
☎ 97.55.64.60

Small unspoilt town amidst pretty countryside of pines and gorse within easy reach of the coastal resorts where the long stretches of wet sand lend themselves to the sport of sand-yachting. As at Carnac close by, there are menhirs to be seen here: the megalithic alignments of Kerzerho with over 1,000 menhirs and the dolmens of Crucuno, Mané-Croch and Mané-Braz, amidst a lovely area for rides and walks.

Leisure
Beach Nearby plage de Kerhillio has 8 km of uninterrupted safe, sandy beach bordered by dunes. Children's beach club and watersports facilities.
Fishing On the River Etel and sea fishing.
Golf See Carnac and Vannes.
Naturism Permitted on the plage de Kerminihy.

Hotels
Auberge du Sous Bois **
route de Pont Lorois
☎ 97.55.66.10
(and restaurant)
Hôtel des Voyageurs **
14 rue de l'Océan
☎ 97.55.64.47
(and restaurant)
Hôtel le Narbon **
route de la Plage
☎ 97.55.67.55
(and restaurant)
Camping
Airotel Kerzerho ****
170 places mid-May-30 Sep
☎ 97.55.63.17
Les Sept Saints ***
200 places 1 May-15 Sep
☎ 97.55.52.65
Ideal Camping ***
35 places 15 Jun-15 Sep
☎ 97.55.67.66
La Groz Villieu **
100 places 15 Jun-15 Sep
☎ 97.55.68.27
Restaurant
Saint-Hubert **
1 rue des Menhirs
☎ 97.55.64.50

DOLMEN DE KERIAVAL

THE BRETON LANGUAGE
There are still some Breton-speaking areas in Lower Brittany where this Celtic language is quite widely spoken. Some Breton vocabulary will be recognized in placenames, much of it reminiscent of Welsh:

aber	estuaire estuary
aod	côte coast, shore
avon	fleuve river
beg	pointe point, cape
coat/goat	bois wood
gwenn/guen	blanc white
iliz	église church
kastel	château castle
ker	ville town
lenn	étang pool, lake
loc	lieu saint holy place
manac'h	moine monk
marc'h	cheval horse
ménéz	montagne mountain
mor	mer sea
nevez	neuf new
penn	point head, top
plou/pleu	paroisse parish
pors	port harbour
roc'h	rocher rock
sant	sainte saint
ter	rivière river
ti/ty	maison house
trez	sable sand
tro/trou	trou valley or hollow

ERQUY
Map ref 124 B2
Pop 4,000
Dinard 37 km
Rennes 98 km
Brest 194 km
Nantes 205 km
Paris 400 km
🛈 boulevard
de la Mer
☎ 96.72.30.12

Small but busy scallop-fishing port and family seaside resort situated within a sheltered bay, with three harbours offering mooring for 400 pleasure boats. There are good beaches at Sables-d'Or-les-Pins (8 km) and at Val-André (11 km) and fine camp sites amongst the typically Breton cottage landscape. The view from Cap Erquy over the Baie de St-Brieuc is beautiful.

Leisure
Boat Trips Out to the Ile de Bréhat during July and Aug. Enquire at the Tourist Office.
Golf See St-Cast-le-Guildo.
Microlight flying Instruction courses and photography flights ☎ 96.72.37.81

Hotels
Hôtel de la Plage **
boulevard de la Mer
☎ 96.72.30.09 (sea view and restaurant)
Hôtel le Brigantin **
square de l'Hôtel de Ville
☎ 96.72.32.14
Camping
La Plage St-Pabu ***
350 places Easter-30 Sep
☎ 96.72.24.65
Les Pins ***
300 places 15 May-15 Sep
☎ 96.72.31.12
Le Vieux Moulin ***

200 places 1 Apr-25 Sep
☎ 96.72.34.23
Bellevue ***
100 places Easter-15 Sep
☎ 96.72.33.04
Les Hautes Grées **
130 places 1 Jun-30 Sep
☎ 96.72.34.78
Les Roches **
120 places Easter-30 Sep
☎ 96.72.32.90
Restaurant
L'Escurial
boulevard de la Mer
☎ 96.72.31.56

A PATH TO THE BEACH

FOUESNANT
Map ref 130 E2
Pop 5,000
Concarneau 13 km
Brest 87 km
Rennes 198 km
Nantes 219 km
Paris 550 km
🛈 rue Kérourgué
☎ 98.56.00.93

FOUGERES FOREST

Riding Carriage driving at Labruyère
☎ 96.72.19.05

Along with Beg-Meil, Cap-Coz and
Mousterlin, this is an area which abounds
in numerous beaches sheltered by
wooded dunes, the south-facing **Forêt-**
Fouesnant at the foot of the bay
stretching between Beg-Meil and
Concarneau and affording peaceful and
pleasant walks.
This is also an important cider-producing
region and the apple orchards are not
forgotten in the annual cycle of ritual and
blessings, celebrated in the Fête des
Pommiers.
Leisure
Golf See Concarneau and Bénodet.
Tradition Fête des Pommiers (third Sun in
July); Pardon de Ste-Anne (Sun following
St-Anne's day, 26 July); Fête de la Mer
(first Sun in Aug).

Hotels
Hôtel Belle Vue **
Cap-Coz
☎ 98.56.00.33 (sea view)
Hôtel Celtique **
plage du Cap-Coz
26 avenue de la Pointe
☎ 98.56.01.79 (sea view)
Hôtel de la Pointe de
Mousterlin **
pointe de Mousterlin
☎ 98.56.04.12 (sea view
and restaurant)
Hôtel de la Pointe du
Cap-Coz **
152 avenue de la Pointe du
Cap-Coz
☎ 98.56.01.63 (sea view)
Camping
L'Atlantique ****
Mousterlin
150 places 1 Apr-30 Oct
☎ 98.56.14.44
Le Manoir de Pen Ar
Steir ****
Forêt-Fouesnant
105 places open all year
☎ 98.56.97.75
St-Laurent ****
Forêt-Fouesnant
300 places mid-May-15 Sep
☎ 98.56.97.65
Le Grand Large ***
Mousterlin
300 places 15 Jun-15 Sep
☎ 98.56.04.06
Kerneuc **
Mousterlin
80 places early Jun-5 Sep
☎ 98.56.07.70
Restaurant
Auberge St-Laurent *
Forêt-Fouesnant
☎ 98.56.98.07

FOUGERES
Map ref 127 E5
Pop 26,000
Rennes 47 km
Nantes 143 km
Brest 275 km
Paris 298 km
🅱 1 place
Aristide Briand
☎ 99.94.12.20

A well-preserved medieval castle, one of the finest examples of military architecture, marks what was for centuries one of the principal frontier fortress towns of the Marches between Brittany and the rest of France. Nearby the thousand-year-old **Forêt de Fougères** offers peaceful walking, cycling and riding paths through beech groves dotted with megaliths.

Leisure
Activity Centre The Ferme de Chénedet, Landéan, 35300 Fougères is set in the middle of forest and offers a number of outdoor activities to the visitor, with instruction, such as riding, cycling and dinghy sailing. There is a beach area and jogging course and basic camp site accommodation, see Camping.
☎ *99.97.35.46*
Art The Musée de la Villéon, 51 rue Nationale has a collection of Impressionist paintings. ☎ *99.99.18.98*
Castle Open Mar-Oct with son-et-lumière in summer.
Fishing Category 1 fishing on the rivers Nançon and Couësnon.
Museum The small shoe museum within the castle represents the town's dominance in the footwear industry
☎ *99.99.18.98*

Hotels
Balzac Hôtel ✶✶
15 rue Nationale
☎ *99.99.42.46*
Hôtel des Voyageurs ✶✶
10 place Gambetta
☎ *99.99.18.21*
(and restaurant)
Hôtel Mainotel ✶✶
route N12
☎ *99.99.81.55*
(and restaurant)
Hôtel du Commerce ✶
place de l'Europe
☎ *99.94.40.40*
(and restaurant)
Camping
Municipal Paron ✶✶✶
90 places open all year
☎ *99.99.40.81*
Ferme de Chénedet ✶✶
Landéan
25 places open all year
☎ *99.97.35.46*
Youth Hostel
11 rue Beaumanoir
open all year
☎ *99.94.23.22*
Restaurant
Au Cellier ✶✶
29 rue Victor Hugo
☎ *99.97.20.50*

HUELGOAT
Map ref 121 F4
Pop 2,000
Landerneau 47 km
Brest 68 km
Rennes 174 km
Nantes 233 km
Paris 513 km
🅱 place de la Mairie
☎ 98.99.72.32

The magical combination of huge mossy boulders, woodland and water make up the legendary attractions of the **Forêt de Huelgoat**, for this is what remains of a vast forest which once used to cover the entire region. Protected today as part of the **Parc Régional d'Armorique**, there are a variety of signposted walks from the village leading to points of beauty and interest, and good river and lake fishing. A popular centre for walkers, the **Monts d'Arrée**, although only 384 m high, are the highest range of hills in Brittany, and lie slightly north-west of Huelgoat. Due south are the **Montagnes Noires**, and both offer magnificent scenery all year round.

Leisure
Horse-drawn vehicles To hire from Locmaria-Berrien, east of Huelgoat
☎ *98.99.73.28*

Hotels
Auberge de la Truite ✶
Locmaria
☎ *98.99.73.05*
(and restaurant)
Hôtel An Triskel ✶
rue des Cieux
☎ *98.99.71.85*
Hôtel du Lac ✶
rue du Général de Gaulle
☎ *98.99.71.14 (lake view)*
Camping
La Rivière d'Argent ✶✶
80 places 15 May-30 Sep
☎ *98.99.72.50*
Municipal du Lac ✶✶
100 places 15 Jun-15 Sep
☎ *98.99.78.80*

JOSSELIN
Map ref 133 D6
Pop 3,000
Vannes 39 km
Rennes 74 km
Nantes 125 km
Brest 175 km
Paris 418 km
🅱 place de la
Congrégation
☎ 97.22.36.43

An attractive old town which boasts the impressive **Château des Rohan** rising photogenically from its own reflection in the waters of the River Oust. Built and added to between the 14th and 17th centuries, this fortress is a remarkable example of medieval architecture. A good base for exploring the area, the Nantes-Brest Canal joins the River Oust here. North-east of Josselin lies the largest forested area in Brittany, the **Forêt de Paimpont**. An exceptionally beautiful place, it is by tradition known as Brocéliande and is bound up in the legendary stories of King Arthur, the Round Table and Merlin the enchanter.

Hotels
Hôtel au Relais de l'Oust ✶✶
Le Rouvran, La Nouée
☎ *97.75.63.06 (river view)*
Hôtel du Château ✶✶
1 rue du Général de Gaulle
☎ *97.22.20.11 (river view and restaurant)*
Restaurant
Blot Hôtel du Commerce ✶✶
rue Glatinier
☎ *97.22.22.08*

THE CHATEAU DE JOSSELIN

Leisure
Museum The family's private doll collection numbers over 500 and is charmingly set within the old stables of the château. Open daily, May-Sep.
Tradition Pardon de Notre-Dame du Roncier, 8 Sep.

JUGON-LES-LACS
Map ref 124 D3
Pop 1,500
Dinan 22 km
Rennes 71 km
Nantes 170 km
Brest 185 km
Paris 385 km
🏛 la Mairie
☎ 96.31.61.62

Lake Jugon is situated a few kilometres west of Dinan, in a region of peaceful rivers and *étangs* or small lakes, rich in fish. The old houses of Jugon-les-Lacs are set between lake and reservoir, an ideal centre for riding, walking and watersports generally. The seaside resorts of St-Malo, Paramé and Dinard are all within 30 km.
Leisure
Fishing Category 2 fishing on the rivers Arguenon and Rosette.
Riding Centre Equestre de la Ville Helle
☎ 96.31.61.66

Hotels
Hôtel de la Grande Fontaine ∗
rue de Lion d'Or
☎ 96.31.61.29
(and restaurant)
Hôtel le Petit Palace ∗
1 rue de Clisson
☎ 96.31.65.24
Camping
Municipal Le Bocage ∗∗
180 places 1 May-30 Sep
☎ 96.31.60.16

LANDERNEAU
Map ref 120 E1
Pop 15,000
Brest 20 km
Nantes 179 km
Rennes 220 km
Paris 548 km

The striking old bridge across the River Elorn is one of the very few inhabited bridges left. Originally a simple bridge allowing the crossing between the Léon and Cornouaille regions, its line of houses date from the 16th century.
A busy agricultural centre, Landerneau is

Hotels
Hôtel Belle Aurore ∗∗
13 rue du Commerce
☎ 98.21.62.62
Hôtel Ibis ∗∗
Mescoat
☎ 98.21.32.32

THE BRETON FLAG
Created in 1923, the *Gwenn ha du,* as it is called, consists of five black bands (*du*) symbolizing the five bishoprics of Upper Brittany: Rennes, Nantes, Dol, St-Malo and St-Brieuc; and four white bands (*gwenn*) symbolizing the four ancient bishoprics of Lower Brittany: Léon, Cornouaille, Vannes and Tréguier. The field of ermine in the top left-hand corner recalls the ancient duchy of Brittany.
The only flag in the world that does not use colour, the *Gwenn ha du* must traditionally be carried in processions at arm's length above the flag-bearer's head.

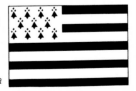

PARISH CLOSES

A parish close is an architectural phenomenon unique to Brittany, and more specifically to Finistère, dating from the 15th to 17th centuries. Each consists of a set of religious monuments which generally includes a triumphal archway, the church itself, a calvary of carved stone saints and martyrs representing scenes from the Crucifixion, and an ossuary for storing the bones of the dead. Some also have a fountain and a graveyard.

The principal closes to see are at Argol, Guimiliau, Lampaul, La Martyre, Pleyben, St-Thégonnec and Sizun. South of Morlaix, there is a motorists' signposted circuit, *Circuit des Trois Enclos*, of the three main ones – Lampaul, Guimiliau and St-Thégonnec – all within a few kilometres of one another.

THE PARISH CLOSE AT ARGOL

⊞ Pont de Rohan
☎ 98.85.13.09
or ☎ 98.21.65.60

LANNION
Map ref 122 B2
Pop 17,000
Morlaix 74 km
Brest 131 km
Rennes 168 km
Nantes 250 km
Paris 489 km
⊞ quai d'Aiguillon
☎ 96.37.07.35

at the heart of that part of Finistère renowned for its parish closes, many of the most impressive being nearby.
Leisure
Golf 18-hole public course set in the grounds of a country park at Golf de Brest-Iroise, Parc des Loisirs de Lann Rohou, 29220 Landerneau ☎ 98.85.16.17
Tradition Kan al Loar, 11-15 July, cultural festival of events.

Founded in the 11th century on the banks of the wide River Léguer, Lannion is in a central position for discovering the big-name beach resorts of the **Côte de Granit Rose**: Perros-Guirec, Ploumanac'h, Trégastel and Trébeurden, as well as some wonderful countryside to the south dotted with chapels, châteaux, manor houses and mills. Its own charm rests in the characteristic half-timbered buildings and the old port area still in use for visiting pleasure boats, the whole best viewed perhaps from the heights of Brélévenez church terrace.

Just to the north is the satellite station at **Pleumeur-Bodou**, its enormous white plastic *radôme* enclosing giant radar equipment. Its siting here in 1962 has caused the development of related industries in Lannion, and also brought a certain economic revival to the region.
Leisure
Cycling Cycles can be hired from the SNCF station and from the Youth Hostel.
Golf See Trébeurden.
Leisure Park Brand new centre offering indoor and outdoor family activities including swimming pool, pedalos, ice skating, bob sleighing. Armoripark, Parc de Bégard ☎ 96.45.36.36, south of Lannion towards Guingamp.
*Loisirs Accueil The rivers of the region, the Léguer, Trieux and the Jaudy, abound in fish and special fly-fishing weeks enable the technique to be learnt or perfected. Tuition, hotel ** accommodation and relevant licences are all included in the cost of 1,950FF per person, Mar-Sep. Contact Loisirs Accueil Côtes-d'Armor (address on page 25).*
Radôme The telecommunications station at Pleumeur-Bodou is open to the public

*Hôtel l'Amandier ***
55 rue de Brest
☎ 98.85.10.89
(and restaurant)
*Hôtel le Clos du Pontic ***
rue du Pontic
☎ 98.21.50.91
Camping
*Municipal ***
40 places 15 May-15 Oct
☎ 98.21.66.59

Hotels
*Château de Brélidy ****
Brélidy
☎ 96.95.69.38
(and restaurant)
*Hôtel Climat de France ***
route de Perros-Guirec
☎ 96.48.70.18
(and restaurant)
*Hôtel de la Porte de France ***
5 rue Jean Savidan
☎ 96.46.54.81
Camping
*Beg Leguer ****
250 places 1 May-30 Sep
☎ 96.47.25.00
*l'Abri Côtier ****
Pleumeur-Bodou
135 places Easter-Sep
☎ 96.91.92.03
Youth Hostel
Les Korrigans
23300 Lannion
Open all year
☎ 96.37.91.28
Restaurants
*La Flambée ***
rue Georges Pompidou
☎ 96.48.04.85
*Ar Vro **
Le Yaudet
Ploulec'h
☎ 96.35.24.21

for guided visits, 26 Mar-31 May and 1
Sep-15 Oct daily, except Sat; daily, Jun,
July and Aug. Close by is a planetarium
open all year ☎ 96.91.83.78

LOCTUDY
Map ref 130 F1
Pop 4,000
Douarnenez 47 km
Brest 96 km
Rennes 222 km
Nantes 244 km
Paris 575 km
⊞ place de la
Mairie
☎ 98.87.53.78
Jun-Sep

A pretty port situated on the estuary of the
Pont l'Abbé river, it is popular as a family
seaside resort and set amidst the
beautiful countryside of the **Pays
Bigouden**. The rhythm of life is marked by
the comings and goings of the fishing
boats and the fish auctions held at 6.30
a.m. and 5.30 p.m. every day.
Leisure
Beach Sandy on the open sea.
Boat Trips Vedettes de l'Odet go to Iles
de Glénan and up the Odet estuary. See
Bénodet.
Fishing Good river and sea fishing.
Golf See Bénodet and Concarneau.
Sailing Renouveau ☎ 98.87.40.22
Windsurfing Cercle Nautique
☎ 98.87.42.84

Hotels
Hôtel Tudy ✶✶
☎ 98.87.42.99 (sea view)
Hôtel de Bretagne ✶
19 rue du port
☎ 98.87.40.21 (sea view)
Camping
Kergall ✶✶
100 places Easter-30 Sep
☎ 98.87.45.93
Les Hortensias ✶✶
100 places 1 July-31 Aug
☎ 98.87.46.64
Cosquer ✶✶
30 places 15 Jun-15 Sep
☎ 98.87.52.92
Les Mouettes ✶✶
74 places 30 Mar-30 Sep
☎ 98.87.43.51

LORIENT
Map ref 138 A2
Pop 65,000
Vannes 56 km
Brest 134 km
Rennes 146 km
Nantes 166 km
Paris 498 km
⊞ quai de Rohan
☎ 97.21.07.84

Taking its name from the establishment
here in the 17th century of the French
equivalent of the East India Company, the
town was created as the headquarters
and base for the Compagnie des Indes et
de l'Orient. The French Navy took over the
company in 1770, establishing a naval
base and dockyards. Its strategically
important location led to the French
submarine base Stosskopf being
constructed here during World War II,
today open only to visits by French
nationals. Occupation by the Germans
followed, and during the Allied liberation
moves of 1944, the city suffered massive
bomb damage which has since resulted
in its almost wholesale reconstruction.
A major Breton harbour at the mouth of
the River Scorff, the lively fishing port is
commercially the third busiest in France
after Boulogne and Concarneau, and
throughout the year fleets of trawlers
leave for a fortnight's fishing at a time, to
return with their huge catches pre-frozen
ready for distribution.
Leisure
Art Contemporary art exhibitions at Galerie
Espace l'Orient, 13 rue Beauvais
☎ 97.21.78.73
Cycling Cycles can be hired from the
SNCF station.
Loisirs Accueil Daily use of courts plus
accommodation at Tennis Résidence
Loisirs at Ploemeur. Prices are based on
weekly rentals with shared accommodation
for 4, 5 or 6 persons. Bookable through
Loisirs Accueil Morbihan (address on
page 25).
Tradition Kan Ar Bobl, held each year at
Easter, is a festival celebrating traditional
Breton singing. The Festival Interceltique
des Cornemuses in early August is one of
the biggest Breton festivals and celebrates
a heritage of bagpipe music that attracts
many performers from the British Isles.

Hotels
Hôtel Mercure ✶✶✶
31 place Jules Ferry
☎ 97.21.35.73
Hôtel Novotel ✶✶✶
Caudan
Centre Hôtelier de Kerpont
☎ 97.76.02.16
Armor Hôtel ✶✶
*11 boulevard Franchet
d'Esperey*
☎ 97.21.73.87
Hôtel Astoria ✶✶
3 rue de Clisson
☎ 97.21.10.23
Youth Hostel
Rives du Ter
41 rue Victor Schoelcher
☎ 97.37.11.65
Restaurants
Le Poisson d'Or
1 rue Martin-Esvelin
☎ 97.21.57.06
Le Pic
*2 boulevard Franchet
d'Esperey*
☎ 97.21.18.29
L'Amphitiyon
*127 rue de Colonel Muller,
Keryado*
☎ 97.83.34.04

BRETON FISHERMEN

MONT-ST-MICHEL
Map ref 126 B3
Pop 100
St-Malo 50 km
Rennes 67 km
Nantes 175 km
Brest 259 km
Paris 323 km
🖪 place Aristide
Briand
☎ 33.60.14.30

A major tourist and historic site, the medieval monastic abbey church crowns the peak of this granite rock in a marvellous silhouette, perfectly justifying the simple French title *la Merveille* or the Marvel. Totally surrounded by the sea at high tide, it is connected to the mainland only by a causeway. The startling speed of the tides makes walking round the sands at low tide quite dangerous. Tidal movements can result in variations of 15 metres or 50 ft on certain days in March and September. One of the strongest and fastest tides in the world, it advances at well over 9 kmph or 6 mph and is capable of overtaking the fastest of runners! A cluster of old buildings flank the rock providing restaurant and hotel accommodation, but with only one road and tiny alleyways through this medieval fortress, summer visitors are virtually cheek by jowl all the way up and all the way down – the price paid for seeing one of the wonders of the world.

Leisure
Abbey Open for visits:
Nov-Feb 10-12 and 2-4.30
Feb-15 June 9.30-12 and 2-5
16 Jun-15 Sep 9.30-5.30
16 Sep-Oct 9.30-12 and 2-5
Riding La Gourmette du Mont-St-Michel
☎ 33.60.27.73

MONT-ST-MICHEL AT DUSK

Hotels
Relais du Roy ***
☎ 33.60.14.25
(and restaurant)
Hôtel la Digue **
La Digue, 2 km south
☎ 33.60.14.02
(and restaurant)
Hôtel Saint-Pierre **
Grande-Rue
☎ 33.60.14.03
(and restaurant)
Camping
Camping du Mont-St-Michel
☎ 33.60.09.33
Restaurant
La Mère Poulard **
Grande-Rue
☎ 33.60.14.01

MORLAIX
Map ref 121 D4
Pop 17,000
Brest 59 km
Rennes 189 km
Nantes 261 km
Paris 510 km
🖪 place des
Otages
☎ 98.62.14.94

A huge railway viaduct treads high across the narrow valley with the old town and harbour of Morlaix beneath it. Though several miles inland, small boats and cruisers can still gain access to the town by means of the pretty Dossen estuary. The quays were once busy with traffic and the many half-timbered houses are evidence of this earlier trading prosperity and importance.
St-Thégonnec, one of the most fascinating of the parish closes, is 13 km southwest of the town. Guimiliau and Lampaul-Guimiliau are also in the vicinity. For a day out at the seaside, there are several small resorts along the attractive coast with pretty beaches such as those at Carantec and Trégastel.

Leisure
Cycling Cycles can be hired from the SNCF station.
Golf See Trébeurden and Landerneau.
Horse-drawn vehicles To hire from Espaces Verts et Bleues, Plougonven, east of Morlaix ☎ 98.78.65.85
Museum History museum and large collection of paintings housed in the 13th-century convent, the Musée des Jacobins, rue des Vignes, closed Tues
☎ 98.88.68.88
Watersports Sailing, windsurfing and scuba diving at C.N.C.H., at the plage du Kélenn at Carantec ☎ 98.67.01.12

Hotels
Hôtel Mini Mote ***
26 allée des Peupliers
St-Martin-des-Champs
☎ 98.88.35.30
Hôtel d'Europe **
rue d'Aiguillon
☎ 98.62.11.99
(and restaurant)
Hôtel du Port **
3 quai de Léon
☎ 98.88.07.54 (river view)
Youth Hostel
route de Paris
☎ 98.88.13.63
Restaurants
Au Passé Simple
21 bis place Ch. de Gaulle
☎ 98.88.71.02
Bisliot Boeuf
7 place de Viarmes
☎ 98.88.61.18

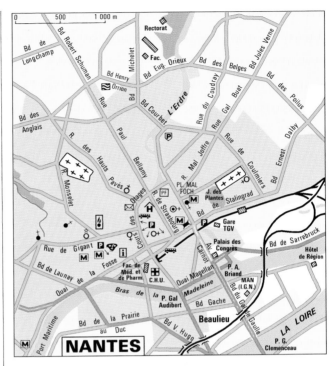

NANTES
Map ref 142 F3
Pop 430,000
Angers 89 km
Rennes 108 km
Brest 292 km
Paris 380 km
🅱 place du
Commerce
☎ 40.47.04.51

Large university and cathedral city on the Loire, and a busy commercial and economic centre. The city's oldest sections are worth exploring as is the **Château des Ducs de Bretagne** which contains three museums. The opera, theatre, concerts and museums make Nantes a great cultural centre, while the attractions of the coast and seaside are within easy reach, with the popular resort of **La Baule** or the small fishing ports of Le Croisic and La Turballe as options.

Leisure
Boat Trips Travel in glass-sided futuristic boats on luxury gastronomic cruises up the River Erdre, passing manor houses and châteaux along the banks. Bookable from Grands Bateaux de l'Erdre, quai de Versailles ☎ *40.20.24.50*
Golf 18-hole private course at Golf de Nantes, 44360 Vigneux de Bretagne ☎ *40.63.25.82*

Hotels
*Le Domaine d'Orvault ✶✶✶✶
chemin des Marais du Sens
Orvault* ☎ *40.76.84.02*
*Hôtel Astoria ✶✶✶
rue de Richebourg*
☎ *40.74.39.90*
*Hôtel de France ✶✶✶
24 rue Crébillon*
☎ *40.73.57.91*
*Hôtel de la Vendée ✶✶✶
allée du Commandant Charcot*
☎ *40.74.14.54*
*Hôtel Mercure Atlantel ✶✶✶
Sautron*
☎ *40.57.10.80*
*Hôtel Novotel ✶✶✶
allée des Sapins, Carquefou*
☎ *40.52.64.64*
*Hôtel Pullman Beaulieu ✶✶✶
3 rue du Docteur Zamenhof*
☎ *40.47.10.58*
Youth Hostel
*2 place de la Manu
Open all year*
☎ *40.20.57.25*
Restaurants
*Les Maraîchers
21 rue Fouré*
☎ *40.47.06.51*
*Le Colvert
14 rue Armand Brossard*
☎ *40.48.20.02*
*Torigoü
Ile de Versailles*
☎ *40.39.06.37*

VEDETTE

PAIMPOL
Map ref 123 B4
Pop 9,000
St-Brieuc 44 km
Brest 136 km
Rennes 144 km
Nantes 240 km
Paris 465 km
🄱 rue Pierre
Feutren
☎ 96.20.83.16

The seas off Paimpol are full of reefs and this small town, once noted for its cod-fishing fleet, now concentrates on oysters. The charming harbour caters almost entirely for pleasure boats and during the summer excursion boats leave for the Ile de Bréhat, a sunny and fertile little island in the Baie de St-Brieuc.

Leisure
Boat Hire Sailing boats available from Loc'Océan ☎ 96.20.17.76
Golf 18-hole private course set in château-hotel grounds at Golf du Boisgélen, Pléhédel, 22290 Lanvollon ☎ 96.22.31.24
*Loisirs Accueil Several imaginative options are avilable for the sea-farer! Enjoy the wonderful coastline while learning to handle a traditional sailing vessel of the last century. Cost 880FF per person, includes two sea outings and hotel ** accommodation and runs every weekend, Apr-Nov. Or relive the life of a corsair Surcouf-style for a weekend. Cost 1,320FF per person, Feb-Nov, includes two outings and **hotel accommodation. Contact Loisirs Accueil Côtes-d'Armor (address on page 25).*
Riding Coat Bruc, Plourivo ☎ 96.55.93.16
Sailing And sea kayaking are popular here, in fact this is the largest kayaking centre in France. Enquire at the Youth Hostel ☎ 96.20.83.60

Hotels
Hôtel le Barbu ★★★
Pointe de l'Arcouest
☎ *96.55.86.98 (sea view and restaurant)*
Hôtel le Relais des Pins ★★★
Pont de Lézardrieux
☎ *96.20.11.05 (sea view and restaurant)*
Hôtel le Repaire de Kerroc'h ★★★
29 quai Morand
☎ *96.20.50.13 (sea view and restaurant)*
Hôtel de la Marne ★★
30 rue de la Marne
☎ *96.20.82.16*
Hôtel du Goëlo ★
le Port
☎ *96.20.82.74 (sea view)*
Camping
Municipal Cruckin Kerity ★★
200 places Easter-30 Sep
☎ *96.20.78.47*
Youth Hostel
Parc de Kéraoul
Open all year
☎ *96.20.83.60*
Restaurants
La Vieille Tour
13 rue de l'Eglise
☎ *96.20.83.18*
La Marne
30 rue de la Marne
☎ *96.20.82.16*

PENMARC'H
Map ref 129 F5
Pop 6,000
Quimper 30 km
Brest 101 km
Rennes 228 km
Nantes 250 km
Paris 580 km
🄱 Syndicat
d'Initiative
☎ 98.58.81.44

Treeless landscape with squat white cottages thick-set against the weather, for this is a wild and windswept coastline where the invigorating salty air lends itself to such pursuits as sand-yachting, windsurfing and riding along the 12 km beach. The enormous, crashing seas in rough weather are very impressive, particularly at St-Guénolé just around the headland where the Eckmühl lighthouse is situated. The little chapel with the long name, Notre-Dame-de-la-Joie-au-Péril-de-la-Mer, stands in rocky isolation at the place where, as the Breton legend and Thomas Malory tell, Isolde landed and seeing that Tristan was dead, she threw herself on his body and died, as he had, of despair.

Leisure
Golf See Bénodet.
Lighthouse The Phare Eckmühl stands 65 m high and its beams carry for 54 km. Open to visitors throughout the year ☎ 98.58.61.17
Riding Centre Equestre de la Joie ☎ 98.58.79.60
Sailing Cercle de Voile ☎ 98.58.64.87

Hotels
Hôtel de la Mer ★★
184 rue François Péron
St-Guénolé
☎ *98.58.62.22 (sea view and restaurant)*
Hôtel le Sterren ★★
St-Guénolé
☎ *98.58.60.36 (sea view and restaurant)*
Camping
La Joie ★★
260 places 1 Apr-31 Oct
☎ *98.58.63.24*
Municipal Toul Ar Ster ★
250 places 1 July-31 Aug
☎ *98.58.86.88*

PERROS-GUIREC
Map ref 122 B2
Pop 8,000
St-Brieuc 69 km
Brest 105 km
Rennes 169 km

An attractive and very popular resort on a coast famed for its rose-red granite rock formations. Good shopping, beaches and lively nightlife attract the crowds, and boats leave daily for trips around the Sept-Iles, a famous nature reserve and

Hotels
Grand Hôtel de Trestraou ★★★
boulevard Joseph Bihan
☎ *96.23.24.05 (sea view and restaurant)*
Hôtel du Levant ★★★

Nantes 260 km
Paris 431 km
🛈 21 place de
l'Hôtel de Ville
☎ 96.23.21.15

THE PORT,
PERROS-GUIREC

bird sanctuary providing shelter for
gannets, puffins, penguins and
quillemots.

Leisure

*Beaches Soft sandy beaches at Trestraou
and Trestrignel. At Ploumanac'h low tide
reveals the extraordinarily-shaped rocks
on the beach.*

*Bird Watching To protect the birds' natural
environment, access to the Sept-Iles is
restricted, but boats circle the islands to
allow closer observation. See also
Trébeurden.*

*Casino Casino de la Côte de Granit Rose,
plage de Trestraou* ☎ *96.23.20.51 Apr-Sep.*

Golf See Trébeurden.

*Sailing Le Centre Nautique de Perros-
Guirec on Trestraou beach offers sailing
tuition to children as well as classes in
windsurfing and boat hire* ☎ *96.23.25.62
Feb-Nov.*

*Walking Follow the old sentier des
douaniers or Customs officers' paths to
Ploumanac'h.*

Port de Plaisance
☎ *96.23.20.15 (sea view)*
Hôtel le Sphynx ***
chemin de la Messe
☎ *96.23.25.42 (sea view)*
Hôtel Printania ***
12 rue des Bons Enfants
☎ *96.23.21.00 (sea view
and restaurant)*
Morgane Hôtel ***
plage de Trestraou
☎ *96.23.22.80 (sea view
and restaurant)*
Hôtel des Rochers ***
chemin de la Pointe
☎ *96.91.44.49 (sea view
and restaurant)*
Hôtel de France **
14 rue Rouzig
☎ *96.23.20.27 (sea view
and restaurant)*
Hôtel du Parc **
Ploumanac'h
☎ *96.91.40.80*

Camping
Camping le Ranolien ****
Ploumanac'h
450 places 3 Feb-13 Nov
☎ *96.91.43.58*
Trestraou ***
180 places Easter-30 Sep
☎ *96.23.08.11*
La Claire Fontaine ***
180 places 15 Jun-15 Sep
☎ *96.23.03.55*
West Camping **
50 places 1 May-30 Sep
☎ *96.91.43.82*

Restaurants
Le Gulf Stream *
26 rue des Sept-Iles
☎ *96.23.21.86*
Les Rochers
chemin de la Pointe
Ploumanac'h
☎ *96.91.44.49*

**PLENEUF-VAL-
ANDRE**
Map ref 124 B2
Pop 4,000
St-Malo 52 km
Rennes 97 km
Brest 175 km
Nantes 196 km
Paris 407 km
🛈 1 rue Winston
Churchill
☎ 96.72.20.55

Great family resort particularly popular
with the British as it has one of the finest
sandy beaches in Brittany and good
watersports facilities for a small town.
Follow the *sentier des douaniers* or
Customs officers' path along the coast for
panoramic views of the Baie de St-Brieuc
and, on the road between Pléneuf and
Erquy, see the 15th-century moated
Château de Bien-Assis surrounded by
formal gardens.

Leisure

*Beach 3 km curving sandy beach ideal
for small children and, at low tide, an
enormous play area.*

Casino La Rotonde ☎ *96.72.85.06
Jul-Sep.*

Golf See St-Cast-le-Guildo.

*Riding Lessons and treks with Club
Hippique de Nantois* ☎ *96.72.25.27 and
La Jeannette* ☎ *96.72.95.79*

*Sailing Centre Nautique offers sailing,
kayaking and windsurfing lessons from its*

Hotels
Grand Hôtel **
rue Amiral Charner
☎ *96.72.20.56 (sea view
and restaurant)*
*Hôtel de France et du Petit
Prince* **
4 rue Pasteur
☎ *96.72.22.52
(and restaurant)*
Hôtel le Clémenceau **
131 rue Clémenceau
☎ *96.72.23.70 (sea view)*
Hôtel de la Mer *
63 rue A. Charner
☎ *96.72.20.44 (sea view
and restaurant)*

Camping
Le Minihy ***
65 places Easter-15 Sep
☎ *96.72.22.95*
*Municipal Les Monts
Colleux* ***

bases at the ports of Dahouët and Piégu
☎ 96.72.95.28, open all year.
Tennis 12 courts to hire at Tennis
l'Amirauté ☎ 96.72.23.25

186 places open all year
☎ 96.72.95.10
Restaurants
Au Biniou **
121 rue Clémenceau
☎ 96.72.24.35
La Cotriade
port de Piégu
☎ 96.72.20.26
Le Panoramique **
80 rue A. Charner
☎ 96.72.20.56

WINDSURFERS

PARDONS

Most Breton towns and villages hold an annual *pardon* when a statue or relic of the local saint is paraded through the streets in a religious procession which culminates in a Mass held at the church. The word *pardon* is used since this is a time for the people to pray for forgiveness of their sins through the intercession of their honoured saint. Though not all of them are recognized by Rome, there are hundreds of local saints who have been venerated over the centuries by these communities, and whose origins generally lie in superstition or legend.

Some are revered as 'healing' saints and are called upon to cure physical ailments or protect in difficult or dangerous conditions, such as St-Yvertin for headaches, Ste-Eugénie for childbirth, St-Languis for backward children, St-Jacut for insanity and St-Doboan for deafness. There are even those associated with the care of particular animals: St-Cornély for cattle and St-Herbot for oxen; and some are patron saints regarded as having special concern for the professions: St-Yves for lawyers, St-Eloi for farriers; or specific towns: St-Malo, St-Brieuc, etc; or locations: St-Michel is patron saint of all high places.

For the casual observer, these processions and subsequent musical festivities provide an opportunity to see many of the local people dressed in their traditional costumes and lace *coiffes* or headdresses. The main events and dates are given below.

DATE	PLACE
Easter	La Trinité-sur-Mer (La Trinité-Porhoët)
May	
13	Penvenan (Pardon aux chevaux sur l'Ile St-Gildas)
20	Tréguier (Pardon de la St-Yves)
June	
Whitsun	Rumengol (Grand Pardon de Rumengol)
end	Le Faouët (St-Barbe)
July	
7/8/9	Goudelin (Fête et pardon de l'Ile Baignade des chevaux) Blessing of the horses
8	Locronan (La Petite Troménie)
21/22	Le Vieux Marché (Pardon des Sept Saints, Pélerinage Islamo-Chrétien)
25/26	Ste-Anne d'Auray (Ste-Anne)
last Sun	Sizun (Pardon de Loïc Ildut)
29	Fouesnant (Pardon Ste-Anne)
August	
1st Sat	Plumeliau (St-Nicodème)
8	Josselin (Notre-Dame du Roncier)
15	Perros-Guirec (Pardon Notre-Dame de la Clarté)
15	Guern (Notre-Dame de Quelven)
15	Porcaro (Pardon de la Madone des Motards)
3rd Sun	Rochefort-en-Terre (Pardon Notre-Dame de la Tronchaye)
3rd Sun	Le Faouët (St-Fiacre)
mid	Callac (Pardon de la Grotte et du Calvaire de Callac)
26	Plonévez Porzay (Ste-Anne la Palud)
end	Tressignaux (Pardon et fête bretonne à l'ancienne)
September	
2	Le Folgoët (Grand Pardon de Notre-Dame)
16	St-Jean Trolimon (Notre-Dame de Tronoën)
end	Gourin (Pardon des Sonneurs)

STE-ANNE LA PALUD

PLOERMEL
Map ref 134 C1
Pop 7,000
Josselin 12 km
Rennes 61 km
Nantes 112 km
Brest 187 km
Paris 406 km
🄳 place
Lamennais
☎ 97.74.02.70

Much fought over in the Middle Ages and bomb-damaged during the last war, this little town still possesses some very fine 16th-century houses, some with sculpted wood carvings. The church, harbouring the tombs of two of the Dukes of Brittany, is dedicated to St-Armel after whom the town takes its name. A particular curiosity to be discovered in the town centre is the exceptional astronomical clock erected by the Ploërmel monks in the last century. Bathing, fishing, bird-watching and a range of watersports take place at the popular Etang au Duc, 3 km north.
Leisure
Horse-Racing First Sun in Sep.
Loisirs Accueil a range of interesting options in this area include: farm stays living on and sharing the daily life of a working farm. Cost: Jun-Sep, 5 days, 4 nights 1,610FF per person. Artistic weekends working alongside a craftsman – potter, sculptor, etc. Cost: weekend 575FF per person; 5 days, 4 nights 1,725FF per person. Also nature excursions combining walks with canoe travel. Cost: weekend 555FF per person; 8 days, 7 nights 2,025FF per person. Gastronomy weekends learning how to make Breton pancakes. Cost: 730FF per person on specific dates throughout the year. For all the above contact Loisirs Accueil Morbihan (address on page 25).

Hotels
Hôtel le Cobh ✱✱
rue des Forges
☎ 97.74.00.49
(and restaurant)
Hôtel du Commerce ✱✱
70 rue de la Gare
☎ 97.74.05.32
Camping
Les Belles Rives ✱✱
135 places Apr-Oct
☎ 97.74.01.22

BRETON PANCAKES

PONT-AVEN
Map ref 131 E4
Pop 3,000
Concarneau 14 km
Brest 99 km
Rennes 176 km
Nantes 198 km
Paris 528 km
🄳 place de
l'Hôtel de Ville
☎ 98.06.04.70

Sung of by Théodore Botrel and immortalized in paint by Gauguin and disciples, Pont-Aven is a charming little town on the banks of the River Aven, at the foot of a lush and wooded rural valley. Signposted trails lead those in quest of the scenery which inspired these painters towards the lovely **Bois d'Amour**, and the museum is devoted to the memory of the artists who worked in the area, especially those of the Pont-Aven School.
It is famous too for its water mills and the delicious butter biscuits which bear the town's name.
Leisure
Golf See Bénodet and Concarneau.
Museum Musée Municipal des Beaux Arts, place de l'Hôtel de Ville open daily, 25 March-6 Jan. Spring exhibitions 10-12.30 and 2-5 ☎ 98.06.14.43
Tradition Pardon de Trémalo, 29 July, and Fête des Fleurs d'Ajoncs, first Sun in Aug.

Hotels
Hôtellerie de Keraven
château-hôtel
50 rue du Coteau
☎ 98.06.16.11 (river view)
Hôtel des Ajoncs d'Or ✱✱
place de l'Hôtel de Ville
☎ 98.06.02.06
(and restaurant)
Restaurants
Le Moulin de Rosmadec
centre ville
☎ 98.06.00.22
La Taupinière
route de Concarneau
☎ 98.06.03.12

PONTIVY
Map ref 134 C3
Pop 15,000
Lorient 55 km
Rennes 108 km
Brest 140 km
Nantes 160 km
Paris 457 km

Numerous buildings of interest vie for attention in the older part of town, but as an example of 15th-century military architecture, the **Château de Rohan**, a fortress intact with moats and two huge towers built by the powerful Rohan family, is the last that remains in the whole of Brittany. High above the River Blavet, the château now hosts a three-month long music festival between June and September.
This is today a prospering agricultural region fed by the waters of canal and

Hotels
Hôtel de l'Europe ✱✱
12 rue de la Mairie
☎ 97.25.11.14
(and restaurant)
Hôtel du Porhoët ✱✱
rue du Général de Gaulle
☎ 97.25.34.88
Hôtel le Rohan ✱✱
90 rue Nationale
☎ 97.25.02.01
Hôtel Martin ✱✱
1 and 3 rue Leperdit

☎ Office de
Tourisme
☎ 97.25.04.10

river. The Nantes-Brest Canal section between Pontivy and Redon offers some of the loveliest cruising country in Brittany – with Rohan, Josselin, Malestroit and La Gacilly worthy ports of call whether waterborne or motoring. The large expanse of water of the **Lac de Guerlédan** to the north is attractively framed by moors and woodland and offers good bathing and a wide range of watersports activities.

Leisure
Château Dating from 1485, the Château de Rohan is open throughout the year as an exhibition centre.
Riding L'Ecurie des Ajoncs in the forested area near Ste-Brigitte.
Watersports The Lac de Guerlédan offers good bathing and watersports activities as well as boat trips.

☎ 97.27.92.20
Chez Robic
2-4 rue Jean Jaurès
☎ 97.25.11.80
Camping
Municipal le Douric **
25 places open all year
☎ 97.25.92.20
Youth Hostel
Ile des Récollets
☎ 97.25.58.27
Restaurant
Le Gambetta
place de la Gare
☎ 97.25.53.70

QUIBERON
Map ref 138 C3
Pop 7,000
Vannes 47
Rennes 152 km
Nantes 157 km
Brest 178 km
Paris 505 km
☎ 7 rue de Verdun
☎ 97.50.07.84

One of the most beautiful parts of Brittany, Quiberon is a popular and interesting town situated on the very tip of the narrow **Côte Sauvage** peninsula, the west coast of which is wildly buffeted by the Atlantic. Boat excursions to the accurately named **Belle-Ile** plus the smaller islands of Houat and Hoëdic reward those seeking more good bathing possibilities. Nightlife is lively and there is a casino too, but traffic congestion at weekends can be horrific.
Leisure
Beaches Numerous safe and sheltered beaches on the east coast but *it is positively dangerous to swim around the rocks or caves on the west even when the*

Hotels
Hôtel Sofitel Diététique ****
pointe de Goulvars
☎ 97.50.20.00 (sea view and restaurant)
Hôtel Sofitel Thalassa ****
boulevard Goviro
☎ 97.50.20.00 (sea view and restaurant)
Hôtel Beau Rivage ***
11 rue Port Maria
☎ 97.50.08.39 (sea view and restaurant)
Hôtel Europa ***
Port Haliguen
☎ 97.50.25.00 (sea view and restaurant)
Hôtel Ker Noyal ***
rue de St-Clement
☎ 97.50.08.41
(and restaurant)
Résidence Orion ***
rue du Port de Pêche
☎ 97.30.42.74
Hôtel Bellevue **
rue de Tiviec
☎ 97.50.16.28 (sea view and restaurant)
Camping
Domisilami ***
170 places 15 Mar-5 Nov
☎ 97.50.22.52
Beauséjour **
150 places 1 Apr-30 Sep
☎ 97.30.44.93
Municipal Conguel **
165 places 15 Jun-3 Sep
☎ 97.50.19.11
Municipal du Bois d'Amour **
335 places 1 May-30 Sep
☎ 97.50.13.52
Municipal Goviro **
200 places open all year
☎ 97.50.13.54
Youth Hostel
Les Filets Bleus
45 rue du Roch Priol
1 Jul-31 Aug
☎ 97.50.15.54

ANNE OF BRITTANY
Anne was the daughter and heir of Francis II, Duke of Brittany. Although small, thin and with a limp, she was well educated and vivacious, and in an age when princes and kings won territories by marriage as well as by force of arms, the heiress to the Duchy of Brittany was a catch indeed.

Betrothed at first to the Holy Roman Emperor, Maximilian of Austria, she was pursued by the young French king, Charles VIII, who saw the alliance of Brittany and Austria as a direct threat to his throne. On the death of her father Anne refused to revoke her betrothal to Maximilian, and the French king then invaded Brittany and laid siege to Rennes where Anne was esconced. When Maximilian failed to come to her aid, and moved by the deprivations of the people of the city, Anne agreed to the annulment of her marriage and on 6 December 1491, at Langeais, she married instead the squat, ugly Charles.

Despite the inauspicious beginnings to this marriage, Anne grew to love Charles and he in turn was devoted to his 'petite Brette'. Though living at Amboise and surrounding herself with artists and writers, the new Queen of France did not forget her native Brittany. As part of her marriage settlement she retained the sovereign title of Duchess of Brittany, and when Charles died her marriage settlement to his successor Louis XII retained this clause.

This devotion to the interests of her Breton subjects is well remembered, and to this day her name is commemorated in some way in every town in Brittany. For by maintaining her sovereignty she allied rather than subjugated Brittany to the French crown, and enabled Bretons to accept the French kings as heirs of their own Duchess.

sea appears to be calm.
Cycling *Cycles can be hired from the
SNCF station. Mopeds and scooters can
be hired from Cyclo-Loisirs, 3 rue de
Manéreur ☎ 97.50.10.69 and from
Cyclomar, place Hoche.*
Golf *See Belle-Ile-en-Mer, Carnac and
Vannes.*
Thalassotherapy *Open Feb-Dec, Institut
de Thalassothérapie de Quiberon, BP 170,
56170 Quiberon ☎ 97.50.20.00*
Windsurfing *And boat hire from
Loc'Evasion, Port de Plaisance.*

Restaurants
*Hoche ✱✱
19 place Hoche
☎ 97.50.07.73
La Chaumine ✱✱
36 place du Manemeur
☎ 97.50.17.67
Les Druides ✱✱
6 rue du Port-Maria
☎ 97.50.14.74
La Roseraie
3 quai de Houat Port-Maria
☎ 97.30.40.83*

QUIMPER
Map ref 130 D1
Pop 60,000
Lorient 66 km
Brest 71 km
Rennes 205 km
Nantes 227 km
Paris 554 km
🏛 place de
la Résistance
☎ 98.95.04.69

The chief town of Finistère and capital of
Cornouaille, Quimper annually hosts one
of the most important festivals in Brittany.
The Festival de Cornouaille with its
thousands of participants, celebrates the
music, dancing and costumes of the
region and is one not to miss if possible.
Pleasantly built along the banks of the
River Odet, Quimper offers a delightful
mix of ancient and modern. Guided tours
of the old quarters are available, where
visitors will be rewarded by the sight of
the beautiful medieval houses and the
faïenceries or pottery studios of the rue
Kéréon, the little River Steir running
behind. The splendid Gothic
St-Corentin cathedral has a peculiarity all
its own – the unusual sloping angle
between choir and nave is said to
represent that of Christ's head on the
cross. Beyond the cathedral and across
the river rises the little hill of **Mont Frugy**.
A short walk to its summit will reveal a
good view over the city.
Leisure
Art *The Musée des Beaux Arts, place
St-Corentin has a collection of European
paintings from the 16th to 19th centuries,
as well as from the Pont-Aven school.*
Boat Trips *The beautiful Odet estuary can
be explored by vedette. See Bénodet.*
Cycling *Cycles can be hired from the
SNCF station.*
Golf *See Bénodet.*
Museum *Interesting local history museum
housed in the Bishop's Palace, rue Roi*

Hotels
*Hôtel le Griffon ✱✱✱
131 route de Bénodet
☎ 98.90.33.33
Hôtel Novotel ✱✱✱
route de Bénodet
☎ 98.90.46.26
Hôtel la Tour d'Auvergne ✱✱
13 rue des Reguaires
☎ 98.95.08.70
(and restaurant)
Hôtel Dupleix ✱✱
34 boulevard Dupleix
☎ 98.90.53.35 (river view
and restaurant)
Hôtel Gradlon ✱✱
30 rue de Brest
☎ 98.95.04.39
Hôtel Ibis ✱✱
rue Gustave Eiffel
☎ 98.90.53.80
Hôtel la Sapinière ✱✱
286 route de Bénodet
☎ 98.90.39.63*
Camping
*L'Orangerie de Lanniron ✱✱✱✱
100 places 1 May-15 Sep
☎ 98.90.62.02*
Youth Hostel
*6 avenue des Oiseaux
Bois de l'Ancien Séminaire
☎ 98.55.41.67*
Restaurants
*Le Capucin Gourmand
29 rue des Reguaires
☎ 98.95.43.12*

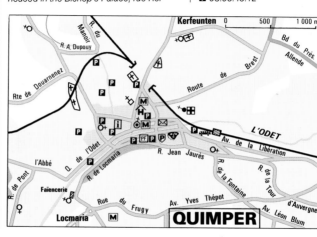

Gradlon, next to the cathedral.
Pottery Those interested in seeing Quimper's traditional earthenware decorators at work can visit the following studios: Faïenceries H-B. Henriot, allées de Locmaria, rue de Bénodet; and Faïenceries Keraluc, 14 rue de Troménie.
Tradition Festival de Cornouaille, fourth Sun of July and week preceding.

QUIMPERLE
Map ref 131 E5
Pop 12,000
Concarneau 31 km
Brest 112 km
Rennes 159 km
Nantes 181 km
Paris 511 km
🏛 Pont Bourgneuf
☎ 98.96.04.32

The town is built on two levels, both parts dominated by churches; Ste-Croix in the lower town amongst cobbled back streets and half-timbered houses is modelled on the church of the Holy Sepulchre in Jerusalem.
Prettily situated where the rivers Ellé and Isole meet amidst a fertile landscape, Quimperlé is edged on the south by the **Forêt de Carnoët** of beech and oak, and from there a picturesque road leads on to the sea. Popular with Gauguin and other painters from the Pont-Aven school, the area is most attractive.
Leisure
Museum The Musée d'Histoire et de Traditions Locales, Maison des Archers explores the lives and work of such as the oyster farmer and the clog-maker.
Tradition At Toulfoën, on the edge of the Forêt de Carnoët, Pardon des Oiseaux, Whit Sunday.

REDON
Map ref 134 F3
Pop 10,000
St-Nazaire 54 km
Rennes 64 km
Nantes 68 km
Brest 232 km
Paris 401 km
🏛 place du Parlement
☎ 99.71.06.04

Redon is the crossroads of the Breton waterway system with the Nantes-Brest Canal and the River Vilaine intersecting and punctuating the town with locks. An attractive and popular area for cruising holidaymakers who can either pick up and hire a boat here, or use the town as a base for further exploration by bicycle. Narrow streets of old buildings, some of them quite impressive, recall the days when the river port area was busy with commercial rather than pleasure traffic and wealthy merchants and ship-owners settled here. A son-et-lumière show celebrates this little town's past fame during June and July, while the Benedictine abbey of St-Sauveur, founded in 832 and reconstructed in the 17th century, now hosts a summer music festival in the cloisters.
Leisure
Boat Hire Several operators are based here. See page 26 for information on cruising holidays in the region .
Cycling Cycles for hire. Enquire at the Tourist Office.
Fishing Category 2 fishing on the River Vilaine and the Nantes-Brest Canal.
Loisirs Accueil Interesting options in the area include: 2-week holidays in leisurely style – one week in a horse-drawn vehicle followed by one week on a canal cruiser. Cost 5,750FF during May, Jun and Sep; 6,950FF in July and Aug. Also riding breaks exploring the Vilaine valley region. Cost including basic accommodation in gîtes d'étape, 2 days 500FF per person; 4

Fleur de Sel
1, quai Neuf
☎ *98.55.04.71*
Le Transvaal
34 boulevard Duplex
☎ *98.90.09.91*

Hotels
Hôtel de l'Ermitage ★★★
2 km south, D49
☎ *98.96.04.66*
(and restaurant)
Camping
Municipal Kerbertrand ★★
40 places 15 Jun-15 Sep
☎ *98.39.31.30*
or ☎ *98.96.01.41 (la Mairie)*
Restaurants
Auberge de Toulfoën ★★
route du Pouldu
☎ *98.96.00.29*
Le Bistro de la Tour
2 rue Dom Morice
☎ *98.39.29.98*
Ty Gwechall (crêpérie)
4 rue Mellac
☎ *98.96.30.63*

Hotels
Hôtel Chandouineau ★★
avenue de la Gare
☎ *99.71.02.04*
(and restaurant)
Hôtel de Bretagne ★★
place de la Gare
☎ *99.71.00.42*
(and restaurant)
Hôtel de France ★★
30 rue du Guesclin
☎ *99.71.06.11*
Camping
Municipal la Goule d'Eau ★★
46 places 15 Jun-15 Sep
☎ *99.72.36.16*

HOLIDAYS IN THE SADDLE

PAUL GAUGUIN (1848-1903)

Considering how lavishly the Bretons painted the interiors of their churches and chapels, it is surprising that they produced no great artists in the centuries from the Renaissance right up to the Impressionist period; nor were artists from elsewhere attracted to Brittany, at least until the mid-19th century. By about 1860, however, artists in search of unspoilt scenery for background and unsophisticated country people for models had started to arrive, settling in and around the riverside village of Pont-Aven, in southern Finistère.

They were joined in the 1880s by Paul Gauguin, one of the greatest of all French artists, whose influence and example at once put Brittany on the artistic map. It was his association with the little town of Pont-Aven that was to result in the creation of the Pont-Aven School of Painting. Gauguin stayed in Brittany on and off for a period of five years, in both Pont-Aven and the seaside village of Le Pouldu along the coast.

BRETON WOMEN, PAUL GAUGUIN

Like the stone calvaries of the *enclos paroissiaux,* his paintings set Biblical scenes in a Breton context. Peasant women, wearing the traditional white lace coif on their heads, tend sheep above a village or drive oxen past a calvary in the snow. In one of the most moving of all his paintings, the *Christ Jaune,* Gauguin took as his model the yellow-painted statue of Christ in the chapel of Trémalo, up the hill past Pont-Aven. Typically, he brought the figure out of the gloom of the chapel and set it among the gentle folds of the Breton countryside.

When Gauguin finally left France for Tahiti and another famous phase in his career, the leaders of the group, Paul Sérusier and Emile Bernard, carried Gauguin's adventurous use of colour and perspective still further, but by the time of the First World War the original impetus had gone. Today there are still plenty of artists painting in and around Pont-Aven, and during the summer the Municipality holds regular exhibitions by artists of the Pont-Aven School, from the time of Gauguin to the present day.

Besides Gauguin and his followers, earlier and later artists, both Breton-born and inspired by Brittany, feature in the extensive collections in the region's art galleries: the Musées des Beaux Arts in Rennes, Quimper and Nantes, in Morlaix the Musée des Jacobins, and in Vannes the Musée de la Cohue. Visitors to Lamballe should also hunt out the small museum devoted to the paintings and drawings of Mathurin Méheut (1882-1958), who was born in the town, studied in Paris, and who spent his long creative life in Brittany.

---

days 900FF. Contact Loisirs Accueil Ille-et-Vilaine (address on page 25).
Tradition Fête de l'Eau, early July; month-long music festival in the abbey cloisters, mid-July.
Watersports Sailing and windsurfing at the Etang d'Aumée.

RENNES
Map ref 135 A6
Pop 200,000
Nantes 108 km
Brest 240 km
Paris 345 km
🄷 Pont de Nemours
☎ 99.79.01.98

The capital of Brittany and very much a mirror of modern Breton life, Rennes is a major industrial and university city as well as a large administrative and commercial centre. Though much has been destroyed over the centuries and subsequently replaced with modern construction, parts of the city remain very old and the Palais de Justice building is one of the most notable, built in the 17th century.
Like a green oasis, the Jardins du Thabor are situated right in the centre and are amongst the finest public gardens in France. Created from the grounds of a former Benedictine monastery, a variety of styles is represented. Other recreational outlets are provided by the waymarked walks and bridle-paths through the **Forêt de Rennes**, where there are also pleasant picnic areas and a lake.

Leisure
Activity Centre Just past Montfort west of Rennes is the Etang de Trémelin en Iffendic, an outdoor activity centre based

Hotels
Hôtel Altea Parc du Colombier ★★★
rue du Capitaine Maignan
☎ *99.31.54.54*
(and restaurant)
Hôtel Anne de Bretagne ★★★
12 rue Tronjolly
☎ *99.31.49.49*
Hôtel le Président ★★★
27 avenue janvier
☎ *99.65.42.22*
Hôtel le Sévigné ★★★
47 avenue janvier
☎ *99.67.27.55*
Hôtel Mercure ★★★
rue Paul Louis Courier
☎ *99.78.32.32*
Le Central Hôtel ★★★
6 rue Lanjuinais
☎ *99.79.12.36*
Hôtel Arvor ★★
31 avenue Louis Barthou
☎ *99.30.36.47*

on the lake and surrounded by pine woods. The centre offers cycling, riding, fishing and sailing, with rowing boat and pedalo hire, a sandy beach and bathing area, children's playgrounds and amusements and a small zoo. There is ** camp site accommodation available, 115 places ☎ 99.09.73.79

Boat Trips Half-day and full-day trips on the rivers Ille and Vilaine.

Château Impressive remains of 15th-century Château de Châteaugiron, 16 km to the south east.

Cycling Cycles can be hired from the SNCF station and from the Youth Hostel ☎ 99.33.22.33

Fishing Category 2 fishing on the River Vilaine, the Ille-et-Rance canal and various lakes. Information from Fédération Départementale des Associations de Pêche, 149 rue d'Antrain, Rennes ☎ 99.63.03.95

Golf 9-hole private course at Golf de Rennes, 35000 St-Jacques-de-la-Lande ☎ 99.64.24.18. Also new 18-hole course at Golf de la Freslonnière, 35650 Le Rheu ☎ 99.60.84.09 with putting green and restaurant.

Museums The Musée de la Bretagne, 20 quai Emile Zola, covers the history of

(and restaurant)

Hôtel aux Voyageurs **
28 avenue janvier
☎ 99.31.73.33

Hôtel de Bretagne **
7 bis, place de la Gare
☎ 99.31.48.48

Garden Hôtel **
3 rue Duhamel
☎ 99.65.45.06

Camping
Municipal les Gayeulles **
100 places Easter-1 Oct
☎ 99.36.91.22

ST-PIERRE CATHEDRAL, RENNES

Youth Hostel
10 Canal St-Martin
Open all year
☎ 99.33.22.33

Restaurants
Auberge St-Sauveur **
6 rue St-Sauveur
☎ 99.79.32.56

Brasserie La Chope **
3 rue de la Chalotais
☎ 99.79.34.54

Le Corsaire *
52 rue d'Antrain
☎ 99.36.33.69

Auberge St-Martin *
230 rue de St-Malo
☎ 99.33.94.89

Du Palais
7 place du Parlement
de Bretagne
☎ 99.79.45.01

HOUSE OF DU GUESCLIN

Breton life and culture ☎ 99.28.55.84; the Musée des Beaux Arts et d'Archéologie, in the same building ☎ 99.28.55.84 houses an important collection of paintings from all periods; and the Ecomusée du Pays de Rennes, Ferme des Bintinays ☎ 99.51.38.15 covers the folk history of the region. These museums close on Tues.
Riding Centre Equestre La Muserolle, opposite St-Jacques golf course, Bruz ☎ 99.64.24.38

Le Pire
18 rue Maréchal Joffre
☎ 99.79.31.41
Chouan
rue d'Isly
☎ 99.30.87.86

Tradition Every two years the Festival des Arts Electroniques is held (early June in 1990) representing the state of the art in this technology. Past events have proved predictably spectacular. Les Tombées de la Nuit or 'Nightfall' festival, held on the first 10 days of July, represents the creativity of Brittany in an interesting combination of music and theatre and is staged outdoors in the streets of the city centre – one not to miss if possible.
Walking ABRI, 9 rue des Portes Mordelaises ☎ 99.31.59.44

PALAIS ST-GEORGES, RENNES

ROSCOFF
Map ref 120 C3
Pop 4,000
Brest 62 km
Rennes 210 km
Nantes 283 km
Paris 531 km
🛈 chapelle
Ste-Anne
☎ 98.69.70.70
(and car ferry)

Little fishing port remarkable for being the richest place in Europe for seaweed, hence the popularity of the two marine therapy treatment centres here. Not unattractive, the austere old stone houses line the busy port area, another major cross-Channel ferry route – from Cork and Plymouth. Boat trips sail every hour to the Ile de Batz, its mild climate and good beaches making it a popular excursion. St-Pol-de-Léon and this part of north Finistère is agriculturally responsible for the greater part of France's cauliflower and artichoke production. A controlling body was set up in the early 1960s to run this local trade and to transport the produce to England. Later to diversify successfully into tourism, that original freight carrier is now better known as Brittany Ferries.

Leisure
Aquarium Part of Paris University's biology research department, the Aquarium Charles Perez, place Georges-Tessier ☎ 98.29.23.25 reveals the underwater life of the Channel.

Hotels
Hôtel le Brittany ***
boulevard Ste-Barbe
☎ 98.69.70.78 (sea view and restaurant)
Hôtel le Gulf Stream ***
rue Marquise de Kergariou
☎ 98.69.73.19 (sea view and restaurant)
Hôtel Regina ***
rue Ropartz-Morvan
☎ 98.61.23.55 (sea view)
Hôtel Bellevue **
rue Jeanne d'Arc
☎ 98.61.23.38 (sea view and restaurant)
Hôtel les Alizés
quai d'Auxerre
☎ 98.69.72.22
Camping
Municipal Perharidy **
200 places Easter-30 Sep
☎ 98.69.70.86
Manoir de Kérestat **
45 places
☎ 98.69.71.92

Beach Sand and shingle on the nearby estuaries.
Botanic Gardens The Jardin Botanique du Rocher de la Maison Rouge boasts tropical plants and views of the Baie de Morlaix.
Cycling Cycles can be hired from the SNCF station.
Fishing Sea-fishing trips on Vedettes Blanches ☎ 98.61.77.75
Market The early morning (8 a.m.) auctions of fresh produce take place daily at the Marché au Cadran, St-Pol-de-Léon.
Thalassotherapy There are two centres: open all year, Clinique de Rééducation Fonctionelle Ker-Léna, BP 13, 29211 Roscoff ☎ 98.24.33.33; and open Apr-Oct, the Institut Marin Rockroum Centre de Thalassothérapie, BP 28, 29211 Roscoff ☎ 98.29.20.00

Restaurant
Le Temps du Vivre
place Lacaze Duthiers
☎ 98.61.27.28

ROOFTOPS IN ROSCOFF

ST-BRIEUC
Map ref 123 E6
Pop 52,000
Dinan 62 km
Rennes 104 km
Brest 144 km
Nantes 192 km
Paris 425 km
🛈 7 rue St-Gouéno
☎ 96.33.32.50

Capital of the Côtes-d'Armor *département*, this is a busy commercial and industrial centre slightly inland from the sea. Founded in the 6th century by the Welsh monk, Brieuc, the town possesses the rather severe and much restored 13th-century cathedral of St-Etienne and a number of very old buildings close by. An ideal base for exploring inland or along the northern coastline, most leisurely perhaps by bicycle, due south is the pretty **Lac de Guerlédan** near Mur-de-Bretagne, which offers a range of watersports activities and boat trips.
Leisure
Cycling Cycles can be hired from the SNCF station and from the Youth Hostel.
Golf See Paimpol and St-Quay-Portrieux.
Museum History museum, closed Mon, in rue des Lycéens-Martyrs ☎ 96.33.39.12
National Stud Created in 1825, and one of the largest and most important in France, the Haras National at Lamballe is renowned for its thoroughbreds. Open July-Feb for guided tours ☎ 96.31.00.40
Tradition Pardon de Notre-Dame-d'Espérance, last Sun in May, and Le Mai Breton, May, devoted to folklore and music.

Hotels
Hôtel le Griffon ✦✦✦
rue de Guernsey
☎ 96.94.57.62
La Pomme d'Or Hôtellerie ✦✦✦
Voie Express RN/2
☎ 96.61.12.10
Hôtel du Guesclin ✦✦
place du Guesclin
(and restaurant)
☎ 96.33.11.58
Hôtel Ker Izel ✦✦
20 rue du Gouet
☎ 96.33.46.29
Hôtel le Chêne Vert Plérin ✦✦
RN12, 22190 Plérin
☎ 96.74.63.20
Hôtel le Pignon Pointu ✦✦
rue J-J. Rousseau
☎ 96.33.02.39
Youth Hostel
Manoir de la Ville-Guyomard
☎ 96.78.70.70 Open all year
Restaurants
L'Amadeus
22 rue du Gouët
☎ 96.33.92.44
Aux Pesked
59 rue du Légué
☎ 96.33.34.65
La Croix Blanche
61 rue de Genève
☎ 96.33.16.97
La Vieille Tour
75 rue de la Tour
Plérin
☎ 96.33.10.30

ST-CAST-LE-GUILDO
Map ref 124 B3
Pop 4,000
St-Malo 31 km
Rennes 86 km
Brest 193 km
Nantes 193 km
Paris 386 km
🛈 place du Général de Gaulle
☎ 96.41.81.52

Popular seaside resort which extends the length of a peninsula with seven well-sheltered beaches of fine sand edged by rocky cliffs. There are good watersports facilities and river and sea-fishing trips available.
Some of the most astounding views are possible from the wild **Cap Fréhel** area where many types of seabirds such as shags, kittiwakes and common guillemots or murres nest in the crevices of the cliffs. In August migrating flocks of puffins,

Hotels
Hôtel les Dunes
rue Primauguet ✦✦
☎ 96.41.80.31
(and restaurant)
Hôtel Ker Louis ✦✦
rue du Guesclin
☎ 96.41.80.77 (sea view)
Hôtel l'Etoile des Mers ✦✦
32 rue du Port
☎ 96.41.85.36 (sea view)

gannets, terns and common scoters can also be seen.

Just around the cape is the **Fort la Latte**, built between the 14th and 17th centuries and commanding an exceptional island position overhanging the sea, with a drawbridge connecting it to the mainland.

Leisure

Cycling Cycles for hire from M Page, rue de l'Isle ☎ 96.41.87.71

Golf Often crowded 9-hole private course suitable for beginners and juniors in a beautiful position facing the sea at Golf de Pen Guen, 22380 St-Cast-le-Guildo ☎ 96.41.91.20; and 9-hole private course, half woodland, half links, at Golf des Sables-d'Or-Les-Pins, 22240 Cap Fréhel ☎ 96.41.42.57

Lighthouse The powerful clifftop Cap Fréhel lighthouse can be visited, Easter-Sep, on contacting the keeper ☎ 96.41.40.03. Its beams carry over a distance of 110 km or nearly 70 miles.

Painting Drawing and watercolour courses, both outdoor and in the studio, from Atelier de Galinée (Monique Rabasté) ☎ 96.41.10.28

Riding Centre Equestre du Bois Bras ☎ 96.41.95.01

Sailing School offering sailing and windsurfing tuition to beginners and improvers at the Ecole de Voile based in the port ☎ 96.41.86.42

Tennis 12 courts to hire at the Tennis Club de la Garde ☎ 96.41.88.16

Walking Follow the coastal paths.

ST-MALO

Map ref 125 B5
Pop 48,000
Rennes 71 km
St-Brieuc 86 km
Nantes 178 km
Brest 220 km
Paris 361 km
🅸 esplanade St-Vincent
☎ 99.56.64.48

A delightful old city of narrow, cobbled streets, once the haunt of pirates, or more properly corsairs. Magnificently situated on a rocky promontory off the mainland, the huge circuiting ramparts of the old town known as **Intra Muros** or 'Within the Walls' are often buffeted by the wild seas, while in gentler weather they provide shelter for the sandy beaches below. The careful restoration programme which followed the massive bomb damage suffered during 1944 reveals the 'new' St-Malo beyond; tall, elegant buildings built again out of the local granite.

The inhabitants of St-Malo, known as Malouins, have a saying: *'Malouin d'abord, Breton peut-être, français s'il en reste'* – A St-Malo man first, a Breton perhaps, a Frenchman if there is anything left. The town has always been fiercely self-sufficient; indeed the castle here was constructed to maintain the independence of the people from the Duke of Brittany. A magnificent 15th-century fortification, it consists of four huge towers and is used to house the present-day museum. An important commercial centre and port, the harbour is busy with shipping of all kinds and sizes from cross-Channel ferries and freighters to yachts and fishing boats, and is the nearest Breton port to Paris.

The city can boast several famous sons.

Camping

Le Châtelet ★★★★
170 places 1 May-20 Sep
☎ 96.41.96.33
La Ferme de Pen Guen ★★
300 places Easter-30 Sep
☎ 96.41.92.18
Municipal les Mielles ★★
220 places mid-May-15 Sep
☎ 96.41.87.60

Restaurant

Bon Abri ★
4 rue du Semaphore
☎ 96.41.85.74

SEAGULLS AND PINK ROCKS NEAR ST-CAST-LE-GUILDO

Hotels

Grand Hôtel des Thermes ★★★
100 boulevard Hébert
☎ 99.40.75.75 (sea view and restaurant)
Hôtel Ajoncs d'Or ★★★
10 rue des Forgeurs
☎ 99.40.85.03
Hôtel Central ★★★
6 Grande-Rue
☎ 99.40.87.70 (and restaurant)
Hôtel de la Digue ★★★
49 chaussée du Sillon
☎ 99.56.09.26
Hôtel du Guesclin ★★★
1 place du Guesclin
☎ 99.56.01.30
Hôtel Elisabeth ★★★
2 rue des Cordiers
☎ 99.56.24.98
Hôtel la Korrigane ★★★
39 rue le Pommelec
☎ 99.81.65.85
Hôtel la Villefromoy ★★★
7 boulevard Hébert
☎ 99.40.92.20 (sea view)
Hôtel le Valmarin ★★★
7 rue Jean XXIII
☎ 99.81.94.76
Hôtel Mercure ★★★
2 rue Joseph Loth
☎ 99.56.84.84 (sea view)

The great romantic writer René Chateaubriand was both born and buried here – on a small island just offshore; and, reflecting its great seafaring heritage, the explorer Jacques Cartier who discovered Canada; the lieutenant-general of the Navy under Louis XIV and scourge of the English, Duguay-Trouin; and, more infamously perhaps, the corsair Surcouf. It was, incidentally, Malouin sailors who first discovered the Falkland Islands and named them Les Malouines, a name reflected in the Argentinian equivalent Las Malvinas. Together with the closely-neighbouring resorts of Paramé, St-Servan and Rothéneuf, this is now a built-up and commercialized coastline which stretches from St-Malo towards Cancale to the east and Val-André to the west.

Leisure

Casino In the chaussée du Sillon
☎ 99.56.00.05
Cycling Cycles can be hired from the SNCF station.
Golf 18-hole private course at Tronchet, ☎ 99.58.96.69; driving range Le Colombier ☎ 99.82.30.38. See also Dol-de-Bretagne.
Loisirs Accueil Summer French language courses lasting 1, 2 or 3 weeks, Jun-Aug. Cost 1,000FF per person per week. Also caters for advanced and literature students. Contact Loisirs Accueil Ille-et-Vilaine (address on page 25).
Museum Set within one of the towers of the castle is the curiously named Quic-en-Groigne exhibition on the corsair lifestyle ☎ 99.40.80.26, open Easter-Sep.
Riding Centre Hippique de St-Malo,

Résidence Orion ✱✱✱
33 rue George V
☎ 99.82.29.40

Camping

Le Petit Bois ✱✱✱✱
180 places 15 May-15 Sep
☎ 99.81.48.36
La Fontaine ✱✱
100 places 15 Jun-15 Sep
☎ 99.81.62.62
Cité d'Aleth✱✱
400 places open all year
☎ 99.81.60.91
Municipal le Nicet ✱✱
250 places 1 May-20 Sep
☎ 99.40.26.32

Youth Hostel

37 avenue R-P. Umbricht
Open all year
☎ 99.40.29.80

Restaurants

Casino ✱✱✱
2 chaussée du Sillon
☎ 99.56.00.05
La Métairie de Beauregard ✱✱✱
Bourg de St-Etienne
Z.I. de La Grassinet
☎ 99.81.37.06
Cap Horn ✱✱
100 boulevard Hébert
☎ 99.40.75.75
La Rochebonne ✱✱
15 boulevard Chateaubriand
☎ 99.56.65.30
Le Servannais ✱✱
4 rue Amiral Magon
☎ 99.81.45.50
Porte St-Pierre ✱
2 place du Guet
☎ 99.40.91.27

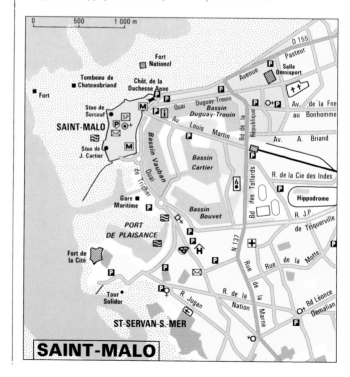

SAINT-MALO

PIRATES AND PIONEERS

With its extensive coastline and sheltered inlets and creeks Brittany, like Devon and Cornwall, has produced generations of fishermen and sailors. With the development of ship-building and navigation in the 16th century, Breton sailors began their journeys of discovery across the Atlantic. In 1534 Jacques Cartier, a native of St-Malo, in his search for the fabled north-west passage to India, discovered the St Lawrence river and claimed Canada for the French crown.

Their adventures were not confined to the North Atlantic however. Sailors from St-Malo – *les malouins* – discovered the islands in the South Atlantic which the British know as the Falklands, the Spanish as Las Malvinas and the French by their original name, Les Malouines.

Although the great French statesman Cardinal Richelieu created Brest as the centre of French naval ship-building, it was St-Malo that attracted more colourful and adventurous enterprises. Smuggling across the Channel was always a lucrative trade in times of peace or war, but the increased shipping off the coasts of France encouraged more daring escapades. St-Malo was home port to privateers – corsairs or pirates with licence from the French crown to prey on foreign shipping provided they passed over a proportion of their spoils to the state. Under the protection of the French government, these commissions allowed men like Duguay-Trouin (1673-1736) and Robert Surcouf (1773-1827) to use their own vessels and men and caused great losses to the English, Spanish and Dutch navies. Despite attempts by the British Royal Navy to reduce the fortress to rubble and destroy this source of illicit income, the fine houses and fortifications of the city today testify to the prosperity which ensued from the success of the corsairs.

38 rue du Chapitre ☎ *99.81.20.34*
Thalassotherapy Open Feb-Dec, Les Thermes Marins, Grande Plage, 100 boulevard Hébert, BP 32, 35401 St-Malo ☎ *99.40.75.75*
Tradition Festival de Musique Sacrée, mid July-mid Aug; Fête du Clos Poulet, mid July is a folk festival; and the Transatlantic Sailing Race between St-Malo and Canada departs at the end of Aug.

A la Duchesse Anne
place Guy la Chambre
☎ *99.40.85.33*
J.P. Delaunay
6 rue Saint-Barbe
☎ *99.40.92.46*
Le Chalut
8 rue de la Corne-du-Cerf
☎ *99.56.71.58*
Robert Abraham
4 chaussée du Sillon
☎ *99.40.50.93*

SLIPPING OVER THE BORDER *into Pays de la Loire*

ST-NAZAIRE
Map ref 141 E4
Pop 69,000
La Baule 17 km
Nantes 64 km
Rennes 118 km
Brest 257 km
Paris 426 km
🛈 place François Blancho
☎ 40.22.40.65

This is a predominantly modern city, having been rebuilt after massive destruction during the last war. Here some of the world's largest ships are constructed in the enormous estuary shipyards, within sight of the impressive toll bridge which crosses the Loire at this point, thus providing swift connection with St-Brévin-les-Pins and the coast beyond. Good shopping and busy markets, fishermen's auctions on the quayside, and the submarine base, scene of a daring and spectacular Anglo-Canadian raid against the German U-boat base on 28 March 1942. The numerous strange and prehistoric megaliths in the surrounding countryside offer a direct contrast with the modern city.

Leisure
Beach Good coastal bathing at numerous beaches and creeks nearby, particularly at St-Marc-sur-Mer.
Boat Trips Fascinating 1 hr 30 min trips around the massive port installations and beneath the elegant new road bridge, and to visit the submarine basin where the French polar submarine l'Espadon is open to the public. Trips by bus are also possible around the shipyard wharves, to observe the construction work in progress.

Hotels
Hôtel du Bon Accueil ***
39 rue Marceau
☎ *40.22.07.05*
Hôtel du Berry ***
1 place de la Gare
☎ *40.22.42.61*
Hôtel de l'Europe **
place Martyrs de la Résistance
☎ *40.22.49.87*
Hôtel du Dauphin **
33 rue Jean Jaurès
☎ *40.66.59.61*

SHIPYARDS, ST-NAZAIRE

These trips are bookable through the
Tourist Office. Numerous outlets offer
guided trips through the Parc de la Brière.
Good places to start from are St-Joachim
and St-Lyphard, typical small villages.
Canoeing On the stretch of water known
as the Etang du Bois Joalland which is also
a pleasant walking area.
Cycling Cycles can be hired from the
SNCF station.
Golf 18-hole private course in the Parc de
Brière at Golf de la Bretesche 44780
Missillac ☎ 40.88.30.03. See also
La Baule.
Riding La Chaussée Neuve, St-André-
des-Eaux ☎ 40.01.24.64 and Manège des
Grands Parcs ☎ 40.61.31.62
Walking Follow the sentier des douaniers
or Customs officers' paths along the coast
and discover the 20 or so beaches and
secluded creeks.

Camping
Camping de l'Eve
400 places mid-May-mid-Sept
☎ 40.91.90.65
Camping les Jaunais
St-Marc-sur-Mer 80 places
June-Sept ☎ 40.91.90.60
Restaurant
Le Margaux
60 avenue Albert de Mun
☎ 40.22.15.16

ST-QUAY-PORTRIEUX
Map ref 123 C6
Pop 4,000
St-Brieuc 20 km
Rennes 121 km
Brest 139 km
Nantes 217 km
Paris 426 km
🏛 Office de Tourisme
☎ 96.70.40.64

Busy and popular family resort on the
Côtes d'Armor with good bathing beaches
and sports facilities, exhilarating cliff
walks and pretty countryside nearby best
explored perhaps by bicycle. For the
children, the zoo at **Trégomeur** with its
variety of wild animals will prove popular.

Leisure
Beaches 5 safe and sandy beaches:
Casino, Châtelet, Comtesse, Port and
Grève Noire.
Casino ☎ 96.70.40.36
Cycling Cycles for hire from M. Guyot,
place d'Armes. Enquire at the Tourist
Office.
Golf Flat 18-hole public course,
interestingly laid out with a lake and raised
greens, at Golf des Ajoncs d'Or, 22410 St-
Quay-Portrieux ☎ 96.71.90.74
Riding Ranch des Ajoncs d'Or, Kerisago,
route de Paimpol ☎ 96.20.32.54
Sailing And windsurfing, sea kayaking,
catamaran, judo, water skiing and other
sports and activities are offered for
children aged between 13 and 20 years.
Tuition is available on a weekly, fortnightly,
monthly or longer basis from the Centre
des Loisirs pour les Jeunes (CLJ) and is
located at 10 boulevard de Gaulle but
bookable through the Tourist Office.
Tennis 9 courts to hire.
Zoo open daily, Apr-Nov, Parc Zoologique
du Moulin de Richard at Trégomeur
☎ 96.79.01.07

Hotels
Hôtel Ker Moor ***
rue du Président le Sénécal
☎ 96.70.52.22 (sea view
and restaurant)
Hôtel le Gerbot d'Avoine **
2 boulevard du Littoral
☎ 96.70.40.09 (sea view
and restaurant)
Hôtel la Jetée *
quai de la République
☎ 96.70.40.52 (sea view
and restaurant)
Hôtel St-Quay *
72 boulevard Foch
☎ 96.70.40.99
(and restaurant)
Camping
Camping Bellevue ***
200 places 1 May-15 Sep
☎ 96.70.41.84

TREBEURDEN
Map ref 121 B6
Pop 4,000
Perros-Guirec
13 km
Brest 104 km
Rennes 183 km
Nantes 274 km
Paris 504 km
🏛 place de
Crec'h-Héry
☎ 96.23.51.64

The Gulf Stream brings its warm waters to
this extremely pretty fishing port and
seaside resort.
There are lovely walks along the
rocky coast with only the sea birds as
company, or inland where megalithic
monuments and historic old chapels
contrast with the ultra-modern white dome
of the satellite communications centre at
Pleumeur-Bodou.

Leisure
Beach Large sweeping sandy beach at

Hotels
Hôtel Ti Al Lannec ***
allée de Mezo Gwen
☎ 96.23.57.26 (sea view
and **** restaurant)
Manoir de Lan-Kerellec ***
allée de Lan-Kerellec
☎ 96.23.50.09 (sea view
and restaurant)
Family Hotel **
85 les Plages
☎ 96.23.50.31 (sea view

Tresmeur. Numerous rocky coves of fine sand stretch along the coast from Landrellec to Pors-Mabo.

Bird-watching Permanent video relay information on the birds at the Sept-Iles reserve. Organized outings for bird spotting and excursions looking at coastal plants, sand dunes and tidal movement. Station Ornithologique Ile-Grande ☎ 96.91.91.40

Golf 18-hole private heathland course with marvellous views at Golf de St-Samson, route de Kérenoc, 22560 Pleumeur-Bodou ☎ 96.23.87.34

Riding Relais Equestre d'Armor ☎ 96.23.63.95

Watersports Sailing from the plage de Tresmeur and skin-diving with the Cap de Trébeurden school ☎ 96.23.66.71

and restaurant)
Hôtel Ker An Nod **
rue de Pors Termen
☎ 96.23.50.21 (sea view and restaurant)
Camping
Kerdual ***
35 places 1 May-30 Sep
☎ 96.23.54.86
L'Espérance ***
40 places 1 Apr-30 Sep
☎ 96.91.95.05
Camping Roz-Ar-Mor **
35 places Easter-15 Sep
☎ 96.23.58.12
Youth Hostel
Le Toëno
Mar-Nov
☎ 96.23.52.22

TREGASTEL-PLAGE
Map ref 121 A6
Pop 2,000
Perros-Guirec 7 km
Brest 108 km
Rennes 176 km
Nantes 267 km
Paris 497 km
🛈 place Ste-Anne
☎ 96.23.88.67

Small seaside resort at the very tip of the Côte de Granit Rose, the naturally pink tinge to the smooth and strangely-formed rocks here makes for an attractive and interesting coastline. Popular for family holidays and for sailing enthusiasts who compete in the 24-hour summer regatta.

Leisure
Beaches 2 main sandy beaches: Coz-Pors and Grève Blanche, but numerous other small coves in the area.
Golf See Trébeurden.
Riding Pony Club, route de Woas-Wen ☎ 96.23.85.29 and Club Hippique, route du Calvaire Crec'h Léo ☎ 96.23.86.14
Sailing Club Nautique school at Grève Rose ☎ 96.23.45.05
Tennis 12 courts to hire.

Hotels
Armoric Hôtel ***
place du Coz-Pors
☎ 96.23.88.16 (sea view and restaurant)
Hôtel Belle Vue ***
20 rue des Calculots
☎ 96.23.88.18 (sea view and restaurant)
Hôtel de la Mer et de la Plage **
place du Coz-Pors
☎ 96.23.88.03 (sea view and restaurant)
Hôtel des Bains **
boulevard du Coz-Pors
☎ 96.23.88.09 (sea view and restaurant)
Hôtel le Beau Séjour **
place du Coz-Pors
☎ 96.23.88.02 (sea view and restaurant)
Camping
Le Golven ***
160 places 1 May-15 Sep
☎ 96.23.87.77
Tourony ***
100 places 1 Jun-30 Sep
☎ 96.23.86.61
Restaurant
La Corniche *
38 rue Charles le Goffic
☎ 96.23.88.15

THE COAST NEAR TREGASTEL

LA TRINITE-SUR-MER
Map ref 139 B4
Pop 2,000
Vannes 30 km
Nantes 141 km
Rennes 159 km
Brest 192 km
Paris 485 km
🛈 cours des Quais
☎ 97.55.72.21

An attractive little fishing port on the River Crach which specializes in oysters. Traditionally a centre for open-sea racing (and notably for local-born Eric Taberly), this is now a popular base for the sailing fraternity with mooring and facilities for 1,000 pleasure boats. Together with nearby Carnac and Quiberon, La Trinité is a busy holiday resort which, because of its sheltered location, boasts a sunshine record on a par with the South of France.

Hotels
Hôtel Le Rouzic **
17 cours des Quais
☎ 97.55.72.06 (sea view and restaurant)
Hôtel Panorama **
route d'Auray
Saint Philibert
☎ 97.55.00.56
(and restaurant)
Hôtel du Commerce *

Leisure
Cycling Mountain bikes for hire from
Morbihan Multicoques, Résidence les
Voiliers, place du Marché; also windsurf
boards, jet-skis and large boats for hire.
Golf See Carnac and Vannes.
Riding Centre Equestre des Menhirs, La
Grande Métairie ☎ 97.52.26.85 or
97.55.73.45
Tennis Tuition and courts to hire at plage
de Kervillen, opposite Camping de la
Plage. Also courts at Tennis Club de
Quéhan, near the Kerisper bridge.
Tradition Pardon at Trinité-Porhoet, Easter.

4 rue de Carnac
☎ 97.55.72.36 (sea view)
Camping
Camping de la Baie ★★★★
170 places 11 May-15 Sep
☎ 97.55.73.42
Camping de la Plage ★★★★
200 places 23 May-15 Sep
☎ 97.55.73.28
Kermarquer ★★★
90 places 1 Jun-15 Sep
☎ 97.55.79.18
Kervilor ★★★
200 places 18 May-15 Sep
☎ 97.55.76.75
Park Plijadur ★★★
200 places 1 Jun-end Sep
☎ 97.55.72.05
Restaurants
L'Azimut ★★★
1 rue de Men-Du
☎ 97.55.71.88
Les Hortensias
4 place Yvonne Sarcey
☎ 97.55.73.69

GARDENS AND RAMPARTS AT VANNES

VANNES
Map ref 139 B6
Pop 45,000
Rennes 105 km
St-Brieuc 105 km
Nantes 111 km
Brest 182 km
Paris 450 km
🛈 1 rue Thiers
☎ 97.47.24.34

Situated at the head of the Golfe du
Morbihan, Vannes is busy and attractive
and as such popular with summer visitors.
A historic town, the 9th-century capital of
the kingdom of Brittany under the Breton
chief, Nominoé, it was also the seat of the
Parliament of Brittany for some years. It
has retained a quite charming medieval
heart around the Saint-Pierre cathedral,
the ancient ramparts providing superb
views over the half-timbered houses and
formal gardens of the old town.
Dine-and-cruise trips operate around the
tidal gulf and there are also pleasure trips
out to the bay's many tiny islands.
Leisure
Boat Trips Regular island services and
pleasure trips offered by Vedettes Vertes
☎ 97.47.10.78, Mar-Sep.
Cycling Cycles can be hired from the
SNCF station.
Fishing Sea and river fishing.
Golf New 18-hole course at Golf de
Kerver, Le Crouesty, St-Gildas-du-Rhuys
☎ 97.45.30.09. See also Carnac.
Museum The Musée de la Cohue, place
St-Pierre devotes itself to the theme of the
sea and the Gulf in particular. Also
possesses engravings by Corot and Goya
and paintings by Delacroix as well as local
artists' works; closed Tues.
Tradition Medieval fête held in the town
centre in early July with street theatre,
music and dancing.

Hotels
Aquarium'Hôtel ★★★
Le Parc du Golfe
☎ 97.40.44.52 (sea view
and restaurant)
Hôtel la Marebaudière ★★★
4 rue Aristide Briand
☎ 97.47.34.29
Hôtel le Roof ★★★
Presqu'île de Conleau
☎ 97.63.47.47 (sea view
and restaurant)
Inter Hotel Manche Océan ★★★
31 rue du Lt-Col Maury
☎ 97.47.26.46
Hôtel Anne de Bretagne ★★
42 rue O. de Clisson
☎ 97.54.22.19
Camping
Municipal de Conleau ★★★
290 places 1 Apr-30 Sep
☎ 97.63.13.88
Restaurants
A l'Image Ste-Anne ★★
8 place de la Libération
☎ 97.63.27.36
L'Epée ★★
2 rue Joseph le Brix
☎ 97.47.10.11
Le Richemont
place de la Gare
☎ 97.42.61.41
Le Pressoir
7 rue de l'Hôpital,
St-Avé
☎ 97.60.87.63

SEA BIRDS

The Golfe du Morbihan, harbouring a greater concentration of sea birds than anywhere else on France's Channel-Atlantic coastline – 60,000 to upwards of 100,000 in some years, is one of the best areas in western Europe for observing over-wintering colonies. For some species, like the barnacle goose, these may include up to 25 per cent of the total world population.

There are numerous reserves along this part of the coast: on the island of Groix, at Rohellan, Theviec, on Belle-Ile island, Meaban, Creizic, Pladic, Er Lannic, Ile-aux-Oiseaux (in the gulf itself), Séné, on the marshy Rhuys peninsula, the islands of Houat and Hoëdic, Kervoyal cove and the island of Bel-Air at Penestin.

Koh Kastell, one of the two reserves on Belle-Ile, is open to the public where, according to the season, colonies of kittiwakes, greater and lesser black-backed gulls and herring gulls, oystercatchers, shags, ravens and choughs can be seen.

Bird-watching is also possible in the swan reserve near the Lasné-Ludré channel on the eastern side of the gulf in Saint-Armel commune, and around Duer Kergeorget near Sarzeau.

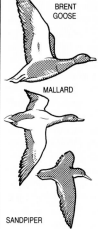

BRENT GOOSE

July-March

Brent geese, duck and shore birds arrive having flown thousands of miles from their breeding grounds in Lapland or Siberia.

July-April

Mallard and red-breasted merganser congregate at the gulf's reserve and may feed as far inland as the Parc Régionale de la Brière to the south.

MALLARD

July onwards

An entire population of shore birds arrive to nest in the marshy areas of the Rhuys peninsula, including many species of sandpipers and curlews, together with larger waders like spoon-bills, stilts, common herons and egrets. Throughout the year there are organized bird-watching outings. Enquire at the local Tourist Offices for further information or call at the Hôtel du Département in Vannes ☎ 97.54.06.56.

Please note that all these sea birds are protected species and holidaymakers are strongly urged not to land on the islands while the birds are nesting, that is between 15 March and the end of July.

SANDPIPER

VITRE

Map ref 137 B5
Pop 14,000
Rennes 35 km
Nantes 148 km
Brest 290 km
Paris 320 km
🛈 promenade
St-Yves
☎ 99.75.04.46

Like Fougères this is another medieval town with a superb castle, one of a line of defences across the eastern Marches of Brittany. Since its original construction in the 11th century, this fortress has undergone much addition and renovation and today presents an impressively powerful face. The small town is attractive, its ancient buildings giving an air of timelessness. Its former manufacturing prosperity is currently undergoing a revival. Just outside Vitré lies the magnificent **Château des Rochers Sévigné** and its exquisite formal gardens, favourite country home of Madame de Sévigné, whose famous *Lettres* have provided invaluable insight into court and country life in the 17th century. Her responsibility here was the creation of the park and gardens.

Leisure

Château Château des Rochers-Sévigné, 6 km south. Though most of the building is private, Mme de Sévigné's workroom and gardens are open all year.
☎ 99.96.76.51
Golf 18-hole private course at Château des Rochers-Sévigné, 35500 Vitré
☎ 99.96.52.52
Riding L'Etrier Vitréen, La Hodyère
☎ 99.75.35.03
Windsurfing On the lake at Chapelle Erbrée.

Hotels
Hôtel la Grenouillère ✳✳
☎ 99.75.34.52
Hôtel le Château ✳✳
5 rue Rallon
☎ 99.74.58.59
Hôtel le Minotel ✳✳
47 rue Poterie
☎ 99.75.11.11
Hôtel le Patio ✳✳
Aire d'Erbrée
☎ 99.49.49.99
Hôtel le Petit Billot ✳✳
5 bis place du Général Leclerc
☎ 99.75.02.10 or
☎ 99.75.68.88
(and restaurant)
Camping
Municipal St-Etienne ✳✳
50 places open all year
☎ 99.75.25.28
Restaurants
Le Pichet
17 boulevard de Laval
☎ 99.75.24.09
La Taverne de l'Eau
12 rue Baudrairie
☎ 99.75.11.09

PRACTICAL INFORMATION

TRAVEL
By air
Airlines with regular scheduled services from UK airports are Brit Air, TAT (Transport Aérien Transrégional) and Air France. All flights to France are handled by Air France, 158 New Bond Street, London W1Y 0AY ☎ 071-499 9511.

By sea
Cross-Channel ferries and hovercraft offer quick and cheap car and passenger crossings throughout the year. Brochures detailing crossings (some only operate during the summer months) and fares are available at travel agents nationwide.

By train
The French railway system is run by the Société Nationale des Chemins de fer Français, or SNCF for short, and is the largest rail network in western Europe. Details of fares, routes and special deals and reductions are available from principal British Rail Travel Centres and continental rail-appointed travel agents. There are, for example, reduced rate tickets for families (*Rail Europ Family*), for senior citizens (*Rail Europ Senior*), for the under 26s (*Carré Jeune/Carte Jeune*), and for everyone there is the *France Vacances Pass* and the *Billet Séjour*. Many stations offer a car hire service and over 280 of them also offer a cycle hire service. SNCF (French Railways) 179 Piccadilly, London W1V 0BA. ☎ 071-409 3518

By car
The international road sign system operates in France. Driving is on the right-hand side of the road and it is important to remember to yield right-of-way to the right when emerging from a stationary position. The French motorway system is run by private enterprise and tolls are levied on all the *autoroutes à péage*. Service stations with full facilities are located every 25 km and there are also *aire de repos* or rest areas where motorists can break their journeys. In the event of a breakdown or accident on a motorway, contact the police by using the emergency telephones sited every 2 km in orange posts. If the car electrics have failed, place the hazard warning triangle 45 m behind your vehicle.
- Speed limits
open road 90 kmph = 55 mph approx
dual carriageways 110 kmph = 68 mph approx
towns and cities 60 kmph = 37 mph approx
motorways 130 kmph = 80 mph approx
Paris ring roads 80 kmph = 49 mph approx
- Seat belts must be worn, by law.
- Helmets must be worn on motorcycles and motorbikes.

The traffic jams at the beginning and end of August, when the whole of France seems on the move, are best avoided. During this period alternative itineraries or *itinéraires bis* (sometimes just *Bis* for short) are signposted which take motorists away from the traditionally congested routes. Up-to-date telephone information on road and traffic conditions in Brittany can be obtained from ☎ 99.32.33.33

Car hire
If you are considering hiring a vehicle while in France, car hire can be arranged locally by enquiring at the Tourist Office, or in advance by contacting any of the following international agencies. Because of the 33% tax levied, however, this will not prove a cheap exercise.

Avis Rent-a-Car
Hayes Gate House, 27 Uxbridge Road, Hayes, Middx
☎ 081-848 8733
Budget Rent-a-Car International
Marlowes, Hemel Hempstead HP1 1LD
☎ 0442 232555
Godfrey Davis Europcar
Bushey House, High Street, Bushey, Watford
☎ 081-950 5050
Hertz Rent-a-Car
Radnor House, 1272 London Road, Norbury, London SW16
☎ 081-679 1799

THE FRENCH RAIL SYSTEM

South East TGV line — New lines under discussion
Atlantic TGV line — Conventional lines
New lines agreed

GENERAL INFORMATION
Banks
Open regular hours, Monday-Friday, 9-12 noon and 2-4 p.m., though most will be open all day in Paris or regional capitals. Some will open on Saturday mornings too if that is market day, but stay closed on Mondays instead. Banks close on some public holidays – see National Holidays, so watch out for notices posted outside giving advance warning of such closures.

Emergencies and Problems
There are two emergency phone numbers:
Police and Ambulance 17
Fire 18
In the event of sickness, *pharmacies* or chemists' shops can provide addresses of local doctors and the nearest hospital casualty department.
Nantes centre hospitalier universitaire ☎ 40.08.33.33
Quimper hôpital Laenec ☎ 98.52.60.60
Rennes centre hospitalier du Pontchaillou ☎ 99.28.43.21
Rennes centre anti-poison ☎ 99.59.22.22
St-Brieuc hôpital de la Beauchée ☎ 96.01.71.23
Vannes hôpital Chubert ☎ 97.01.41.41

Theft or loss
● Of car or personal belongings
Go to the nearest local or national police station, the *gendarmerie* or *Commissariat de Police.*
● Of passport or identity papers
Go to the nearest local or national police station, consulate or embassy, or administrative police headquarters, the *préfecture.*
● Of credit cards
Go to the nearest local or national police station or to the *Mairie* or town hall and immediately notify:
Diner's Club ☎ (1) 47.62.75.00
Carte Bleue (Barclaycard and Visa) ☎ (1) 42.77.11.90
American Express ☎ (1) 47.08.31.21
Europcard (Mastercard and Access) ☎ (1) 43.23.46.46
After reporting a theft or loss you will need a copy of the police's official report for a claim against your insurance company.

National Holidays
Administrative offices and most shops close on public holidays.
New Year's Day, January 1
Easter Monday, date varies
Labour Day, May 1
Ascension Day, varies, according to Easter
VE Day, May 8
Whit Monday, varies, according to Easter
Bastille Day, July 14
Assumption Day, August 15
All Saints' Day, November 1
Remembrance Day, November 11
Christmas Day

Shops
Food shops tend to open early, close at around midday for a lengthy lunch period, then re-open in the afternoon for another four hours or so. Many will open on Sunday mornings, but close on Mondays instead.

Market days
Brest daily in les Halles
Nantes daily except Monday
Quimper Wednesday and Saturday morning
Rennes Saturday morning, place des Lices
St-Brieuc Wednesday and Saturday morning
Vannes Wednesday and Saturday morning

THE MARKET AT RENNES

WHERE TO STAY

Out of season you can usually find accommodation en route and as the fancy takes you. The local Tourist Office, which is known either as an *Office de Tourisme* or a *Syndicat d'Initiative* can provide on-the-spot advice and information on accommodation availability. However, if your visit coincides with the peak holiday period, you should make advance reservations for accommodation.

The *Comité Régional du Tourisme* as well as the Tourist Board for each of the *départements* within the region (*Comité Départmental du Tourisme*) will supply, on request, specific brochures detailing hotel, camping and self-catering *gîte* accommodation in their areas, from which you can make your choice.

General information on the region can be obtained by telephoning or writing to:
Comité Régional du Tourisme
3 rue d'Espagne, BP 4175,
35041 Rennes Cedex
☎ *99.50.11.15*
Specific information on the individual *départements* can be obtained by telephoning or writing to:
Côtes-d'Armor (22)
Comité Départemental du Tourisme
29 rue des Promenades, BP 620,
22011 Saint-Brieuc Cedex
☎ *96.62.72.00*
Finistère (29)
Comité Départemental du Tourisme
11 rue Théodore le Hars, BP 125,
29104 Quimper Cedex
☎ *98.53.09.00*
Ille-et-Vilaine (35)
Comité Départemental du Tourisme
1 rue Martenot,
35000 Rennes Cedex
☎ *99.02.97.43*
Morbihan (56)
Comité Départemental du Tourisme
BP 400, 56009 Vannes Cedex
☎ *97.54.06.56*
Loire-Atlantique (44)
Comité Départemental du Tourisme
Maison du Tourisme,
place du Commerce, 44000 Nantes
☎ *40.89.50.77*

CAMPING
There are probably more camp sites in France than in any other country in Europe, and they enjoy an excellent reputation. Living under canvas can be wonderful fun as many of the sites are more like holiday camps in their provision of on-site shopping facilities and entertainment, and with such activities as riding, tennis, canoeing, etc. all laid on. Amenities do vary though, and camp sites are officially star-graded as follows:

* basic but adequate amenities
** good all-round standard of amenities
*** first class standards with emphasis on comfort and privacy
**** very comfortable, low-density and landscaped sites

All sites must display their grading and charges at the site entrance (for a family of four with tent, allow about 60FF for a * site and 150FF for a **** site per day). They must have roads connecting with the public highway, and be laid out so as to respect the environment, with at least 10 per cent of the ground devoted to trees or shrubs. They must also have adequate fire and security arrangements, permanent and covered washing and sanitary facilities linked to public drainage, and daily refuse collection. The maximum number of people per hectare, or about two and a half acres, is 300. However, at peak periods, when all sites are under considerable strain, there may be some relaxation in the regulations. Sites graded ** and above must have communal buildings lit (and roads lit for *** and ****), games areas (with equipment for *** and ****), a central meeting place, points for electric razors, surrounding fence with a day guard (night watchman for *** and **** sites). Sites graded *** and **** must also have washing facilities in cubicles, hot showers, safe deposits, telephones and good shops on or close to the site.

Camping +
Lists a selection of 29 *** and **** sites across Brittany.
Contact *Comité Régional de Tourisme, 3 rue d'Espagne, BP 4175, 35041 Rennes*
☎ *99.50.11.15*

GITES
These are Government-sponsored, self-catering rural properties, rarely near the sea, which can be anything from a small cottage or village house to a flat or part of a farm. Reasonably priced, they are ideal for families travelling by car, and offer an economical way to meet and mix with the locals. The owner will be on hand to greet you when you arrive.
A small membership fee entitles you to a fully illustrated official handbook and free reservation service from the official London booking office.
Contact *Gîtes de France, 178 Piccadilly, London W1V 9DB* ☎ *071-493 3480.*

THE MANOIR DE KERESTAT, ROSCOFF (see p.95 camping)

Many tour operators also offer *gîte*, villa, chalet or apartment accommodation in Brittany. These may be located at the coast, or in rural areas, and are frequently sold as packages with flights included, but may also be accommodation only. More specific details for a particular location can be obtained by writing to the *Relais des Gîtes Ruraux de France et de Tourisme Vert* for each *département*, the addresses for which are listed below.

Côtes-d'Armor (22)
5 rue des Promenades, BP 556, 22010 Saint-Brieuc Cedex
☎ *96.61.82.79 (guide costs 50FF)*

Finistère (29)
5 allée de Sully, 29322 Quimper Cedex
☎ *98.52.48.00 (guide costs 55FF)*

Ille-et-Vilaine (35)
1 rue Martenot, 35000 Rennes Cedex
☎ *99.02.97.41 (guide costs 35FF)*

Morbihan (56)
2 rue du Château, BP 318, 56403 Auray Cedex
☎ *97.56.48.12 (guide costs 45FF)*

Loire-Atlantique (44)
Maison du Tourisme, place du Commerce, 44000 Nantes Cedex
☎ *40.35.35.48 (guide costs 22FF)*

Chambres d'Hôte
Bed and breakfast accommodation in private homes, usually in rural locations. Local information on these available at the Tourist Offices.
Contact *Gîtes de France Ltd, 178 Piccadilly, London W1V 9DB* ☎ *071–408 1343 and 071–493 3480*
In France *contact the addresses given above.*

Rented accommodation
Local Tourist Offices will supply details of apartment rental agencies or rentals with private individuals in the resort of your choice. In addition, Loca + lists agents and their services throughout Brittany.
Contact *Loca +, Comité Régional de Tourisme, 3 rue d'Espagne, BP 4175, 35041 Rennes* ☎ *99.50.11.15.*

HOTELS
The French Government Tourist Office (FGTO), 178 Piccadilly, London W1V 0AL publishes a full list of hotel groups with details of booking offices in the UK, as well as those French chains with whom you book direct. They can also offer further advice, and personal callers have a choice of three video terminals from which to select hotels of all categories. The official government star rating of hotels (Homologation Officielle du Ministère Chargé du Tourisme) is

GITES ARE OFTEN CONVERTED OLD HOUSES

determined by the quality of accommodation, amenities and service. There are five grades, from * to **** luxury and the prices quoted below are the minimum and maximum one might expect to pay per room.

****L	: Luxury hotel (palace)	520FF upwards
****	: Top class hotel	315–475FF
***	: Very comfortable hotel	210–365FF
**	: Good average hotel	125–260FF
*	: Simple but fairly comfortable hotel	95–140FF

Prices are quoted per room, though a few offer a reduction for single occupancy.
Just as at camp sites, hotel prices must be displayed outside and inside the establishment. Most hotels with their own restaurant expect you to take dinner when staying the night. Full board or *pension* terms, i.e. room and all meals, is offered for a stay of three days or longer; half-board or *demi-pension* terms for room, breakfast and one meal are available outside the peak holiday period and many hotels offer this in season too. Breakfast is not mandatory and you should not be billed for it if you haven't had it! Breakfast will be charged as a supplement varying between 15–77FF. When reserving accommodation, make sure the amount of *arrhes* or deposit is clearly stated, and ask for a receipt for any sum paid.
When making telephone reservations, ensure that you state your arrival time, as hotels may reallocate rooms after 7 p.m. If you find yourself delayed en route, make a courtesy phone call to the hotel, stating your revised arrival time.
A selection showing the variety of hotel accommodation follows.

Where possible, the British representative of a French hotel chain is given.

Brittany Hôtels
31 mainly ** hotels in Brittany.
Contact *M. Mercier, hôtel le Herel, 50100 Granville* ☎ *33.90.48.08.*

Campanile
Small modern ** hotels. Guide provides good street location maps.
Contact *Campanile, Unit 8, Red Lion Road, Hounslow TW3 1JF*
☎ *081-569 5757.*
In France *Campanile, 40 rue de Villiers, 92300 Levallois-Perret* ☎ *47.57.11.11.*

Châteaux et Manoirs de Bretagne
Top level accommodation as private guests in some of the most stylish manor houses and châteaux of Brittany. For details see page 110.

Châteaux, Hôtels Indépendents et Hostelleries d'atmosphere
Stylish private establishments such as châteaux, hotels and castles, offering hotel-type accommodation and services, but unaffiliated to any overseeing body. The illustrated guide book includes a section on restaurants.
Contact *M. Farard, BP 12, 41700 Cour Cheverny (no telephone).*

Climat de France
Chain of 140 ** hotels throughout France.
Contact *Voyages Vacances Ltd, 197 Knightsbridge, London SW7 1RB*
☎ *071-581 5111.*
In France *Climat de France, BP 93, 91943 Les Ulis Cedex* ☎ *(1) 64.46.01.23.*

France Accueil – Minotel Europe
Family-run ** and *** hotels, many with pools. Guide lists 160.
Contact *France Accueil Hotels (UK) Ltd, 10 Salisbury Hollow, Edington, Westbury BA13 4PF* ☎ *0380 830125.*
In France *85 rue de Dessous des Berges, 75013 Paris* ☎ *(1) 45.83.04.22.*

Ibis **
240 ** hotels throughout France.

GRAND HOTEL DES THERMES, ST-MALO (see p.97)

Contact *Resinter, c/o Novotel, Shortlands, Hammersmith, London W6 8DR*
☎ *071-724 1000*
In France *6–8 rue du Bois Briard, Courcouronnes, 91021 Evry*
☎ *(1) 60.77.27.27.*

Ilôtels
15 ** hotels situated on the islands surrounding Brittany.
Contact *Inter France Reservation, 3 Station Parade, London NW2 4NU*
☎ *081-450 9388*
In France *45 rue Jean Jaurès, 56400 Auray* ☎ *97.56.52.57.*

Logis de France
Small and medium-sized family-run hotels often with restaurant. Ideal for short breaks or motoring holidays, these are mostly * and ** hotels and are almost always rurally situated, providing good and reasonably priced accommodation.
Contact *FGTO, 178 Piccadilly, London W1V 0AL for guide enclosing 80p in stamps.*
In France *Logis de France, 83 avenue de l'Italie, 75013 Paris* ☎ *(1) 45.84.70.00.*

Mapotel Best Western
160 *** and **** privately owned hotels throughout France.
Contact *Best Western Hotels, Vine House, 143 London Road, Kingston-upon-Thames KT2 6NA* ☎ *081-541 0033.*
In France *74 avenue du Dr Arnold-Netter, 75012 Paris* ☎ *(1) 43.41.22.44.*

Moulin Etape
Though only a few are located in Brittany, this is a chain of 36 * to **** hotels with a difference – they are all located within converted mills. Some have restaurants, most are on or near water, all are beautiful. The brochure details the history of each, price guide, exact location and address and the telephone number for direct bookings.
Contact *FGTO, 178 Piccadilly, London W1V 0AL for brochure.*
In France *Moulin Etape, Auberge de Moulin de Chaméron, 18210 Bannegon*
☎ *48.61.83.80.*

Relais du Silence
Though only a handful are in Brittany, this chain of 139 hotels specializes in offering locations of total peace and tranquillity for restful stays. There is a multi-lingual brochure as the chain operates in many European countries.
Contact *Hôtels Relais du Silence, 2 passage du Guesclin, 75015 Paris*
☎ *(1) 45.66.77.77.*

Relais et Châteaux
Luxury hotel accommodation and restaurant guide.
Contact *FGTO, 178 Piccadilly, London W1V 0AL enclosing 80p in stamps.*
In France *Relais et Châteaux, Château Hôtel de Locquénolé, 56700 Hennebont*
☎ *97.76.29.04.*

Relais St-Pierre
This is a chain of 48 hotels, 6 of which are in Brittany, which specialize in offering

A LINE OF SMALL FISHING BOATS

good local fishing possibilities and flexible meal times to those who are on fishing holidays. They will also prepare what you catch for your dinner or freeze it for a later date. Non-fishing members of the party are often catered for too, with a selection of tours and excursions.
Contact *FGTO, 178 Piccadilly, London W1V 0AL.*

LOISIRS ACCUEIL
Many *départements* in France, roughly equivalent to the English county, put together fully illustrated brochures under the title **Loisirs Accueil** in which are detailed hundreds of local *gîtes*.
Having received the brochure, one phone call – there are usually English-speaking staff available – will ascertain the availability of the *gîte* of your choice and the organization provides a free direct booking service. They can also book camp sites and hotels.
In addition, their brochures offer options for holidaymakers who are seeking something different. Unusual and interesting short break ideas with accommodation, arranged in local *gîtes*, hotels and camp sites. Further details, with addresses are given on page 25.

YOUTH HOSTELS
This type of accommodation has always provided a cheap and cheerful means of visiting another country. An International Youth Hostels membership card must first be obtained from:
The Youth Hostels Association (YHA), Trevelyan House, St Albans, Herts ALM1 2DY ☎ *0727 55215.*
Details of location of hostels in Brittany available from
Association Bretonne des Auberges de Jeunesse, 41 rue Victor Schoelcher, 56100 Lorient ☎ *97.37.11.65.*
Other useful addresses:
Fédération Unie des Auberges de Jeunesse (FUAJ), 27 rue Pajol, 75018 Paris ☎ *(1) 42.41.59.00.*
Ligue Française pour les Auberges de Jeunesse (LFAG), 38 boulevard Raspail, 75007 Paris ☎ *(1) 45.48.69.84.*

BIENVENUE AU CHATEAU

Châteaux et Manoirs de Bretagne
The participating members of the Châteaux et Manoirs de Bretagne chain offer a selection of châteaux, manor houses and traditional Breton residences where visitors can appreciate a luxurious style of living.

Whether your stay is for a night, a weekend or longer, the owners will treat you as their personal guests. Each château or manor has its own character and history and, carefully selected for its architectural features as well as its natural surroundings, will provide all the comfort and amenity of a high-class home.

Reservations can be made direct with the owners or through: Seratour, 33 boulevard Solferino, 35000 Rennes ☎ 99.35.01.02. Fax: 99.30.59.78

❶ Manoir de Kerguereon
Lannion 10 km
Perros-Guirec 20 km
Contact M. and Mme de Bellefon.
Ploubezre, 22300 Lannion ☎ 96.38.91.46
Open Easter-Nov, 2 rooms (480 FF),
Attractive Breton manor house dating from the 15th century set amidst farming land, 8 km from the sea. Fishing and golf available close by.

CHATEAU DE LA BOURBANSAIS

❷ Château de Kermezen
Tréguier 7 km
Perros-Guirec 20 km
Contact M. and Mme de Kermel,
Pommerit-Jaudy, 22450
La-Roche-Derrien ☎ 96.91.35.75
Open all year, 2 rooms and 1 apartment (400-700 FF), evening meal on request.
A fine 17th-century manor house close to the sea and set in a pleasant valley. Leisure activities include tennis, golf, fishing and riding.

❸ Manoir de Kergrec'h
Tréguier 7 km
Perros-Guirec 20 km
Contact M. and Mme de Roquefeuil,

22820 Plougrescant ☎ 96.92.56.06
Open all year, 3 rooms and 2 suites (350-550 FF). 17th-century manor house situated close to the sea on the lovely Côte de Granit Rose. Golf, tennis, fishing and riding are offered.

❹ Manoir de Keringant
Perros-Guirec 4 km
Contact M. and Mme Piers de Raveschoot, Saint-Quay Perros, 22700
Perros-Guirec ☎ 96.48.09.87
Open all year, 3 rooms, 1 small house, 3 studios, 1 duplex flat (225 FF upwards), evening meal on request.
This is a fine manor house rurally located yet close to the sea. Leisure activities include golf, tennis, riding, fishing and swimming. Games room for children.

❺ Manoir de la Noë Verte
Lanloup
Contact M. and Mme Léon Boutbien,
22580 Lanloup ☎ 96.22.33.03
Open Easter-Oct, 4 rooms and 1 cottage (250-600 FF), evening meal on request.
15th-century manor house on the edge of a lake and within parkland. Golf, tennis, riding and fishing available.

❻ Château du Val d'Arguenon
St-Cast-le-Guildo
Contact Mme de la Blanchardière, Notre-Dame-du-Guildo, 22380 St-Cast
☎ 96.41.07.03
Open Mar-Nov, 5 rooms and 2 apartments (310-500 FF).
Beautiful house dating from the 16th to 18th centuries, set in parkland leading directly on to the sea. Tennis, golf, fishing and riding available.

❼ Château de Kerminaouët
Tregunc 4 km
Pont-Aven 4 km
Contact M. and Mme de Calan, 29910
Tregunc ☎ 98.97.62.20 or ☎ 98.97.62.71
Open Easter-30 Sep. 14 rooms. 2 suites and 1 apartment (450 FF upwards).
Large elegant château set in its own 70 acres of parkland close to the coast. Golf, tennis, riding and fishing available.

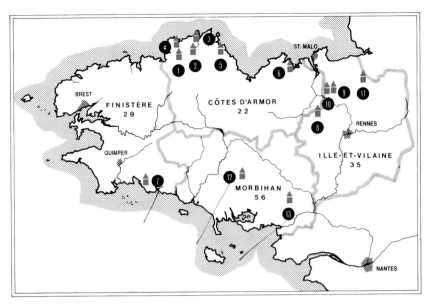

⑧ Château de Léauville
Paris-St-Brieuc-Brest 7 km from the Paris-Brest RN12
Contact M. and Mme Gicquiaux, Landujan, 35360
Montauban-de-Bretagne ☎ 99.61.10.10
Open 15 Mar-15 Nov, 7 rooms (470-570 FF), evening meal on request.
Graceful Breton château dating from the 11th to 17th centuries, surrounded by peaceful woodland. Swimming pool, golf, tennis and riding available.

⑨ Château de la Bourbansais
Pleugueneuc
Contact M. and Mme de Lorgeril, 35720
Pleugueneuc ☎ 99.69.40.48
Open all year, 2 apartments (750 FF).
Splendidly built château dating from the 16th to 18th centuries and set in traditional French gardens. Golf, tennis and fishing available.

⑩ Château de la Motte Beaumanoir
400 m from the RN Rennes-St-Malo
Contact M. and Mme Bernard, 35720
Pleugueneuc ☎ 99.69.46.01
Open all year, 5 rooms, 1 apartment and 2 suites (680-880 FF), evening meal on request.
Beautiful château dating from the 15th to 18th centuries set amidst its own parkland. Golf, tennis and fishing available.

⑪ Château des Blosses
Avranches 25 km
St-Malo 48 km
Contact M. and Mme Barbier, 35460
Saint-Ouen-La-Rouerie ☎ 99.98.36.16
Open 15 Feb-10 Nov, 4 rooms and 1 apartment (350-550 FF), evening meal on request.
Charming 19th-century château in large woodland area. Golf, tennis, riding and fishing available.

⑫ Château du Resto
Locminé
Contact M. and Mme de Kersabiec, Moustoir Ac, 56500 Locminé
☎ 97.44.12.04
Open 15 Jun-15 Nov. 5 rooms and 2 apartments (300 FF), evening meal on request.
19th-century château in rural setting. Golf, tennis, riding and fishing available.

⑬ Château de Talhouet
Rochefort-en-Terre
Contact M. Jean Pol Soulaine, Pluherlin, 56220
Rochefort-en-Terre ☎ 97.43.34.72
Open all year (except 5 Jan-15 Feb) 8 rooms (500-800 FF), evening meal on request.
Château dating from the 16th and 17th centuries set within its own large grounds. Golf and fishing available.

CHATEAU DE LEAUVILLE

ATLAS

Easy to handle and full of useful information, you will find this 26-page atlas of IGN mapping an invaluable travelling companion.

It begins with a double-page general map of the region (scale 1:1,200,000) enabling you to identify all the towns and major places of interest as well as estimate the distances between them. Page references to the more detailed maps of the area (scale 1:250,000) are shown on the grid of this general map.

The legend on page 115 lists all the symbols used on the maps, particularly those denoting places of interest to the tourist: churches and châteaux, historical buildings and curiosities, panoramic views and natural features. A colour code is used on the maps to differentiate between sites judged to be "an absolute must", "interesting" and "worth seeing". Beside each town listed in the gazetteer, you will find the corresponding map reference. The gazetteer section also includes street plans of the main towns. Used in conjunction with the rest of the guide book, this accurate, easy-to-read map section is your key to the region of France you are about to explore.

LEFT THE CHAPEL OF ST-NICHOLAS, LE FAOUET, MORBIHAN **ABOVE** HARVEST TIME

IGN MAPS

As the French saying goes: 'He who travels far cares for his horse . . .', to which one could equally add '. . . and takes with him his IGN maps!' Essential to your travels in France, IGN maps, through their extensive and definitive range, meet every conceivable requirement.

FRANCE IN 16 MAPS
The Red Series
These maps are perfect for driving tours when getting to know a region. Scale 1:250,000 (1 cm = 2.5 km).

FRANCE IN 74 MAPS
The Green Series
Ideal for sporting use such as horse-riding, mountain-biking, canoeing, etc. Scale 1:100,000 (1 cm = 1 km).

FRANCE IN 2,000 MAPS
The Blue Series
These highly-detailed topographical maps are popular for walking, climbing and countryside exploration off the beaten track. Scale 1:25,000 (1 cm = 250 m).

From these have been developed a new practical series called the 'TOP 25': top for topographical and 25 short for the scale size 25,000. The particular qualities of these maps are their redesigned large format covering one specific tourist area (one 'Top 25' map replacing four or five conventional Blue Series maps). They carry a large amount of tourist and practical information enabling visitors to pinpoint with great accuracy the natural and other landmarks of the area. There are at present 90 titles with another 300 planned for the near future.

FRANCE FROM THE AIR
With their unique view of towns, holiday areas and sites of particular interest, the beautifully coloured IGN aero-posters and aerial photographs provide a detailed perspective of the French landscape.

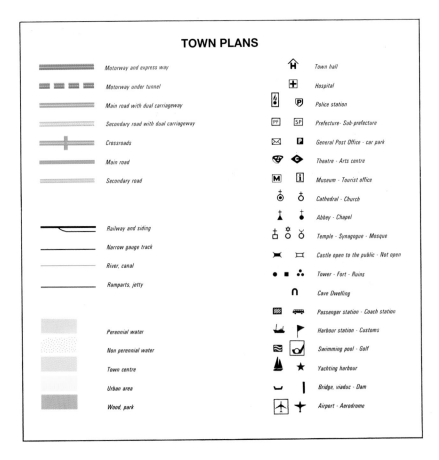

TOWN PLANS

Motorway and express way	Town hall
Motorway under tunnel	Hospital
Main road with dual carriageway	Police station
Secondary road with dual carriageway	Prefecture - Sub-prefecture
Crossroads	General Post Office - car park
Main road	Theatre - Arts centre
Secondary road	Museum - Tourist office
	Cathedral - Church
	Abbey - Chapel
Railway and siding	Temple - Synagogue - Mosque
Narrow gauge track	Castle open to the public - Not open
River, canal	Tower - Fort - Ruins
Ramparts, jetty	Cave Dwelling
	Passenger station - Coach station
Perennial water	Harbour station - Customs
Non perennial water	Swimming pool - Golf
Town centre	Yachting harbour
Urban area	Bridge, viaduc - Dam
Wood, park	Airport - Aerodrome

LEGEND

Motorway (1) - motorway standard (2) `1` `2`

Main road with separate roadways (1), Main roads (2) (3) `1` `2` `3`

Secondary roads

Other roads : regularly maintained (1), not regularly maintained (2), Footpath (3) `1` `2` `3`

Distances in kilometres (between ○ or two outlined cities) 2.5 3.5 6

Railways : double track (1), single track (2) - Station or stopping place (3), open to passenger traffic (4) `1` `2` `3` `4`

Boundary of region (1), of departement (2), of State (3) `1` `2` PF `3`

Navigable canal (1), non navigable canal (2) - Salt pans (3) - Marsh or swamp (4) `1` `2` `3` `4`

Area exposed at low tide : Beach (1) - Rocks (2) `1` `2`

Wood

Airports : international (1), with hard runway (2), without hard runway (3). `1` `2` `3`

TOURISM

Cathedral - Abbey - Church - Chapel

Castle - Castle open to public - Prominent building

View point - Curiosity

District of interest to tourists - Spa - Winter sports resort

Civil architecture (ancient house, bastide, covered market) - Rampart

Ancient remains - Interesting ruins - Memorial

Pilgrimage - Traditional festival - Museum

Military cemetery - Cave - Shelter - Lighthouse

Tourist railway - Rack railway - Aerial cableway, cable car or chair lift

Custom-houses : French, foreign

ITINERARIES

Drive

Walk

Cycling tour

Canal-river cruise

PLACES OF INTEREST

Not to be missed

Interesting

to see

Scale 1: 250 000

Kilomètres 5   3   1   0   5   10   15 Kilomètres

INSTITUT GÉOGRAPHIQUE NATIONAL

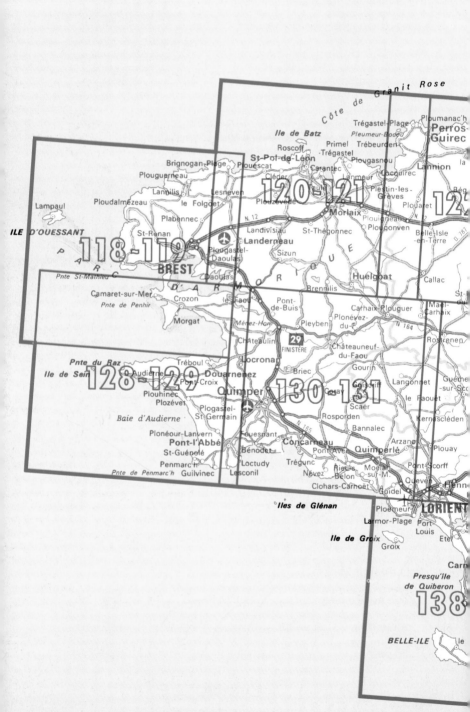

CHANNEL

GUERNSEY
(GUERNESEY)
St-Peter Port
Sark
(Sercq)

ISLANDS
ILES ANGLO-NORMANDES

JERSEY
St-Helier

Alderney
(Aurigny)

Beaumont
Cherbourg
St-Pierre-Eglise
Maupertus
Barfleur
Pte de Barfleur
Tourlaville
la Glacerie
Quettehou
St-Vaast-la-Hougue
les Pieux
Bricquebec
Valognes
Montebourg
Barneville-Carteret
50
MANCHE
Portbail
St-Sauveur-le-Vicomte
Ste-Mère-Eglise
N 13
Carentan
Isigny-s-M
St-Jean-de-Daye
la Haye-du-Puits
St-Clair-sur-l'Elle
Lessay
Périers
Marigny
St-Lô
D 900
St-Sauveur-Lendelin
St-Malo-de-la-Lande
Coutances
N 174
Agon-Coutainville
Cerisy-la-Salle
Tessy
Montmartin
D 971
Percy
Gavray
Brehal
Villedieu-les-Poêles
St-Sever-Calvados
N 175

Ile-de-Bréhat
Ploubazlanec
Paimpol
Plouézec
GOLFE DE ST-MALO
Iles Chausey
Granville
la Haye-Pesnel
St-Pôl
Baie de
Côte d'Émeraude
Carolles
Sartilly
Brécey
St-Quay-Portrieux
Sables d'Or
Erquy
C. Fréhel
Pnte du Grouin
Cancale
St-Jean-le-Thomas
Avranches
Juvigny-le-Tertre
Etables-sur-M.
le Val-André
St-Briac
St-M
le Mont
St-Michel
Poidic-André
St-Cast
le-Guildo
Pléneuf
Matignon
St-Malo
Dinard
St-Lunaire
Portbaultault
Ducey
Isigny-le-Buat
les Rosaires
Plérin
Châteauneuf
St-Brieuc
Lamballe
Ploubalay
Plancoët
N 176
Dol-de-B.
Pontorson
N 176
22
CÔTES-DU-NORD
124-125
Plélan-le-Petit
Jugon-les-Lacs
Dinan
Antrain
D 155
St-Brice-en-Coglès
Fougères
Ploeuc-sur-Lié
Moncontour
Evran
Combourg
Louvigné-du-Désert
Landiv
Collinée
Broons
Caulnes
Bécherel
Tinténiac
35
ILLE-ET-VILAINE
Hédé
Plouguenast
Mérdrignac
Montauban
St-Aubin-d'Aubigné
St-Aubain-du-Cormier
-133
Plémet
N 164
St-Méen-le-Grd
Liffré
Châteaubourg
Vitré
la Chèze
Montfort
RENNES
56
MORBIHAN
la Trinité-Porhoët
Mauron
Mordelles
Argentré-du-Plessis
Josselin
Plélan-le-Grand
Bruz
Châteaugiron
Locminé
Ploërmel
Guichen
Janzé
Rétiers
la Guerche-de-B.
134-135
Guer
Maure-de-B.
le Sel-de-Bretagne
Martigné-Ferchaud
Craon
St-Jean-Brévelay
136-137
Bain-de-B.
St-Aignan-sur-Roë
Grd-Champ
Pipriac
Rougé
Renazé
Elven
Gacilly
le Grand-Fougeray
Questembert
Rochefort-en-Terre
Redon
Derval
Châteaubriant
Pouancé
D 775
Vannes
Allaire
St-Nicolas-de-R.
Guéméné-Penfao
Moisdon-la-Rivière
St-Julien-de-Vouvantes
rmariaquer
Muzillac
Plessé
Nozay
St-Mars-la-Jaille
Cande
la Roche-Bernard
Missillac
Blain
44
LOIRE-ATLANTIQUE
Rialllé
140-141
St-Gildas-des-Bois
Nort-sur-E.
Méng
St-Joachim
Pontchâteau
Ligné
142-143
Ancenis
Guérande
Montoir-de-B.
Savenay
Donges
la Chapelle-sur-Erdre
Carquefou
Champtoceaux
St-Florent-le-Vieil
la Baule
Pnte du Croisic
le Croisic
le Pouliguen
Pornichet
ST-NAZAIRE
Paimboeuf
St-Brévin
St-Père-en-Retz
St-Étienne-de-M.
NANTES
le Loroux-Bottereau
Montrevault
Baupreau
de Hoedic
Pornic
Bouaye
Rezé
Côte d'Amour
Pnte St-Gildas
Côte de
D 751
Vallet
Montfaucon
N 249

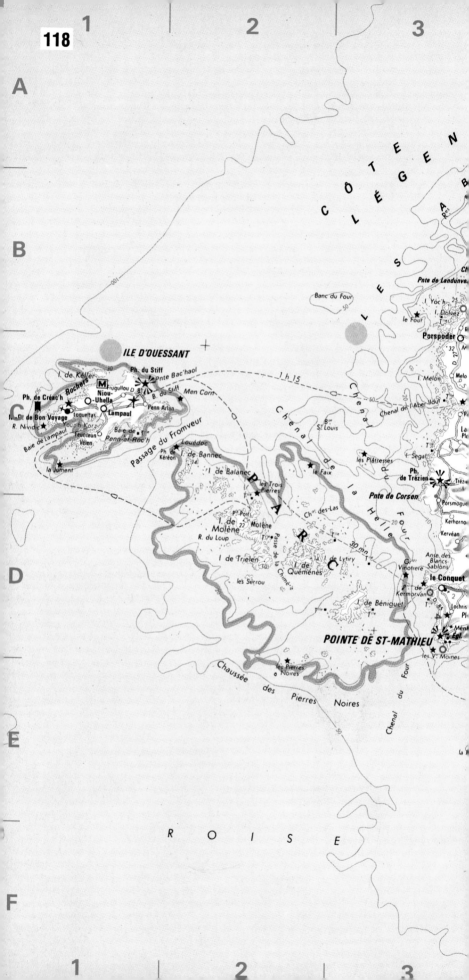

CÔTE

LÉGEN

LES

Banc du Four

Pnte de Landunve

I. Yoc'h   25

I. Doléez

le Four

Porspoder

Porspoder

D 27   32

I. Melon   Melo

ILE D'OUESSANT

I. de Keller

Bochers   Ph. du Stiff

Ph. de Créac'h   Trugullou   Pnte Bac'haol

Niou-Uhella   D 81

N.-D. de Bon Voyage   B. du Stiff

Loquettas   Lampaul   Men Corn

R. Nividic   Youc'h Korz   Penn Arlan

Teuñteun   Baie de

Baie de Lampaul   Vélen   Penn-ar-Roc'h   50

Chenal de l'Aber-Ildut

I. Melon

I. de Ligerc'h

B. St. Louis

la Pli

les Plâtresses   T. Segat

I. Segat

Ph. de Trézien   Trézien

la Jument

Passage du Fromveur

Louëdoc

Ph. de Kéréon   I. de Bannec

I. de Balanec   P   A   R

les Trois Pierres

T. Porsmogue

Pnte de Corsen

Chenal de la Helle

le Faix

Chenal du Four

Porsmogue

P. Pol   I. de   Molène   22   Molène   Ch. des Las

R. du Loup   T.   Passe de la Chimé'a   Kerhorno

Kervéan

I. de Trielen   I. de   I. de Lytiry   30 mn   Anse des

les Serrou   Quéménès   Blancs-Sablons

Gr. Vinotréra

le Conquet

P. de   I. de Béniguet   Kermorvan   T.   2

Lochris   Pl

POINTE DE ST-MATHIEU   Méni

T.   Égl.

les V. Moines

Chaussée   des   Pierres   Noires   les Pierres   Noires

R   O   I   S   E

la E

1 h 15

30

1   **2**   **3**

A

B

Ile de Batz

Ile-de-Batz

F. Verte

Roscoff

Santec

St-Pol-de-Léon

Kérestat

C

Menh.

Brignogan-Plage

Plouénour-Trez

Chât. de Kérouzeré

Manoir de Traonjoly

Cléder

Manoir de Kerlan

Sibiril Plougoulm

Kéromnès

Goulven

Plouescat

Kerlizien

Tréflaouénan

Mespaul

Plouénan

Plouider

Chât. de Kergornadeac'h

Maillé

Plounevez-Lochrist

Berven

Trézilidé

St-Catherine

Plouvorn

D

Lesneven

Plouzévédé

St-Vougay

Chât. de Kerjean

Lanhouarneau

Plougar

Lambader

le Folgoët

Cim. All.

St-Méen

Plougourvest

Plounéventer

Trégarantec

St-Derrien

Ploudaniel

Locméar

Bodilis

Kermat

Guiclan

St-Thég.

E

Trémaouézan

Lanneuffret

St-Servais

Crx des Marmoutiers

Landivisiau

Roc h

Guimiliau

St-Thonan

Ploudern

Abb. de Kerbéneat

Lampaul-Guimiliau

Chât h'ar Bleiz

la Roche-Maurice

Loc-Eguiner

Loc-Eguiner St-Thégonnec

St-Divy

Landerneau

Ploudiry

la Martyre

Locmélar

St-Sauveur

la Forest-Landerneau

Pencran

Queff

Min de Kérouat

Commana

St-Jean

Dirinon

St-Urbain

Tréflévénez

Sizun

le Tréhou

Mougau Bian

Allée Couverte

Plougastel-Daoulas

Loperhet

Irvillac

Pen-ar-Hoat ar-Gorré

Toussainet

Daoulas

St-Eloy

les Létiez

Mais. du Parc

St-Cadou

Quéménén

St-Rivoal

Roudouhir

Menez-Meur *Parc animalier*

Bodinger

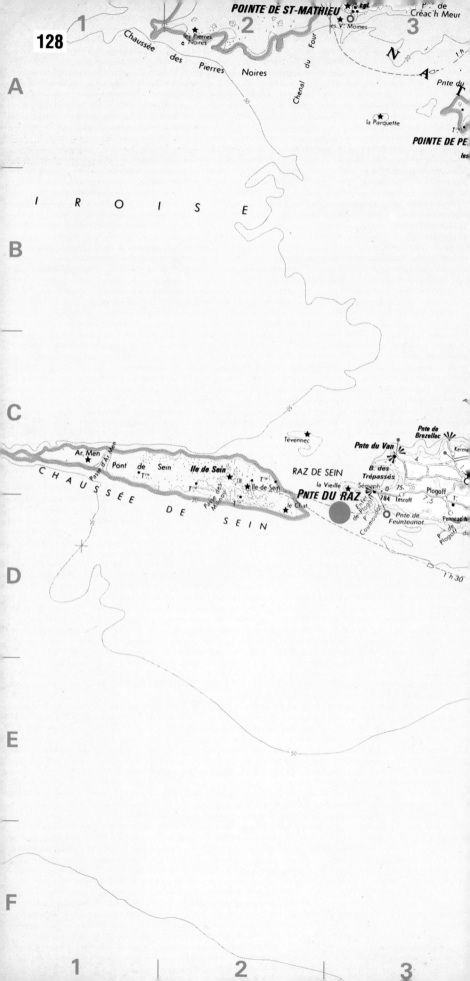

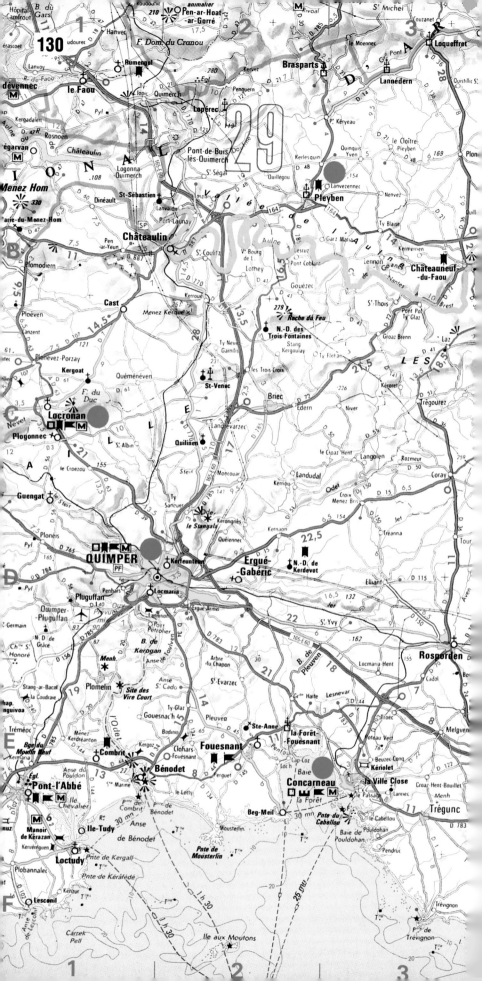

138

Maurice Ch⁵
les 5 Chemins
D 306
Gestel
Caudan
Hennebont

Parc
Zoologique
Quéven
Kerdual
Lanester
le Resto
St Gilles
Branderion

Anse du
Pouldu
le Fort
Bloqué
Fort Bloqué
Carr⁻
de Kaolin
Ploemeur
LORIENT
Base
SP M
Kervignac
Merlevenez
Nostang
Larmor

Larmor
Plage
Port-
Louis
Citadelle
Locmiquélic
Riantec
Plouhinec
St-Cado
Belz

A

B
Réserve
Naturelle
Pen-Men
Grd Phare
Groix
Port-Tudy
Kerohet
Locmaria
Locqueltas
Réserve
Naturelle
Ile de Groix
Roches
de Magouero
Etel
Erdeven
Keravéo
Align
Kerzerho
Plouharne

C
Plateau des Birvideaux
Beg en Aud
Pnte du Percho
PRESQU'ILE
DE QUIBÉRON
Côte Sauvage

D
Beg er
Houlanec
Quiberon

E
Pnte des Poulains
Réserve
Naturelle
Grte de l'Apothicairerie
BELLE-ILE
Sauzon
Grte de
Port Fouquet
le Palais
Citadelle
Pnte de Tail
Rade
Kerledan

Port de Donnant
Iles de
Baguenères
Port Coton
Aiguilles
Port de Goulphar
Grd Phare
Bangor
Port du
Pouldon

F

1   2   3

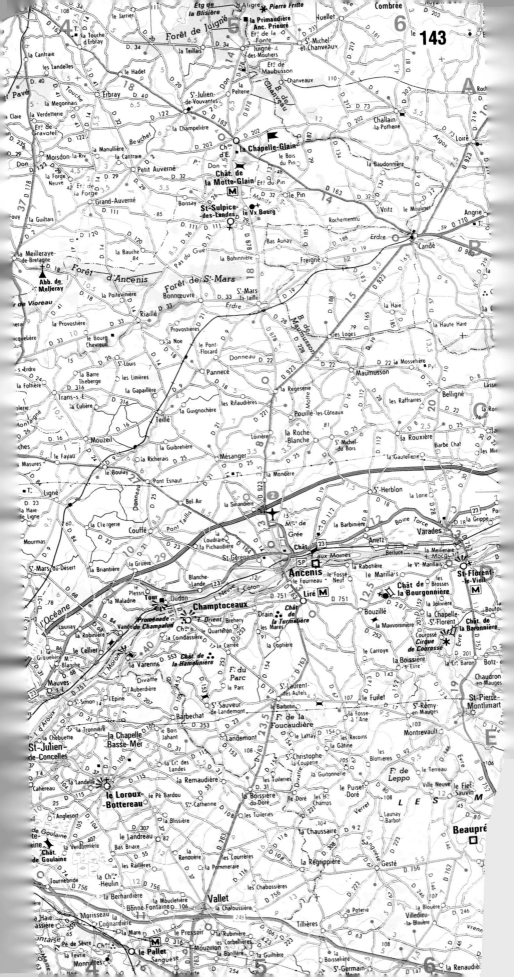

INDEX